Psycholo

Psychology and crime
An introduction to criminological psychology

Clive R. Hollin

First published 1989
by Routledge
11 New Fetter Lane, London EC4P 4EE
29 West 35th Street, New York, NY 10001

Routledge is an imprint of the Taylor & Francis Group

Reprinted 1991, 1992, 1993, 1994, 1996, 1997, 1998 and 1999

Reprinted 2001 and 2002
by Routledge
27 Church Road, Hove, East Sussex BN3 2FA
29 West 35th Street, New York, NY 10001

© 1989 Clive R. Hollin

Typeset in 10pt Times by Mews Photosetting, Beckenham, Kent
Printed and bound in Great Britain by
TJ International Ltd, Padstow, Cornwall

100 2877036

British Library Cataloguing in Publication Data

Hollin, Clive R.
    Psychology and crime: an introduction
    to criminological psychology.
    1. Man. Criminal behaviour. Psychological
    aspects
    I. Title
    364.2′4

Library of Congress Cataloging in Publication Data

Hollin, Clive R.
    Psychology and crime.
    1. Criminal psychology. I. Title.
    HV6080.H64 1989   364.3   88–26371

ISBN 0–415–01807–2

Contents

For Gregory

Figures and tables

Figures

Tables

Preface

Looking back, there were a number of antecedents which led to my interest in crime, so to speak, and so to the writing of this book. These are mostly personal in nature, reflecting the various qualities of those with whom it has been my fortune and misfortune to meet, work with, and learn from. Of those who had a particular impact I must include my doctoral research supervisors, John Radford and Brian Clifford at North East London Polytechnic: both were influential in their own different ways. Of my former colleagues in the Directorate of Psychological Services in the Home Office, Felicity Clarkson, Head of the Psychology Unit at HM Borstal, Feltham, guided my uncertain first steps in the world of real offenders. At that same institution I profited greatly from many long discussions with Graham Huff, which moulded much of my thinking on clinical intervention with offenders. In the world of teaching and research my colleagues, and I hope friends, Monika Henderson, Martin Herbert, and Kevin Howells have influenced my work in many ways. In terms of the written word, Philip Feldman's 1977 book, *Criminal Behaviour: A Psychological Analysis*, had an enormous impact in fostering my appreciation of the way in which psychology could be applied to the study of crime.

I am aware that it is something of a cliché in any book written by an academic, but the undergraduate students who have taken my Forensic Psychology course at the University of Leicester over the past five years have been significantly instrumental in both sharpening my thinking and broadening my reading in the area of psychology and crime. Indeed, the writing of this book directly stems from my teaching. The Forensic course demands of students a great deal of reading, both within and outside mainstream psychology, and I have been aware of the lack of a single source which gathers the bulk of the material which I include on the course. The primary function of this book is therefore to gather material which covers the range of psychology and crime, so providing a text for all those concerned with criminological psychology. (I shall, I think, change the name of my course; as discussed later, the term *criminological* may well be preferable to *forensic*.) Given the aim of a general text, I have tried not to let my own theoretical leanings show too much, although in one or two of the 'perspectives' the sound of galloping hobby-horses is clearly audible. During writing it quickly became apparent that it was impossible to cover everything which might justifiably be called criminological psychology. In consultation with the publishers it was therefore decided not to cover specifically the large field of juvenile delinquency, given the excellent recent text by Michael Rutter and Henri Giller (1983) which reviews this topic in great depth; of course, the discussion of theories and prevention of offending does include many references to delinquents. For the many topics which are included, I have always tried to give an overall picture of the field concerned, although limitations of space have often precluded a full literature review. For this reason I have given a large number of references in the text; the interested reader should always be able to follow up any topic in greater detail from the references given.

In the process of writing I accumulated a number of debts. The second edition of *Criminology* by Larry J. Siegal was an invaluable source to which I referred countless times. A number of friends and colleagues provided references to guide my reading, while some were kind enough also to read parts of the manuscript and suggest improvements; my thanks to Ron Blackburn, Ray Bull, Gisli Gudjonsson, Kevin Howells, Sue Ledwith, Barry McGurk, Lizzie Noon, and Derek Perkins. Sheila Wesson typed the references with awesome speed. Any errors in any part of the text are, of course, of my own making.

The research and writing for this book took a year or so of my life, perhaps one of the hardest year's work I have experienced. My partner in life, Felicity Schofield, gave both the space and the support throughout to see the book through to its completion. It was a year which we started with one child and ended with two: demanding as my labours were, they pale to insignificance compared to hers.

Clive Hollin.
January 1989

Chapter one

Psychology and crime

One of the challenges of crime is that any attempt at its understanding demands knowledge across a wide range of disciplines. Writers and researchers from anthropology, economics, jurisprudence, medicine, philosophy, psychology, and sociology have all contributed to the study of crime. As the study of crime became more refined so it evolved into the specialism of criminology: an integrated approach to the study of crime, in which the elements of other disciplines are used to develop theories and explanations for the phenomenon of crime. There is some debate as to whether criminology has achieved the status of an independent discipline. Critics suggest that as criminology relies so heavily on other disciplines its independence is doubtful and so it would be better considered as a specialization within another established field such as, say, sociology. This argument may have had some force in the past but seems altogether less tenable in the 1980s. I am persuaded by the arguments of writers such as Wolfgang and Ferracuti (1967) who claim that criminology has achieved the status of an independent discipline with its own data base, methodologies, and theories.

With this in mind, I am able to set this book into perspective. I make no imperialist claims on behalf of psychology; crime cannot be explained solely by psychological theory. However, what I believe psychology can do is to contribute to criminology both in terms of its methodology, and by the application of some of its own data base and theory. Further, crime and criminals raise a number of practical issues, principally in two fields. First, how can it be determined whether or not an individual has committed an offence when so accused? Second, when an individual has committed an offence how, if at all, are we to respond to that person? Psychology on its own cannot provide all the answers but, once again, I believe it has a contribution to make. In this light, therefore, the emphasis of this book will be the *contribution* psychology can make to the study of crime. Of necessity the bulk of each chapter is concerned with psychological research and theories as applied to some aspect of crime. Each chapter ends with a short section labelled 'Perspective'. The function of these sections is precisely as the name suggests: to provide a sense of perspective by addressing some point raised in the preceding material.

At the outset, however, there are three fundamental points which must be addressed: What is psychology? What is crime? What is the relationship between psychology and crime?

What is psychology?

There are a number of popular books which attempt to answer the question, what is psychology? (e.g. Colman 1981).To appreciate in full the depth and scope of psychology the best strategy is to peruse an introductory text (Atkinson *et al.* 1983; Berryman *et al.* 1987; Radford and Govier 1980). Simply, psychology is the study of people, although there is a branch of psychology concerned with animals. In the main, psychologists are engaged in the study of *individual* qualities such as perception, memory, thinking, learning, intelligence, creativity, and personality. Further, some psychologists study these human qualities in a particular way: *developmental psychology* is concerned with the study of human growth from infancy to old age; *abnormal psychology*, sometimes called *psychopathology*, is concerned with understanding disturbances such as anxiety, depression, and schizophrenia; *social psychology* is the study of interactions between people, say at work or as part of a family; while *psychophysiology* is the study of the relationship between psychological and physiological processes, as in the interaction between behaviour and aspects of brain functioning.

While these are the mainstream areas of psychology, typically found in undergraduate degree courses, there are also a number of specialist areas of psychological practice. These specialities, developed from the main body of psychological inquiry, are generally studied at postgraduate level. *Educational psychology* is concerned with many aspects of teaching and the educational system. *Occupational psychology* is the application of psychological theory and expertise to the world of organizations, business, management, and so forth. *Clinical psychology* is the extension of abnormal psychology to the treatment, as well as study, of psychological disturbances; treatment methods would include, for example, behaviour therapy, counselling, and psychotherapy (Kovel 1976).

Finally, in this brief gallop through psychology, it is important to note that there are a number of theories prevalent in mainstream psychology (e.g. Chapman and Jones 1980; Price 1978). These theories very much influence the type of research, interpretation of findings, and style of practice of any psychologist. The principal distinction is illustrated by the titles of two psychology books: George Miller's (1962) title is *Psychology: The Science of Mental Life*; while B.F. Skinner (1953) prefers that psychology is about *Science and Human Behavior*. The 'mind' versus 'behaviour' controversy, while not strictly dichotomous, is central to theories of psychology. Recourse to mental processes in seeking to understand human functioning is found in psychological theories both old and new. Freud's theories involved the notion of psychic energies, or psychodynamic forces, driving or compelling human actions (see Kline 1984). More recently cognitive theories have become popular: such theories suggest that human action is determined by a range of mental processes such as reasoning, beliefs, schema, information processing, and so on (see M.W. Eysenck 1984). Such theories would also take into account the force of such 'internal' states as arousal, anger, despair, and self-control as being of fundamental importance in accounting for our actions. The primacy these theories place on mental or 'private' events in determining human functioning contrasts sharply with the position of behavioural theories where emphasis is laid on environmental, not internal, events as determinants of behaviour (Skinner 1974; 1985). This is not to say that behaviourists ignore or deny the existence of internal, private events; rather, that such phenomena are seen as an integral part of human behaviour which, like overt behaviour, can be reinforced or punished by environmental contingencies. The evolution of Social Learning Theory (Bandura 1977) has gone some way towards combining the behavioural and cognitive positions (although differences remain), as also have other multicomponent models of human functioning such as Argyle's (1967) skills model. While there is disagreement about the role of mental events in determining behaviour, it is probably true to say that the majority of psychological theories acknowledge the importance of genetic, neurological, and other biological factors in human functioning.

These theories assume crucial importance when applied to criminal actions. Is a crime committed because the criminal is a rational being, able to make the decision to offend as an act of freewill? Does the crime occur because environmental influences — parents, peer group, culture, and so on — determined the act would invariably happen? Or is the real clue to be found in the genes: are criminals born, not made? The issue goes yet further; if crime is an act of free will, or determined by environmental conditions, or by biological influence, then the solutions to crime demanded by these different perspectives will be very different. These issues will be of concern in this book, but first they need to be set in context alongside some basic facts about crime and criminology. Two points are of particular importance: approaches to defining crime; and the measurement of the amount of crime.

What is crime?

Definitions of crime

The following section examines the three major approaches to defining crime. This is not to say that these are the only approaches, or even the best approaches; rather that they are the most widespread. New ways of viewing crime are continually being developed, such as the critiques presented from a feminist perspective (Heidensohn 1985). However, for the present purpose the three main approaches will suffice.

The consensus view The consensus approach to defining crime stems from the functionalist school within sociology (J. Shepherd 1981). The basic tenet of this school of thought is that society functions as an integrated structure, its stability depending upon agreement, or consensus, among its members about the norms, rules, and values which are to be uniformly respected. Thus, a society's legal system is a reflection of the consensus of what, within that particular society, will and will not be tolerated as acceptable conduct. A crime is therefore a violation of the criminal law, an act which meets with the disapproval of the majority. A definition of crime following this tradition would be of the style exemplified by Williams: 'A crime is an act that is capable of being followed by criminal proceedings, having one of the types of outcome (punishment, etc.) known to follow these proceedings' (G. Williams 1955: 21).

This definition clearly has a number of important consequences. First and foremost an act has to be committed before a crime can be said to have occurred; thought without some action is not a crime. Further, the act must be legally forbidden; 'anti-social' behaviour in itself is not a crime unless specifically and explicitly prohibited by law (*actus reus*). In keeping with this, in the majority of instances the individual must also

4

have had criminal inten* in committing the act (*mens rea*), the exception being crimes of *strict-liability* such as health and safety regulations. An interesting discrepancy arises here between what might seem *morally* wrong, as opposed to 'wrong' in the legal sense. Racism and sexism, for example, may raise great moral issues, but are not well established in criminal law. This is not to preclude the possibility that they might: criminal law has to have the flexibility to accommodate shifting societal values. Sutherland and Cressey (1960) illustrate this latter point, noting that at various times in the past activities such as printing a book, having gold in one's house, or driving with reins have all been criminal acts. More recently abortion, suicide, and consenting homosexual behaviour in adults over the age of 21 years have all been removed from the criminal law domain (or *decriminalized*). The reverse can also happen: acts once not punishable by law are turned into crimes. In the USA it was perfectly legal to own and sell marijuana until the federal law was amended in 1937. In this country changes have been made regarding the sale of solvents to certain age groups, criminalizing a once legal activity — within, of course, the specific boundaries of the law itself. In other instances, technological advances are at present proving challenges to the law-makers: video piracy and computer fraud are contemporary acts which criminal law is having to address.

While there are those acts which may pass in and out of criminal law, and can be thought of as 'statutory' crimes (*mala prohibitum*), there are other acts which are almost universally deemed 'wrong' or 'bad in themselves' (*mala in se*). Such acts would include those which inflict harm on another's person, for example murder, assault, and rape; or would inflict harm on the other person's property, for example burglary, malicious damage, and trespass.

Thus the function of criminal law is to ensure the maintenance of these agreed aims of society, that is to protect the individual's person and property. However, as N. Walker (1965) points out, criminal law adopts a wider brief in seeking to achieve this aim. Laws also exist for the defence of the Realm, and to prevent public acts which might shock, corrupt, or deprave. It can be seen that such laws can be comfortably accommodated within a consensus framework: they act to preserve the stable society within which the individual lives and his or her possessions exist.

An important part of criminal law is the delivery of retribution to those who transgress the commonly agreed boundaries of acceptable conduct. The concept of punishment is not a simple one, raising many

5

practical, legal, and ethical issues (e.g. Ginsberg 1965). For example, most people would agree that not all crimes merit the same punishment. Some system is needed which can differ between crimes of varying severity and magnitude. The tradition in this country is to distinguish between serious offences, sometimes referred to as *indictable* or *notifiable* offences, such as theft, fraud, and violence against the person; and less serious, or *non-indictable* or *summary*, offences such as minor traffic offences and petty damage to property (although some crimes are 'triable either way'). This dichotomy of serious and non-serious offences can be broken down still further: for example Siegal (1986) summarizes findings from the American National Survey of Crime Severity of public perceptions of crime seriousness. In this survey the five most serious crimes, as nominated by a sample from the American public, were all crimes of violence against the person. The most serious of all was: 'Planting a bomb in a public building. The bomb explodes and twenty people are killed.' The crimes judged least serious were being drunk in public, trespass, and least serious of all the 204 crimes in the survey was a 'youngster under sixteen years plays hooky from school'. If criminal law reflects the consensual views of society, then the punishments it delivers must also reflect the consensual view of the seriousness of different types of crime.

The conflict view The conflict view of crime stands directly opposed to the consensus view. It argues that rather than functioning as an integrated unit, society is best seen as a collection of competing diverse groups — professional bodies, unions, students, industrialists, and so on. These groups are in conflict with each other on a range of fronts as, given the unequal distribution of wealth and power within society, some are poor and dissatisfied while others are wealthy and powerful. This inequality in the distribution of power creates a social atmosphere based on conflict, which in turn, it is argued, promotes crime.

The conflict view of crime grew in both popularity and sophistication in the late 1960s and early 1970s. It is most closely associated with the writings of criminologists such as Turk (1969), Quinney (1970), and Chambliss and Seidman (1971); although the contribution of earlier writers such as Vold (1958) and Dahrendorf (1959) should not be neglected.

The conflict view of crime developed into a distinct branch of criminology with the introduction of Marxist theory, a merger generally credited to the book *The New Criminology* by I. Taylor, Walton, and Young (1973). Specifically Marxist or new criminology views crime as a function of a capitalist system which produces those who have wealth and power and those who do not. While each group, or class, within society commits crimes, the type of crime is dictated by the system: the poor commit crimes within their scope, such as theft, murder, and burglary; the middle class commit typical 'white-collar' crimes such as tax evasion and theft from employers; while the wealthy and powerful upper class indulge in activities such as exploitation, profiteering, and environmental pollution and damage — acts which are not accorded the status of crime.

As theories based on conflict are clearly political and economic in orientation, the function of the criminal justice system is viewed in very much the same terms. Criminal laws exist for the express purpose of protecting the rich and powerful from the remainder of the population. In Marxist terms, the 'justice' system exists to preserve capitalist interests — that is the interests of the capitalist bourgeoisie — ensuring power remains with the wealthy and not the proletariat. Thus inequalities in sentencing can be used to support the position of conflict theories. Laws which exact harsher penalties for offences against property rather than against people, and cases in which the poor are imprisoned for minor offences while the rich receive lesser sentences for more serious crimes, appear to offer evidence for a conflict view of crime. Conflict theories have attracted a great deal of criticism. Klockars (1980) has pointed specifically to a number of gaps and flaws in Marxist theories: for example the neglect of individual differences — why do not all people within a capitalist system commit crimes? It should be noted that Marxists have responded to these criticisms and are seeking to refine their theories of criminology (T. Platt 1985).

The interactionist view While the consensus and conflict view of crime stand directly opposed, the interactionist view falls between these two camps. With its beginnings in a school of thought within sociology known as *symbolic interactionism* (Blumer 1969), this view of crime rests on a number of critical assumptions. The first of these assumptions is that each individual's behaviour is guided by their interpretation of reality and the meaning which events hold for them. The second assumption has its focus on the learning of meaning, a process seen as resulting from the way in which other people react, either positively or negatively, towards any given individual or situation. Finally, the third assumption holds that the evaluation of one's own behaviour is made according to the meanings learned and acquired from other people.

In focusing so sharply on meaning, the interactionist view of crime

7

moves away from the moral stance of 'right' and 'wrong' central to the consensus view. Thus, while taking the life of another person is a criminal act, this does not *always* have to be the case: self-defence, in battle during war, and state execution are examples of 'legitimate' killing. The decision as to when an act becomes a crime is not a matter of consensus, rather a statement of the preferences of those who hold social power and are able to impose their preferred definition on society. However, unlike the conflict views of crime, the interactionist view does not suggest that economic and political considerations are the driving motivations for those in power. Becker (1963) used the term 'moral entrepreneurs' to describe those individuals who advance to positions in society which allow them to influence the rule (that is law) making process. Thus the interactionist view is concerned with the way in which changing moral standards — not therefore seen as fixed or absolute — relate to changes in legal standards.

Interactionist views were at their most influential in the 1960s but have rather declined in popularity since then within the criminological community. Some of those who held interactionist views have moved to a conflict position while others shifted to a consensus view: it is probably true to say that in the 1980s the conservative consensus view is once again gaining the ascendancy.

Theories of crime

The three views discussed above have clearly placed very different constructions around the phenomenon of crime. The view taken by the individual criminologist, together with his or her own background in sociology, psychology, and so on, will influence the way in which research evidence is gathered, data interpreted, and theories constructed. The following section briefly examines how the three views noted above have been translated into theories of crime.

Classical and positivist theories The consensus view of crime is linked to two schools of thought within criminology. The *classical* theorists hold central the concept of free will in explaining why a person commits a crime. When the opportunity for crime arises, the individual has a free choice between criminal and non-criminal behaviour. If the payoffs for the criminal act are greater than the retribution it will bring, so the probability of a crime increases. At its most basic this suggests that severe retribution will deter people from any criminal act. Indeed, this simple philosophy was one which guided the process of justice through to the mid-1700s and even into the early 1800s, when acts such as stealing or vagrancy were punishable by severe physical punishment such as flogging or even death. The eighteenth-century Italian economist Cesare Beccaria was in accord with the general view of the time that humans are rational beings, able to choose and control their behaviour. Beccaria was also concerned that the punishment should fit the crime and so argued, with eventual success, that extreme measures are unnecessary and, indeed, may be counter-productive. There is more than a grain of truth in the saying that 'it is as well to be hung for a sheep as a lamb'. Around the turn of the eighteenth century, the British philosopher Jeremy Bentham similarly argued that a balance between profit and pain guided the free choice of a criminal act. Bentham formulated a number of rules by which to regulate the administration of punishment; with the justification for punishment always presented in terms of its preventing a greater evil than it creates.

Classical theory, as presented by Beccaria and Bentham, was the dominant force in Europe and America in the late eighteenth and nineteenth centuries, guiding both judicial philosophers and criminal justice system of the time. With the advent of positivist theories (see next paragraph) the classical school waned in popularity and influence throughout the twentieth centry. However, the 1970s and 1980s have seen a renewed interest in classical criminology. The *neoclassical* or *conservative* criminologists have emerged as a strong voice in contemporary theorizing (e.g. Bayer 1981; Van Den Haag 1982). Fuelled by a general failure of positivist theories to discover the causes of crime and to develop effective strategies for controlling crime, some of the basic ideas associated with classical theories are beginning to return. The call for greater deterrence in the form of longer prison sentences, the return of the death penalty (in Britain), and the notion of 'just deserts' for lawbreakers, has been heard increasingly over the past decade.

The *positivist* theorists, while sympathizing with the consensus view of crime, differ from classical theorists with respect to the role of free will in determining behaviour, including criminal behaviour. Positivist theories grew from the arguments, advanced from the mid-nineteenth century onwards, that influences outside the realm of free will are the most important in determining behaviour. As theories have advanced and fallen so these influences have ranged from biological factors such as genetic transmission, to psychological constructs such as personality, learning, and moral development. While from a more sociological perspective, there are *social structure* theories which emphasize concepts such as 'anomie', and 'strain' which result from class structure and poverty; and *social process* theories which focus on the effects of, for example, education, peer relationships, and the family. Positivist theories are generally seen as more liberal in orientation, with their suggestions that some form of helpful intervention — be it welfare at a social level or treatment at an individual level — is the optimum strategy for reducing crime.

Radical criminology While conflict views of crime encompass a range of opinions, it was those theorists who emphasized the Marxist position who advanced the framework for a new model within criminology. The new criminology promised by I. Taylor *et al.* (1973) quickly became more popularly known as radical criminology. It is incorrect to say that radical criminology represents a unified theory; rather since 1973 it has put forward a series of associated coherent statements which combine to form a body of knowledge and opinion.

While radical criminology has its roots in the writings of Marx and Engels, it was theorists such as Willem Bonger who began to formulate a full Marxist critique of crime. In contrast to classical theories it is proposed that no act in itself is naturally immoral or criminal; definitions of crime are socially determined, reflecting current social values. This emphasis on social determination also runs counter to those positivist theories which incorporate genetic or other biologically based explanations of crime. Within a radical framework, criminal law is designed to suit the purposes of the dominant ruling class, those within society who hold wealth and power. In a capitalist system, the unequal distribution of wealth means that those without finance have to resort to crime to enjoy the luxuries and advantages seen to be enjoyed by others. Crime therefore is in some instances a function of poverty. The rich also commit crimes for the purpose of gaining further wealth and power. However, as the rich control the means of regulating crime, their legal sysem will discriminate against the poor. So while the poor, the proletariat, may commit the same number of crimes as the wealthy, the bourgeoisie, they are arrested and punished with much greater frequency.

A number of modern writers have clarified, elaborated, and extended the position defined by Bonger and articulated by I. Taylor *et al.* (Quinney 1975; Schwendinger and Schwendinger 1979; Spitzer 1975; Sykes 1974; Young 1986). In terms of a solution for crime, radical criminology suggests that changes must occur at economic, political, and social levels. Specifically if progress from the present capitalist system to monopoly capitalism can be made, then redistribution of wealth can take place.

It is argued that crime will then no longer be necessary; any crimes which do occur will be the result of individual psychopathology. T. Platt (1985) presents a blueprint for the formulation of alternatives to the present system of 'law and 'order' which follow a radical criminological approach. As noted previously, radical criminology has been subjected to fierce criticism, with some carefully constructed commentaries (Klockars 1980) and others with more than a touch of naivety (e.g. Washbrook 1981).

Labelling theory The interactionist view of crime gave rise to a theory of criminology which relies on a mixture of social and semantic processes to explain deviance. In common with conflict theories, labelling theory suggests that the law is applied to the benefit of those who hold social and economic power. Thus disadvantaged groups within society, such as the lower socioeconomic classes and minority groups, are more likely to be prosecuted and to receive harsher penalties (Chilton and Galvin 1985; Visher 1983). An individual becomes a criminal when the people who hold power — judges, parents, police, teachers, etc. — decide to confer the label 'criminal'. As Becker notes: 'Deviant behaviour is behaviour that people so label' (1963: 9). Here there is a clear contrast with a moral view: behaviour is not seen as 'right' or 'wrong', rather 'deviant behaviour' is a judgement by certain sections of society towards certain classes of behaviour. This argument does not, of course, apply only to criminal behaviour: the same reasoning has been used to explain the creation of groups variously labelled 'alcoholic', 'mentally ill', 'sexually deviant', and so on.

While writers such as Gove (1975) have offered explanations within a labelling theory framework to account for the involvement of people in criminal acts, the main force of labelling theory has been to examine the consequences of labelling. Two consequences are emphasized — the creation of stigma and modification of self-image.

The term *stigma* refers to the public attitude of condemnation of the deviant and the associated exclusion of the labelled individual from some parts of society. The label 'criminal' is associated with undesirable traits and so, in the public eye, the criminal is a person to be avoided and treated with suspicion. Thus the criminal will find that he or she is barred from certain types of employment; the young offender may find that their school or their family is unwilling to offer a welcome; those with criminal records may attract an undue amount of attention from the police. The force of these social pressures can lead to the second major consequence of the label: the individual comes to believe society's judgement and so modifies his or her self-image to match the label. The prophecy becomes self-fulfiling: the individual becomes the person described by the label. As the label becomes a role for the labelled individual, so the role is reinforced so that the person's life changes to suit the role. More crimes are committed, the peer group changes to others playing the same role, the person's identity becomes that of a 'criminal' with all its associated values, attitudes, and beliefs. Lemart (1951) calls this process *deviance amplification*. The irony of any attempt at intervention, either by punishment or treatment, is that it serves only to reinforce the individual's self-perception of him- or herself as a criminal.

Like all other theories of crime, labelling theory has its critics. There are a range of objections from a failure to specify why some individuals set off on a path of crime, to a failure to acknowledge that some crimes such as murder and rape are universally judged as 'wrong' (Tittle 1975; Wellford 1975). As Siegal (1986) points out, several criminologists who were at one time strong advocates of labelling theory have in the 1970s and 1980s shifted ground to favour more radical theories, principally the conflict theories.

In summary, it can be seen that the three influential theories discussed above explain crime in very different ways. It is true that there is a degree of overlap between certain aspects of some theories, which has been examined by experimental methods (e.g. Bales 1982), but in the main the theories remain independent of each other. While these theories offer explanations for crime, they do not inform us as to the numbers of crimes committed. Knowledge of the numbers of crimes committed is important both theoretically and practically: if crime is a low frequency behaviour then criminals may differ in some important way from those who do not perform such acts; if on the other hand it is a high frequency behaviour this may mean quite the reverse. The practical reasons are concerned with the allocation of finance to those establishments concerned with controlling crime: if there is a great deal of crime, and it is society's wish to control it (however 'society' may be defined), then the forces of law and order will demand a proportion of the public purse — the higher the frequency of crime, the greater the demand on the purse.

How much crime?

In England in the late 1700s the practice began of gathering court statistics in order to gauge the moral health of the country. This preoccupation with figures persists to the present day, although in 1856 the *Judicial Statistics* was for the first time compiled using 'crimes known to the police', rather than court convictions or numbers imprisoned, as the standard measure of quantity of crime. This measure is still favoured and reported annually in the Home Office publication *Criminal Statistics*, which presents a record of the number and types of crime recorded by the police in England and Wales. In the USA the *Uniform Crime Reports*, collected annually by the FBI, serve a similar function. Wolfgang (1971) suggested a number of uses for official statistics: to measure the total volume of crime; to measure the effectiveness of preventative measures; to detect changes in rates of crime; and to provide data for policy decisions.

If the crimes recorded in *Criminal Statistics* are viewed in this light an ominous trend appears: the annual figure for recorded crime has risen from approximately 500,000 in the 1950s, to about 1 million in the mid-1960s, around 2 million by the mid-1970s, and had touched 3 million in the early 1980s. If these figures are reliable, the crime rate is rising rapidly. The logical extension of this argument is that the present methods of crime control are not working and it may seem that policy changes are urgently needed. However, before making this leap from statistics to policy, the reliability of the figures must be questioned. How accurate is the official figure as a measure of the real amount of crime in society? In attempting to answer this question researchers have turned to the three agents involved in crime: the police, the offender, and the victim.

Police recording of crime

If an offence is reported to the police is it guaranteed to appear in the official statistics? An American study cited by Hood and Sparks (1970) suggests not: only about two-thirds of serious crimes which victims claimed to have reported to the police were actually recorded in police files. A British survey similarly found that there were discrepancies between reported crime and police-recorded crime: the percentage shortfall — crimes reported but not recorded — ranged from 75 per cent for robbery to 27 per cent for bicycle theft (Hough and Mayhew 1985). However, three offence categories — sexual offences, thefts of motor vehicles, and theft in a dwelling — showed no shortfall between reporting and police recording. While human error may play a part in mis-recording or 'losing' crimes, and the exact figures involved may be open to question, it is also true that the police have considerable discretion over the recording of reported crime. Bottomley and Pease (1986) present a full discussion of police work and criminal statistics; however, for present purposes the emphasis will be on the process of recording.

As Hough and Mayhew (1985) note, the police may, with justification, feel that a reported 'crime' is a mistake, or there is a lack of evidence to support the report. In other instances an informal caution may be given in which case the offence will not appear in the official figures. In a similar vein, the criminal incident may be satisfactorily resolved by the appearance of a police officer: family disputes and arguments in public houses are examples of this type of situation in which the crime is reported but goes unrecorded. Alternatively it could be that after reporting a crime the injured party asks for the crime to be dropped and so the incident is written off as 'no crime' — again failing to appear in the criminal statistics. In a survey of three London areas, Sparks et al. (1977) found that 'no crime' cases accounted for between 18 per cent and 28 per cent of all initially recorded crimes. The time lapse between the committing of the crime and its reporting to the police is also important; those judged as being too 'stale' to merit investigation may fail to be recorded (Farrington and Bennett 1981). Thus for these and perhaps other reasons the discrepancy between the number of crimes actually committed and the number recorded by the police suggests that the official statistics are not telling the full story — at least for some types of crime.

While crimes can be 'lost' and so distort official figures, variations in police activity can also cause fluctuations in the crime statistics. A crackdown on some criminal group, say drug offenders, can cause a 'bulge' in the figures. Of course this does not mean that there has been a dramatic increase in that type of crime — despite what some newspaper headlines might say — rather that, to use an experimental metaphor, improved sampling has given a better estimate of the true population. In other words, the official figure moves closer to reality. Similarly a change in public attitude or improving the means of communication — it is more convenient to telephone the police at 2 am than to walk to the station — may shift both the quality and quantity of crimes reported to the police. So while, say, the real amount of violent crime in society is decreasing, higher levels of reporting can cause an *increase* to appear in the official figures (McClintock et al. 1963).

The first British Crime Survey (Hough and Mayhew 1983) showed that victims were selective in the crimes they reported to the police: there was, for example, a high rate of reporting for theft of a motor vehicle but a low rate for theft in a dwelling (theft inside a home by someone who is there legitimately, such as a workman, party guest, and so on). M. Hough and Mayhew (1983) also examined the reasons offered by victims for not reporting a crime. The main reasons were the view that the crime was too trivial, or that the police could do nothing, or that it was appropriate to deal with the matter personally. In total these explanations show why victims may decide not to report a crime, although other factors can also be considered. The victim, or perhaps witness, may not realize an act is criminal: physical violence, for example, may be perceived as bullying rather than assault. In cases of fraud or theft from an employer the victim might be unaware of the crime. Alternatively the individual may be a 'willing victim': for example, some homosexual behaviour, drug dealing, and prostitution all involve willing victims. Finally there are 'victimless crimes': if a telephone box is vandalized, or a false income tax return submitted, who is the victim to report the crime?

In summary, crimes are committed, some serious, which fail to appear in the criminal statistics. The amount of this 'unknown' crime is traditionally referred to as the *Dark Figure*. In attempting to shed light on the magnitude of the Dark Figure researchers have turned away from official bodies towards the other two parties involved in crime — the offenders and the victims.

Offender surveys

In the 1960s a number of offender surveys were carried out for which reviews are available (Box 1971; Hood and Sparks 1970; West 1967). The most commonly employed methodology was to select a sample either on the basis of age or geographical location, then to ask the members of the sample whether they had committed any crimes, either detected or undetected. This information was gathered either by questionnaire or interview, conducted with the target person themselves or with someone who knew them well. A British study of theft conducted by Belson (1975) illustrates a typical survey. A sample of 1,445 boys, aged from 13 to 16 years, was randomly selected from a large sample of London households. Interviews with the boys revealed that approximately 70 per cent of the sample had stolen from a shop, and about 17 per cent had stolen from private premises. Thus the majority of boys had committed an offence for which, had they been caught, they would have been liable to prosecution.

The general picture which emerges from the self-report studies is that the official figures underestimate the true extent of crime, especially amongst the young. Indeed, Hood and Sparks (1970) suggest that the official figures represent on average only one-quarter of those who actually commit offences; in other words, they estimate that the Dark Figure is actually about four times greater than the official figure.

The initial impact of the self-report studies was to give pause for thought about whether crime, especially in the young, can legitimately be considered a deviant activity. If so many people are committing offences perhaps that is the norm rather than remaining within the limits of the law. Critics of self-report studies pointed to several shortcomings, the principal one being confidence in the veracity of the data. Does the respondent always tell the truth? Are some crimes withheld, others invented or exaggerated? Further research showed that a number of interviewer and interviewee characteristics — age, sex, socioeconomic status, and race — could influence the quality of information. Additionally there may be sampling problems: if a survey is carried out at a school, for example, it will lose those absent or playing truant — who may be engaged in committing the more serious crimes. Advocates of self-report studies pointed to the advantages of the methodology in that it not only gives a picture of crime involving victims, but also includes 'victimless' crimes such as drug abuse and vandalism. Such doubts led a number of investigators to refine the self-report methodology to include reliability checks on the data.

The most frequently used verification technique is to compare self-report with police records. Studies using this check have found high degrees of agreement between the two measures of offending (Blackmore 1974). Other verification methods include using peer informants to ensure reports match; testing respondents twice to determine if their answers remain constant; and including lie questions in the schedule as a general check on honesty. Hindelang et al. (1981), following a comprehensive review of self-report methodology, conclude that the match is a good one between self-report data and official recording. However, despite the assurances of researchers such as Hindelang et al., the trend in recent times has moved away from offender surveys to victim surveys. One reason for this is that not only can victim surveys reveal information about crime, but also they can be used to gather data on other issues such as public attitudes towards crime and public fear of crime.

Victim surveys

The first contemporary victim surveys were carried out in the USA in the late 1960s (Biederman *et al.* 1967; Ennis 1967; Reiss 1967), followed by the first American national survey in 1972. Similar surveys were carried out in other parts of the world including Australia (Congalton and Najman 1974) and the Scandinavian countries (Aromaa 1974). Smaller-scale victim surveys have been conducted in specific parts of a country, for example in England surveys have been conducted in the Midlands (Farrington and Dowds 1985), in Islington in London (Jones *et al.* 1986), and on Merseyside (Kinsey 1984); or in areas of the same city, such as the survey in different parts of London (Sparks *et al.* 1977).

Victim research has a range of available methodologies (Sparks 1981), but *household surveys* offer perhaps the most important means of data collection. This methodology is typified by the first British Crime Survey (M. Hough and Mayhew 1983). This survey selected 16,000 households from the Electoral Register, with the aim of interviewing one person aged 16 years or older from each household. The survey achieved an 80 per cent success rate in striving to achieve that particular sample. In the context of an interview respondents answered questions about any crimes in which they had been the victim, gave details of the crime (if any), and answered questions on their attitudes towards crime. Surveys such as the British Crime Survey have thrown up a vast amount of data, but across studies a consistent pattern of findings emerges. The most notable is the extent of crime, as Sparks notes: 'Criminal victimization is an extremely rare event . . . crimes of violence are extremely uncommon' (1981: 17). The first British Crime Survey was in agreement with Sparks's observations. As shown in Table 1.1, trivial crimes such as theft from a motor vehicle are the most common, while serious offences such as assault and robbery have a very low frequency of occurrence. Indeed, M. Hough and Mayhew (1983) estimate that the 'statistically average' person over the age of 16 years can expect to be burgled once every 40 years, and to be robbed once every 500 years.

Crime is not, however, a random event and crime surveys illustrate this point. The majority of respondents, Sparks (1981) estimates about 90 per cent, report no experience of crime. On the other hand, some people report being involved in a series of incidents, having been the victims of two, three, four, or even more crimes. This leads to the important distinction between the *incidence* of victimization and the *prevalence* of victimization. The incidence is the average crime rate over

Table 1.1 Offences in England and Wales: British Crime Survey (1983) estimates (after Hough and Mayhew 1983)

Household offences	Best estimate	Rate per 10,000 households
Vandalism	2,650,000	1,494 ± 182
Theft	1,240,000	700 ± 88
Burglary	726,000	410 ± 70
Theft of motor vehicle	277,000	156 ± 34
Bicycle theft	209,000	118 ± 24
Theft in a dwelling	139,000	78 ± 36
Other household theft	1,480,000	835 ± 114
Personal offences		Rate per 10,000 people aged 16+
Common assault	1,490,000	396 ± 94
Theft from the person	422,000	112 ± 32
Wounding	368,000	98 ± 34
Robbery	160,000	42 ± 28
Sexual offences	30,000	16 ± 10
Other personal theft	1,560,000	413 ± 64

Source: *British Crime Survey, Home Office Research Study No. 76*, reproduced with the permission of the Controller of Her Majesty's Stationery Office.

the whole population; the prevalence is that percentage of the population who actually experience crime. Thus surveys reveal that burglaries are most prevalent in inner city areas; cars parked on the street at night are more likely to be stolen; and that it is not the elderly but young males, who typically have assaulted others themselves, who are the most likely victims of assault.

If surveys are repeated over regular periods trends in crime rates may be described. Sparks (1981) discusses some figures from the American National Crime Survey over the period 1973–79: rates for burglary and robbery dropped over that period, while rates for household and personal larceny (without contact) fluctuated over that time. In Britain such trends cannot be calculated as only two national crime surveys have been completed (Hough and Mayhew 1983; 1985). The second of these showed rises in almost all categories of offence as detailed in Table 1.2. It can also be seen that the rises detected by the survey closely parallel changes in the amount of crime recorded by the police.

Victim surveys provide a good picture of the type and amount of crime but they are not without drawbacks. The figures they produce will always underestimate the amount of crime: they focus on offences against the person and against property, omitting the whole area of 'white-collar

Table 1.2 Offences in England and Wales: percentage change in British Crime Survey estimates (1983-85) and offences recorded by the police in the same period (after Hough and Mayhew 1985)

Offences	Survey estimates (% Change)	Recorded offences (% Change)
Vandalism	+ 9	+ 15
Theft from a motor vehicle	+ 7	+ 12
Burglary in a dwelling	+ 21	+ 24
Theft of motor vehicle	0	- 2
Bicycle theft	+ 34	+ 13
Theft in a dwelling	+ 2	+ 13
Theft from a person/robbery	+ 9	- 1
Total	+ 10	+ 12

crime' such as fraud and embezzlement (e.g. Levi 1984). The problems of respondent accuracy, as with offender surveys, also apply to victim surveys. Other factors such as the type of interview (by telephone or in person), interviewer characteristics (such as age and sex), and the use of multiple interviews can all influence the quality of information gained by the survey. Similarly Sparks *et al.* (1977) found that the amount of crime reported was related to the respondent's level of educational achievement. Nevertheless, the figures produced by crime surveys are an important source of information about crime: as such they therefore have great potential for shaping theories of crime and influencing political and social policies towards managing and controlling crime.

In summary, surveys of both offenders and victims confirm that the Dark Figure exists, and that it is substantially greater than official figures. However, given the methodological limitations of surveys, it is prudent to exercise caution in attempting to ascribe exact numerical values to the Dark Figure.

Psychology and crime

The interface between psychology and crime has been given a number of titles including *forensic psychology, legal psychology,* and *criminological psychology.* (The British Psychological Society has a Division of Criminological and Legal Psychology.) In considering the title for this book I selected 'criminological' as the most suitable for my purpose. 'Forensic' and 'legal' are too narrowly defined for use here, properly meaning psychology as applied to courts, legislation, and the like. Criminological, on the other hand, strikes me as suitably all encompassing: if the term is used to refer to all matters related to crime, then it includes courts and so on, but also allows other material to be gathered under its banner. Therefore criminological psychology, as I have used the term, refers to that branch of psychology concerned with the study of criminal behaviour and the functioning of various agencies charged with managing this behaviour.

Thus Chapter 2 is concerned with setting out psychological approaches to understanding crime, noting the range of psychological theories and explanations applied to this task. This topic is extended in Chapter 3 specifically to psychological approaches to understanding serious crime such as murder and sexual violence. While it can be argued that most crimes are committed by perfectly sane people, some crimes are carried out by those who are mentally disturbed. Chapter 4 addresses the issue of the mentally disordered offender. Moving from the criminal to the social agencies responsible for responding to crime, Chapter 5 discusses the application of psychology to the study of the police. This includes psychological studies of the police, and psychology as applied to police work. In a similar vein, Chapter 6 looks at psychology in the courtroom, with particular emphasis on the psychology of the eyewitness and of the jury. Chapter 7 returns to the offender with the topic of psychology and crime prevention, paying particular attention to the application of clinical psychology to crime prevention.

Throughout all these topics I have tried to balance input from criminology and psychology: criminological research is cited to give an understanding of a topic, say a particular type of offence; then research is presented to try to illuminate that topic from a psychological perspective. In giving even a flavour of the areas in which psychology has been applied to the study of crime a substantial literature has been covered from a range of disciplines. Yet, in total, this is but a limited selection from a vast field: for reasons of space a number of areas were omitted or covered only briefly: more might have been included on delinquency — particularly the longitudinal studies which suggest a 'natural lifespan' to juvenile offending (Farrington 1983; Mulvey and LaRosa 1986; Rutherford 1986); on white-collar crime; on penology; on victimology; on drugs and crime; and on offences such as hostage-taking, arson, and bombing. Similar restrictions limited coverage of criminological theories, social control of offenders, the politics of crime, the social role and functioning of the courts, sentencing, and economic crimes. However, my task was to cover psychology and crime; in selecting material two criteria were used: that a reasonable amount of psychological literature existed on a given topic, and that there was no duplication of recent sources such as Rutter and Giller's (1983) masterful text on delinquency. The final product should be greater than simply the sum of the two parts, so that ideally criminology informs psychology and vice versa to produce the hybrid of criminological psychology. The feasibility of this ideal is discussed in the final pages.

Chapter two

Psychological approaches to understanding crime

Theories of crime will be determined, to a greater or lesser degree, by the discipline of the theorist concerned. Thus sociologists draw upon sociological concepts to explain and understand crime, economists upon economic concepts, psychologists upon psychological concepts, and so on. However, this is not to say that, for example, all sociologists will agree in their explanations: the concepts an individual selects as important will be determined by their particular theoretical stance within their discipline. Thus within sociology there are theories of crime which emphasize social structure and draw on concepts such as anomie and subcultures; other theories which stress the importance of social processes, using concepts such as control and labelling; while yet another theory draws on social conflict, calling on concepts such as class structure and class struggle. In some respects the variety of explanations may share common elements; in other instances they stand diametrically opposed. This chapter will examine the variety of psychological explanations which have been offered to attempt to understand crime. Given the close relationship which has always existed between psychology and biology, the starting-point will be those psychobiological theories which have emphasized the primacy of biological factors in explaining crime. Moving from this position, the contribution of the three major standpoints within psychology — psychoanalytic theory, learning theory, and cognitive theory — will be discussed in turn. Finally, it should be made clear that it is not the aim to present here all the evidence pertaining to the various theories; nor to discuss every single variable associated with crime. Such an exercise would demand volumes in its own right. Bartol (1980) and Feldman (1977) provide extensive summaries of a great deal of evidence, while Rutter and Giller (1983) give a concise overview of the whole field. The aim here is to introduce the range, and hint at the depth, of psychological approaches to understanding crime.

Psychobiological theories

Genetic transmission

In its most pure form a theory of crime based solely upon genetic transmission would hold that crime is a direct product of heredity — a criminal is born not made. While such a view would not be seriously entertained by contemporary theorists, who generally prefer interactionist theories, such thinking played a major part in the theories of Cesare Lombroso. Lombroso, a nineteenth-century Italian physician and 'criminal anthropologist', argued that criminals were the product of a genetic constitution unlike that found in the non-criminal population. However, Lombroso also invoked the notion of 'indirect heredity', suggesting that criminality could be acquired through contact with other 'degenerates' such as insane people or alcoholics. Further, in addition to indirect heredity, Lombroso extended his views still wider with the suggestion that environmental conditions such as poor education could also be numbered among the causes of crime. In his later writings Lombroso concluded that about one-third of offenders were born criminals: the remainder had to be accounted for by some other means of explanation.

There was lively debate among Lombroso's contemporaries as to the accuracy of his views. Charles Goring, for example, studied 3,000 English convicts and found that they were less intelligent than expected: as the wisdom of the time held that intelligence was genetically determined, so crime nevertheless had its roots in the genes. A strong genetic argument was evident in relatively recent work (Hooton 1939) and, indeed, is occasionally found in some contemporary work (L. Taylor 1984).

With its emphasis on genetic forces rather than free will, Lombroso's views fall clearly within the positivist school: the act of crime being determined by forces, in this case genes, outside the individual's control. Lombroso's research methods (and those of his contemporaries) had design faults such as the lack of any non-criminal controls, and the use of highly unrepresentative criminal populations which contained mentally disturbed people and others with chromosomal abnormalities. Yet Lombroso can with some justification be hailed as the 'father of modern criminology' (Schafer 1976) as his later theories encompass the three major strands — biology, environment, and psychology — evident in much contemporary research. In addition, by stressing the importance of data and theory, Lombroso played a significant part in shifting the study of crime towards an empirical scientific methodology and away from purely religious and philosophical debate.

While modern theories have moved well away from the notion of a 'criminal gene' which irrevocably sets the criminal apart from the non-criminal, the possibility of some role for genetic constitution in explaining crime has been the subject of a great deal of recent research. This research has focused on three populations — the family, twins, and adoptees.

Family studies In criminological research the family has been studied primarily for two reasons: first to examine the processes within a criminal family to see if they differ in functioning from non-criminal families; second to estimate the degree of similarity between the behaviour of the criminal and their biological relatives. The former strategy has provided a wealth of information about the family backgrounds of delinquents (Offord 1982), especially when longitudinal data are gathered (Farrington *et al*. 1986; West 1982). However, to answer questions of heredity, it is evidence from the consanguinity studies which is important.

The argument behind family studies is that as biological relatives share varying degrees of genetic constitution (the closer the biological relationship, the greater the genetic similarity), so that if criminality is inherited, criminal families will tend to produce criminal children. Looking back to the time of Lombrosian theory, a number of studies were reported which showed that convicted offenders came from families with a criminal history (Dugdale 1910; Estabrook 1916). More recent studies have reached similar conclusions: Osborn and West (1979), for example, found that about 40 per cent of the sons of criminal fathers were criminal themselves, compared with a figure of 13 per cent for sons of non-criminal fathers. Hurwitz and Christiansen (1983) provide a thorough review of this research. While the early researchers claimed their findings as evidence that crime was inherited, and some used it as grounds to argue for the sterilization of criminals, it is evident that there is a major flaw in this conclusion, as contemporary researchers have been at pains to point out.

A correlation between two variables — family criminality and offspring criminality — does not prove that a causal relationship exists between those two variables. It may be that a third variable, perhaps environmental rather than genetic, causes *both* the parents and their children to commit crimes. Thus it is not shared genes which cause high correlations in the criminality of family members, but the fact that all the family members had poor schooling, or inadequate diets, or were unemployed, or lived in the same city area, or were of the same social class, and so on. Alternatively it may be that social and psychological factors within the family are involved in the transmission of criminal values, behaviour, and so on. Clearly what is required is a means of study which would allow the effects of either heredity or environment to be controlled so that the effect of the other can be accurately assessed. One of the traditional methodologies, dating back to Sir Francis Galton, is the study of twins.

Twin studies The basis of twin studies lies in the difference between the two types of twins. Monozygotic (MZ) twins develop from the splitting of a single egg at the time of conception and so share exactly the same genetic constitution: they are *identical* twins. Dizygotic (DZ) twins develop from two different fertilized eggs and are therefore no more alike than any other pair of siblings, sharing about 50 per cent of their genetic constitution. Now, *if* it is assumed that the two members of a twin pair — MZ and DZ alike — experience on average the same environment, then any major differences between members of a pair must be due to genetic variation. As MZ twins have identical genes then it would be predicted that their behaviour would show greater concordance than that of DZ twins. (Concordance can be seen as the degree to which related pairs of subjects within a study population display the same behaviour. It is usually expressed as a percentage: a 50 per cent concordance would indicate that in half of the total sample each member of a twin pair showed the same target behaviour, a 75 per cent rate that three-quarters of the twin pairs showed the same behaviour, and so on.) The twin study method has been widely used in seeking to determine the influence of heredity in, for example, intelligence, and also in disturbances such as alcoholism, depression, and schizophrenia.

The first twin study concerned with criminal behaviour was reported in 1929 by the German physician Johannes Lange giving rise to a number of studies up to the 1940s. The general finding was that MZ twins showed a much higher degree of concordance than DZ twins for criminal behaviour. Indeed the seven studies in Table 2.1 up to and including 1941 show a mean concordance rate of 75 per cent for MZ twins compared to a mean of 24 per cent for DZ twins. A number of reservations have been expressed about the findings of these early studies. The sample sizes are small, only four pairs in two studies; and the sampling is open to question. However, the main reservation lies in the method used by the studies to determine zygocity. If the twins are of the same sex then it can be difficult to distinguish DZ from MZ twins simply on the basis of appearance. Thus typing on the basis of appearance, as in the early studies, may confuse MZ and DZ pairs leading to errors in the concordance rates: although, as Eysenck (1973) explains, this error is as likely to decrease concordance as it is to increase it.

Later studies were able to capitalize on technological advances such as fingerprints, blood typing, and serum protein analysis to make exact determinations of zygocity. The five studies in Table 2.1 reported from 1961 onwards show a mean concordance of 48 per cent for MZ twins, compared to 20 per cent for DZ twins. Thus while the magnitude of the concordance is less in the later studies, which might also reflect improved sampling and different definitions of crime in these studies, the difference between MZ and DZ twins is in general in keeping with a genetic hypothesis.

Table 2.1 Summary of twin study data

	MZ Twins		DZ Twins	
	No. of pairs	% concordant	No. of pairs	% concordant
Lange (1929)	13	77	17	12
Legras (1932)	4	100	5	0
Rosanoff et al. (1934)	37	68	60	10
Kranz (1936)	31	65	43	53
Stumpfl (1936)	18	61	19	37
Borgstrom (1939)	4	75	5	40
Rosanoff et al. (1941)	45	78	27	18
Yoshimasu (1961)	28	61	18	11
Yoshimasu (1965)	28	50	26	0
Hayashi (1967)	15	73	5	60
Dalgaard and Kringlen (1976)	31	26	54	15
Christiansen (1977)	85	32	147	12

Critics of the twin study method rightly point out that the assumption that twins share the same environment can also work against a genetic hypothesis. It may be that MZ twins elicit more similar social responses than DZ twins, meaning that they share a more similar social environment than DZ twins. It may also be the case that MZ twins, again because of their similarity, share a closer relationship with each other than DZ twins and so exhibit similar behaviours — crime included. The answer to this might be found by studying twins reared apart: while the separated twin methodology has been used in other fields of research, it has not been used with criminal behaviour.

In much social science there is a suspicion of explanations which rely upon or incorporate genetic explanations for behaviour. The genetic versus environmental argument is often one in which the proponents of each side stand opposed, arguing that it is their explanation which accounts for the greater degree of the variance in explaining the behaviour in question. Rowe and Osgood (1984) took the position that while genetic arguments for crime were once of the type which stressed the 'defective' nature of genetic material, and hence the person, this 'defective explanation' is not the only available hypothesis. Contemporary genetic theory is concerned with the role of *normal* genetic variability in accounting for differences in behaviour. Further, such genetic influences cannot be accounted for in terms of a single gene; rather the behaviour is associated with many genes. The search for a 'criminal gene' is a fruitless occupation; any tenable explanation for crime which incorporates a genetic element will have to be presented in terms of a polygenetic influence.

Rowe and Osgood (1984) tested this hypothesis with a sample of MZ and DZ twins, measuring the relative influence on delinquent behaviour (self-reported) on three factors: genetic variation, that is type of twin pair; shared environmental influences that affect all family members equally, for example home broken or intact; and specific environmental influences unique to the individual concerned, for example peer group. Following a behavioural genetic analysis, Rowe and Osgood estimated that the genetic component accounted for over 60 per cent of the relationship between the three factors; the shared environment component accounted for about 20 per cent of the relationship; and specific environmental factors for just less than 20 per cent of the total relationship. In keeping with previous work (Rowe 1983), they conclude that genetic factors have a role to play in explaining crime. However, as they stress, this is not to say that delinquency is the inevitable result of a biological difference: rather that individual variations in genetic constitution are the beginnings of a *potential* for the development of criminal behaviour.

An alternative strategy to the use of twins is to study children separated from their parents and raised in another family. The study of adopted children offers a means to do this and so avoid some of the difficulties associated with twin studies.

Adoption studies The procedure in a typical adoption study involves identifying the parents of adopted children and then comparing the criminal behaviour of the biological parents and their children. If the behaviour of the children is more similar to their biological parents than to that of the adoptive parents who are part of the child's environment, then a strong case for a genetic component emerges. Of course should it be the other way around — that children match their adoptive parents — then an environmental position is favoured. This assumes that the adoptive parents are not criminal themselves, a point which a number of studies have shown to be of importance.

In one of the first adoption studies Crowe (1974) found that with a sample of adopted children whose biological mothers had a criminal record, almost 50 per cent of adoptees had a criminal record by 18 years of age. In a matched control group of adopted children born to mothers without a criminal record, only about 5 per cent of the adoptees had been convicted of a criminal offence. Hutchings and Mednick (1975) carried out a large-scale adoption study, involving over 1,000 male adoptees. They found that if the biological father had a criminal record and the adoptive father did not, then the number of adoptees who became criminal was twice that found in cases where the adoptive father was criminal and the biological father non-criminal. However, if *both* fathers had criminal records the percentage of adoptees with criminal records climbed higher still. In summarizing the findings of adoption studies Hutchings and Mednick (1977) concluded that while genetic factors play an aetiological role, the importance of environmental influences cannot be neglected.

More recent research has continued to confirm the importance of genetic and environmental influences. Mednick *et al.* (1983a), with a sample of almost 14,500 adoptees, showed that having a biological parent who is a criminal does lead to a higher number of criminal (male) adoptees. However, as shown in Table 2.2, there is an interactive effect in that the percentage of criminal adoptees is highest when both fathers are criminal. (See Mednick *et al.* 1983b for a discussion of these data within the broader framework of inheritance of deviance.)

While the tendency has been to concentrate upon the genetic factors, a developing line of research has stressed both the primacy and the potency of the interaction between genetic and environmental factors. A study by Cadoret *et al.* (1983) is illustrative of this general approach. Cadoret *et al.* investigated the effects of a range of genetic (e.g. criminality of biological parent) and environmental (e.g. disturbed adoptive

Table 2.2 Percentage of male adoptees with criminal records according to criminality of parents (after Mednick *et al.* 1983a)

Adoptive parents	Biological parents	
	Criminal	Non-criminal
Criminal	24.5% (n = 143)	14.7% (n = 204)
Non-criminal	20.0% (n = 1,226)	13.5% (n = 2,492)

sibling) variables on the development of antisocial behaviour in a sample of adoptees. (It should be noted that the term 'antisocial' — which is used in several of the studies cited immediately above — covers a range of behaviours which might not be considered criminal; this includes being rebellious or difficult to discipline, being destructive, playing truant, fighting, and bullying.) They found that while previous studies had emphasized the influence of genetic factors (Cadoret and Cain 1981), their work favoured environmental variables as the better predictors of antisocial behaviour. In total, however, the genetic and environmental factors alone had a relatively small effect but there was a 'dramatic increase in antisocial behaviours when individuals are exposed to both genetic and environmental factors' (1981: 309). As confirmed by Mednick *et al.* (1983a), the interaction between genes and environment appears to be crucial.

The pathway by which the genetic influence might work has been the subject of a number of studies. In an investigation with Swedish adoptees, Bohman (1978) suggested that the genetic predisposition was to alcoholism; this, in turn, increased the probability of criminal behaviour. Cadoret and Cain (1980) similarly showed, with an adoptee sample, that the genetic variables which best predict antisocial behaviour are having a biological relative who is antisocial or alcoholic. They also found that two environmental variables, having psychiatrically ill or divorced adoptive parents, and having spent time in residential care ('discontinuous mothering'), were also significant predictors of antisocial behaviour. While there is support for the alcohol-crime association, the genetic effect for criminal behaviour is maintained in the absence of alcoholism in the adoptee's biological relatives (Bohman *et al.* 1983).

Van Dusen *et al.* (1983) found that the adopted child's social class has a significant effect on the development of later criminal behaviour.

29

The genetic effect of a criminal biological parent is still present, but is particularly associated with the lower social classes. Van Dusen *et al.* also found a sex effect, such that for male adoptees the environmental factors were more influential than the genetic factors; for females this position was reversed. While this pattern was maintained for male property offences, it was not found for violent male offences (there were too few convicted female offenders for analysis in this study).

Thus the evidence from family, twin, and adoption studies strongly suggests that genetic factors do have a role to play in understanding crime. While some studies favour genetic influences as the most powerful (Rowe and Osgood 1984), and others maintain that environmental factors exert the greater force (Cadoret *et al.* 1983), there is overall agreement that it is the *interaction* between genetic and environmental factors which is crucial. Genetic factors are important but do not predetermine a life of crime — only with certain environmental events is the genetic potential realized. Even given favourable genetic and environmental events as understood by research to date, the outcome is by no means totally predictable. There are children born to criminal parents who experience adverse environments and yet do not commit crimes: other children are born to non-criminal parents, experience seemingly the best of environments, yet commit crimes. The process by which the inherited factors work is also uncertain although a number of hypotheses have been advanced. These include for example a genetic predisposition toward low intelligence, personality type, learning capability, a link with alcoholism, and other biological factors. These qualities react in turn with environmental variables such as the family or school, in a chain of events which eventually culminates in the criminal acts. As Rutter and Giller note, 'The question of just *what* is inherited remains unanswered. It is unlikely to be criminality as such' (1983: 179).

XYY syndrome While contemporary theory has moved away from the notion of a single 'criminal gene' towards polygenetic considerations, the 1960s saw the emergence of an explanation for violent crime in terms of an individual, identifiable genetic abnormality — the XYY syndrome. Chromosomes are structures within cell nuclei which carry the genes: humans normally have 46 chromosomes, of which 44 determine the shape and constitution of the body and two determine sex. A human female would be designated 46,XX; a human male 46,XY. There are a variety of chromosomal abnormalities, some of which involve the presence of extra chromosomes. One such condition, designated 47,XYY, involves the presence of an extra Y chromosome in males.

The extra Y chromosome may be linked to above average height and borderline intelligence; the controversial suggestion is that it is linked to violent crime.

The association between the XYY syndrome and crime came from studies which suggested that XYY males had a disproportionate inclination to violent offences (Sandberg et al. 1961). Owen (1972) reviewed the evidence and suggested otherwise, describing a number of shortcomings with the research: these included difficulties with karyotyping (identification of the extra Y chromosome); the fact that the rate of XYY males in criminal populations is not radically different from non-criminal (at least non-convicted) populations; poorly controlled measures of aggression and violence; and that sexual rather than violent offences appear to be more frequent with XYY males. However, another review by Jarvik et al. (1973) favoured the view that XYY males are overrepresented in criminal, convicted populations as compared to non-criminal populations. A study by Witkin et al. (1976) involved testing over 4,000 men for the presence of the extra Y chromosome. Only twelve cases were identified: while these twelve men were more likely to be involved in crime than might be predicted on the basis of chance, this was not found to be violent crime. Contemporary writers are mixed in their conclusions. Bartol comments that 'The data provide strong support for the relationship between *criminal* behaviour and the extra Y chromosome' (1980: 203). However, following a review by Zellweger and Simpson (1977), Rutter and Giller are of the opinion that 'An extra Y chromosome . . . probably [carries] a slightly increased risk of behavioural problems' (1983: 177). Bartol and Rutter and Giller do agree that the link specifically with violent crime remains without substantive support: also, and more importantly, that some of those individuals with XYY syndrome are not criminal, and the vast majority of criminals do not have any chromosomal abnormality at all.

Biochemical/neurological theories

Over the past decade or so a considerable body of research has accumulated which indicates that the development of criminal behaviour may be related to a range of biochemical and neurological factors. One such area of biochemical research has focused upon the role of vitamin and mineral deficiencies in criminal behaviour. Hippchen (1978) suggested that a deficiency of the vitamin B3 is a major cause of hyperactivity in children and adolescents; Weiss (1983) argued that hyperactive children have an increased risk of later delinquency. Other studies have examined dietary factors such as levels of protein, carbohydrate, and sugar in relation to criminal behaviour (Schoenthaler and Doraz 1983). Yet further studies have focused upon the effects of hormonal influences (Rada 1983), allergic reactions (Mawson and Jacobs 1978), food additives (Hawley and Buckley 1974), and lead pollution (David et al. 1976).

Another line of research has concentrated upon neurophysiological correlates of criminal behaviour. The typical strategy in this research is to compare the neurophysiological functioning of criminal and non-criminal groups. The measure of functioning is usually made via the electroencephalogram (EEG), an instrument which records the electrical activity of the cortex. The EEG can be used to detect unusual patterns of activity, or to search for some type of neurological dysfunction. Historically abnormal EEG has been associated with unusual crimes such as murder by the insane (D. Hill and Pond 1952). However, a number of studies have failed to show any long-term correlation between abnormal EEG and future behaviour (Loomis et al. 1967). Similarly, while some studies have linked EEG abnormality with violence (D. Williams 1969), others have failed to replicate this finding (Moyer 1976) or, indeed, to show any relationship at all between EEG and delinquency (Hsu et al. 1985). Other brain dysfunctions such as Minimal Brain Damage and tumours have also been linked with crime (Kletschka 1966; Monroe 1978).

While some of the more unusual conditions, such as brain lesions, may explain extreme individual cases, the case for a more general biological theory of crime is not well formulated at present. This is partially due to the lack of a sound data base, serious biochemical research has only been underway in this field for about a decade. There are also difficulties with precise neurological measurement, the EEG can be problematic in terms of providing objective information.

Constitutional theories

A theory which sought to combine biological and psychological variables in explaining crime was based on Sheldon's (1942) constitutional theory. Sheldon's theory was concerned with the association between body-build and personality. Simply, Sheldon described three basic body types, or *somatotypes*: these somatotypes are the broad and muscular *mesomorph*, the thin and bony *ectomorph*, and the large and heavy *endomorph*. Some individuals are 'pure' types, while others are hybrids incorporating elements from two or even three builds in their physique. Sheldon further suggested that each body-build is characterized by a particular type of personality: the mesomorph is an adventurous, aggressive person; the ectomorph a restrained, introverted individual; the endomorph a sociable, outgoing character. Each individual will display a mixture of these personality traits according to his or her own particular somatotype.

Sheldon (1949) studied the somatotypes of a sample of almost 400 males in a rehabilitation establishment. The delinquents were characterized by a preponderance of mesomorphs, some indication of endomorphy, and a marked lack of ectomorphs. As this pattern differs from that found in non-criminal populations, Sheldon concluded that there were differences in the physiques of delinquent and non-delinquent males. Subsequent studies by S. Glueck and E. Glueck (1950; 1956) and by Cortes and Gatti (1972) agreed with Sheldon in finding that delinquent populations appear to have more than their fair share of mesomorphs. However, other studies, such as by McCandless et al. (1972), failed to support this conclusion; while a review by Rees (1973) suggested that a link between body-build and crime was not well established.

Although reservations might be expressed about the proposed link between body-build and personality it would be unwise to dismiss totally constitutional theories of crime. As Feldman (1977) suggests, certain aspects of physical appearance, including body-build, may be instrumental in attracting police attention or influencing sentencing decisions. If stereotypes of the appearance of criminals exist — and there is strong evidence that they do (Bull 1982; A.G. Goldstein et al. 1984) — then those individuals who match the stereotype may be being over-selected from the criminal population. As well as this 'selection effect', Feldman suggests various other ways in which body-build might be related to crime: the muscular individual may be more likely to be invited by peers to participate in criminal acts; or certain body-builds may be more likely to be successful at crime.

In total, while biological research may illuminate our understanding of crime — perhaps going some way towards explaining the path which may lead from genetic potential, to difficulties with learning, education, and socialization, and so to a criminal career (Keilitz and Dunivant 1986) — it is unlikely that crime itself will be reduced to a biological explanation. The role of social and individual variables will always have to be included in a full understanding of crime. Constitutional theories combined the biological factors of body-build and the psychological construct of personality, with a reasonably equal balance between the two. Another style of theorizing about crime has moved away from (although not neglected) biological factors to concentrate upon the role of psychological factors in criminal behaviour. The following sections examine theories of crime which have focused on psychology rather than the interaction between biology and psychology.

Psychological theories

Psychoanalytic theory

In formulating psychoanalytic theory, Sigmund Freud was destined to become one of the two major figures to date in the short life of psychology. The ideas and concepts central to his theory have become a part of our everyday life, influencing the way in which many people understand themselves and other people. Terms from the theory have passed into our language — ego, id, the unconscious, regression, rationalization, and any number of others — and through this familiarity they have become 'real', accepted as part of our existence. The complexities of Freudian theory have been expounded in countless texts: Kline (1984) gives a thorough account. There are, of course, various refinements and variations to Freud's theory, offered by post-Freudians such as Carl Jung, Alfred Adler, and Erik Erikson (W.C. Brown 1961). The psychoanalytic tradition gave rise to a philosophy based on psychodynamic concepts which has a number of contemporary variations (Blatt and Lerner 1983) but with the general standpoint that it is inner, dynamic forces which are used to account for human behaviour.

August Aichhorn was one of the first to use psychoanalytic principles to explain criminal behaviour and so exemplifies the style of approach taken by other theorists such as Friedlander (1947). As a teacher working with disturbed and delinquent children, Aichhorn was concerned both to understand and treat these young people and their families. Influenced heavily by the ideas of Freud, which were relatively new at that time, Aichhorn (1925/1955) concluded from his study of delinquents that environmental factors alone could not adequately account for crime. Some underlying predisposition, which he termed *latent delinquency*, psychologically prepares the child for a life of crime. The latent delinquency is seen as partially innate but also in part determined by the child's early emotional relationships. Aichhorn starts from the position that each child is asocial in his or her first dealings with the world: a position which follows Freud's concept of the 'pleasure principle', the view that the infant is only concerned with its own comfort and well-being. In the course of normal development the child's behaviour becomes more socialized with the emergence of the ego and the operation of the 'reality principle'; that is, the child begins to behave in keeping with the rules of its environment. However, in some children the process of socialization goes astray, allowing the latent delinquency to become dominant: a state which Aichhorn describes as 'dissocial'. The criminal behaviour is therefore the result of a failure of psychological development, thereby allowing the underlying, latent delinquency to govern the behaviour.

The reality principle was also central in the explanation of crime offered by F. Alexander and Staub (1931) and F. Alexander and Healy (1935). The criminal from this perspective is someone who is unable to postpone immediate gratification in order to achieve greater long-term gains. In other words, the criminal is one who has failed to progress from the pleasure principle to the reality principle. The antisocial, criminal behaviour in adulthood is seen as a display of characteristics formed during childhood. Healy and Bronner (1936) applied another psychoanalytic concept, *sublimation*, to the explanation of crime. Sublimation is the process by which instinctual impulses are channelled into other thoughts, emotions, and behaviours. Thus the criminal act, it is argued, results from inner unsatisfied desires and dissatisfactions; these unsatisifed wishes, in turn, stem from a failure to experience strong emotional ties with another person, usually a parent. Thus the delinquency is an 'acting out' or sublimation of inner processes. Healy and Bronner provided evidence to support their theory with two groups of children from a child guidance clinic. Compared to a non-delinquent group, the children who had committed offences had less stable families and also showed greater signs of emotional disturbance. Other psychoanalytic explanations for crime have focused on the inability to control impulsive, pleasure-seeking drives (Abramson 1944); unconscious parental permissiveness which gives approval to delinquent behaviour, hence leading to a poorly developed superego and thereby a lack of control over antisocial impulses (Johnson and Szurek 1952); and acting out of feelings of oppression and helplessness (Halleck 1971). Redl and Toch (1979) and R.J. Marshall (1983) provide reviews of the psychoanalytic perspective on crime.

Other theories have moved away from a psychoanalytic view but have remained within a psychodynamic framework. Reckless and Dintz (1967) argued that *self-concept* plays a vital role in the development of criminal behaviour. Studies within this tradition have shown, for example, that offender populations tend to be lower in self-esteem than non-offender populations (L. Bennett et al. 1971), although the evidence is mixed (Gendreau et al. 1973). Similarly, explanations for crime have been offered using concepts taken from reality therapy (Glasser 1965), interpersonal-maturation theory (Warren 1983), socioanalytic theory (Cheek and Hogan 1982), and transactional analysis (Jesness et al. 1972).

Psychoanalytic and psychodynamic theories are concerned to stress the role of inner processes and conflicts as determinants of behaviour. This is not to say that such theories ignore or neglect the importance of social and other environmental factors, rather that they favour the dynamic processes as playing a major role in the development of criminal behaviour. Thus the psychoanalytic model incorporates unresolved inner conflict, a lack of emotional stability, and childhood events in seeking to explain criminal behaviour. The emphasis on childhood is central is perhaps the most influential of all psychoanalytically oriented theories of crime — Bowlby's theory of maternal deprivation.

Maternal deprivation and crime The empirical basis for Bowlby's views on crime came from his study of forty-four juvenile thieves referred to a child guidance clinic (Bowlby 1944; 1946). This group of children were compared with a matched group of non-delinquent children also referred to the clinic. A much higher level of early maternal separation was found in the delinquent group, such that 39 per cent of these children had experienced complete separation from their mothers for six months or more in the first five years of their life. The comparable figure was 5 per cent in the non-delinquent group. A later study failed to provide such clear evidence (Bowlby et al. 1956), but a review of all the available studies had already led Bowlby (1951) to formulate the theory that early maternal deprivation was causally related to antisocial behaviour. This theory rested on two key postulates: a warm, close, and unbroken relationship between child and mother (or permanent mother substitute) is essential for mental health; separation and rejection from and by the mother accounts for most of the more intractable cases of delinquency (Bowlby 1951; Bowlby and Salter-Ainsworth 1965).

Bowlby's theory has been criticized on two fronts, the first with regard to the experimental methodology employed in the two major empirical studies. Morgan (1975) and Feldman (1977) catalogue the research flaws and shortcomings, ranging from the unrepresentative nature of the samples, to poor control group matching, and less than reliable methods of assessment. The second line of criticism, principally from sociologists, was directed at the theory itself rather than the supporting research (see

Hall Williams 1981). Wootton (1959), for example, argued that there is no evidence that the damage from separation is irreversible, and that the type of delinquent with which Bowlby was concerned forms only a small minority of the total delinquent population. Although, to preserve a sense of balance in the debate, Prins cautions, 'Bowlby never made the more extravagant claims for his results that some of his critics have suggested he did' (1982: 85).

Whatever the case, Bowlby's theories were the impetus for a body of research which investigated the effects of maternal deprivation on childhood development. As the evidence accumulated so the theory was used to account for a range of childhood disorders and to generate policies for the treatment of the effects of deprivation. A number of key publications encapsulate the theory, the research, and the controversy it generated (Bowlby 1979; Rutter 1972; 1981; Sluckin *et al.* 1983). Specifically within the field of delinquency, Bowlby's theory heralded a spate of studies concerned with the role of the broken home in the aetiology of delinquency (Grygier *et al.* 1970; Little 1965). While these studies produced findings indicating that a broken home may well play a part in the development of delinquent behaviour, longitudinal studies have shown that the important family influences are much more complex than simply maternal deprivation alone (West 1982). This growing sophistication is, or course, not the sole province of research into crime: A. Clarke and A. Clarke (1976) refer to the 'myths' surrounding early childhood experience, suggesting that attention should be directed at the actual *quality* of upbringing, rather than hypothesized causal links between maternal separation and childhood disturbance in general. Nevertheless, recent research on public explanations of crime has shown that broken homes are popularly seen as a cause of crime (Furnham and Henderson 1983; Hollin and Howells 1987).

In summary, psychoanalytic and psychodynamic theories, like all other theories, have their critics. Objections include the lack of scientific method in formulating the theories, the vague and untestable nature of many of the central concepts, and the reliance on the interpretative skills of the analyst in understanding any given behaviour. These criticisms can all be countered, generally in terms of offering a theory other than a 'scientific' one to understanding human functioning. This response is, in my opinion, a perfectly legitimate one; the real issue is where this approach places the determinants of human behaviour — that is *inside the person*. From this theoretical perspective behaviour is seen, in large part, as a manifestation of inner processes, conflicts, needs, and defences; yet further, inner processes which may be working at an unconscious level. To accept analytic and dynamic approaches, one must therefore be prepared to accept this basic principle. In terms of explaining crime, theorists working within this framework have made a number of valuable contributions in pointing to important variables in the aetiology of criminal behaviour; although, of course, the findings can be explained using a variety of theoretical constructs. My impression from reading the literature is that the use of psychoanalytic and psychodynamic concepts in formulating theories of crime is waning. Rutter and Giller have little doubt why this might be so: 'The [psychoanalytic] theories have not proved to be particularly useful either in furthering our understanding of crime or in devising effective methods of intervention' (1983: 257).

Learning theories

Differential association theory Although it is categorized as a sociological theory in some texts, differential association theory has such clear links with learning theory approaches to explaining crime that it merits a place in any discussion of this nature. Differential association was first described by Sutherland (1939) and later modified slightly (Sutherland 1947); more recent refinements have since been made (Sutherland and Cressey 1970; 1974). The strength of the theory is that it not only describes the necessary social conditions to produce crime, but also attempts to explain the processes by which the individual becomes criminal. Thus, 'crime' is seen as politically defined by those with the power to do so: however, while some people behave in accordance with these definitions, others act outside them. This latter group of people are 'criminal' in that their favoured 'definitions' of acceptable behaviour are seen as deviant by the law-makers. The means by which an individual acquires these definitions conducive to a life of crime merits a detailed account. Sutherland (1947) states nine postulates to account for the process of acquisition:

1 Criminal behaviour is learned.
2 The learning is through association with other people.
3 The main part of the learning occurs within close personal groups.
4 The learning includes techniques to execute particular crimes and also specific attitudes, drives, and motives conducive toward crime.
5 The direction of the drives and motives is learned from perception of the law as either favourable or unfavourable.

6 A person becomes criminal when their definitions favourable to breaking the law outweigh their definitions favourable to non-violation.

7 The learning experiences — differential associations — will vary in frequency, intensity, and importance for each individual.

8 The process of learning criminal behaviour is no different from the learning of any other behaviour.

9 Although criminal behaviour is an expression of needs and values, crime cannot be explained in terms of those needs and values. (For example, it is not the need for money which causes crime, rather the method used to acquire the money; the method is learned.)

Therefore differential association theory is an attempt to explain crime in terms of learning, and social learning at that: it proposes that through contact with other people who hold favourable definitions towards crime that similar definitions are learned. It is important to note that the theory does *not* propose that the learning has to occur through association with criminals, but rather with people who hold definitions favourable to crime. Parents who steadfastly tell their children it is wrong to steal may, nevertheless, show examples of dishonesty such as not informing a shop assistant if they receive too much change in error. Further, varying definitions can co-exist: an individual might argue that it is perfectly reasonable to falsify a tax return, but would define burglary as a crime.

Despite various attempts at empirical validation there are problems with the theory in its original form. These problems include difficulties with the term 'definition', and a lack of detail as why, given similar conditions, some individuals adopt criminal definitions while others do not. Sutherland and Cressey (1974) respond to the criticisms in two ways: the first is to dispel various misconceptions such as that crime is learned through association with criminals (see above); the second is to point out that shortcomings, such as the role of individual differences, define areas for further research rather than refuting the theory. Indeed, in the time since the formulation of differential association theory great advances have been made in the study of learning and so it may now be possible to place some flesh on the bones of Sutherland's theory.

Operant learning If Freud is one of the two major figures in the history of psychology, then the other is certainly the American psychologist Burrhus F. Skinner. Skinner's (1938; 1953) formulation of the principles of operant learning, leading to the emergence and growth of behaviourism, has had a significant effect on both psychology and philosophy (Zuriff 1985), although not without fierce debate and controversy (Modgil and Modgil 1987). At the heart of operant theory is the principle that behaviour is determined by the environmental consequences it produces for the individual concerned. Behaviour which produces desirable consequences will increase in frequency, in which case the behaviour is said to be *reinforced*; behaviour which produces aversive consequences will decrease in frequency, the behaviour is said to be *punished*. In other words, behaviour *operates* on the environment to produce changes which may be reinforcing or punishing. Any such behaviour, driving a car, writing a letter, talking to a friend, setting fire to a house, is *operant* behaviour. Behaviour does not occur at random; environmental cues signal when certain behaviours are liable to be reinforced or punished. Three elements give the concept of the *three-term contingency* which is central to behavioural theory: the *A*ntecedent conditions prompt the *B*ehaviour which in turn produces the *C*onsequences — the ABC of behavioural theory. The operant behaviour of answering the telephone provides a simple example: the ringing tone is the antecedent to the operant behaviour of lifting the receiver, which in turn results in the consequence of speaking to the person at the other end of the line: as we persist in lifting the receiver when the telephone rings, the consequences are clearly reinforcing the behaviour.

Skinner defined two types of reinforcement contingency: with *positive* reinforcement the behaviour produces a rewarding consequence; with *negative* reinforcement the behaviour *avoids* an aversive consequence. Similarly there are two punishment contingencies: with positive punishment the consequences are aversive; with negative punishment the behaviour leads to the removal of something desirable. In both cases the consequences lead to a reduction in the frequency of the behaviour. To summarize, if a behaviour is being maintained or is increasing in frequency it is being reinforced; if a behaviour is decreasing in frequency it is being punished.

The force of this position is that as the consequences of an individual's behaviour are to be found in the environment in which the behaviour occurs, then the determinants of behaviour are to be found *outside* the person — not inside as with psychoanalytic and psychodynamic theories. While the potential for learning, Skinner suggests, is principally a matter of genetic constitution, the acquisition of behaviour can be explained entirely in terms of the individual's learning history via environmental reinforcement and punishment. Before looking at operant explanations of crime, it is as well to tackle the popular misconception that operant theory ignores or denies the existence of thoughts, feelings, emotions, and other 'private events'. Skinner (1974) explores this issue in full, while Blackman expresses the position with clarity:

> Contemporary behaviourists adopt a philosophical position which does not commit them to the assertion that people are no more than puppets, pushed and pulled by forces beyond their control and unable to enjoy or suffer private experiences. Instead they adopt a way of looking at behavioural phenomena which emphasizes the functional importance of environmental influences on what we do, which seeks to find an appropriate way of incorporating private experiences, and which sets these elements within a dynamic and interactive system. (Blackman 1981a: 15)

The precise role of private events in the behavioural sequence is a matter of conjecture, although, as Blackman stresses, cognitions are not afforded the status of autonomous causes of behaviour: for example it is the ringing sound which causes the telephone to be answered, not the thought 'there's the telephone', important as this is in the chain of events. This once orthodox position has been challenged from within behavioural theory (Killeen 1984), although Skinner (1985) remains steadfast and forceful in his views.

Following Sutherland's inclusion of learning into theories of crime, Jeffery (1965) offered a refinement of the notion of differential association by incorporating operant principles into Sutherland's original theory. Jeffery suggested, following Sutherland, that criminal behaviour is operant behaviour: crime is maintained directly by the consequences it produces for the individual concerned. It follows therefore that to understand crime, it is necessary to understand the consequences of the act. The majority of crimes are concerned with stealing where the consequences are clearly material and financial gain: the gains may therefore be seen as positively reinforcing the stealing. Alternatively, the gains may be negatively reinforcing the stealing, as in cases where the proceeds from stealing are used to avoid the effects of poverty such as loss of a home, break-up of a family, and so on. The rewarding consequences of crime can be social as well as material gain: for example, within delinquent groups repeated misconduct is related to social approval and status (Short 1968). Other crimes can be explained in a similar manner: violence, for example, may be positively reinforced by the consequences it produces, or negatively reinforced by removing some unwanted event such as resistance to theft. As well as reinforcing outcomes, crime can also have aversive consequences — being arrested, being sent to prison, having a probation officer, family problems, and so on — which might have a punishing effect on the criminal behaviour (punishing in the operant sense of suppressing the behaviour). As Jeffery notes:

> The theory of differential reinforcement states that a criminal act occurs in an environment in which in the past the actor has been reinforced for behaving in this manner, and the aversive consequences attached to the behaviour have been of such a nature that they do not control or prevent the response. (Jeffery 1965: 295)

In the final analysis it is the balance of reinforcement and punishment in an individual's learning history which will dictate the presence or absence of criminal behaviour. The important point is that each act must be considered in its own right for each individual: some individuals will have been previously rewarded for criminal acts, others will have suffered aversive consequences depending on their social environment. Further, the patterning of reinforcement and punishment is unlikely to have been constant over time, leading to a complex learning history in terms of antecedents to crime and reinforcement schedules (the rate at which reinforcement occurs — not every criminal act is successful). Similarly even within broadly similar social groups or subcultures differences will exist at an individual level in peer group interactions, family processes, schooling, official policies towards crime, and so on. This individual analysis offers one way of explaining why even within similar environments there are some people who become criminal while others do not.

While operant learning stresses the importance of environmental consequences on behaviour, further developments led to a form of learning theory which sought to expand upon the role of 'inner' processes in learning. This approach, termed *social learning theory*, has also been applied to the understanding of criminal behaviour.

Social learning theory Although formulated by Rotter (1954), social learning theory is more generally associated with the American psychologist Albert Bandura. Social learning theory is an extension of operant principles, although there are differences, mainly concerned with the status of cognition. While operant theory maintains that behaviour is acquired through reinforcement and punishment from the environment, social learning theory holds that behaviour can also be learned at a cognitive level through observing the actions of other people. Once learned the behaviour may be reinforced or punished by its consequences like any operant behaviour. Another extension of operant theory lies in the concept of *motivation*: Bandura (1977) suggests that there are three aspects to motivation — external reinforcement (as in operant theory), vicarious reinforcement, and self-reinforcement. Vicarious reinforcement is the observation of other people's behaviour being reinforced or punished. This observation then motivates the observer to behave in a similar manner themselves when the opportunity arises. Self-reinforcement refers to a sense of pride, achievement, or meeting of standards in one's own behaviour. Self-reinforcement motivates the individual to behave similarly in the future.

In total, social learning theory suggests that through observation, especially if the model is someone regarded as successful or of high status, we learn at a cognitive level how to perform the observed behaviour. Given the opportunity, the behaviour may be practised and refined; the behaviour is then reinforced or punished both internally and externally, so motivating future behaviour. Additionally, if a certain behaviour has been reinforced in the past, this creates an *expectancy* that the same behaviour will be reinforced in the future.

The applicability of social learning theory to understanding crime was seen by both psychologists (Bandura 1973a; 1973b; Nietzel 1979) and sociologists (Akers 1977; Akers *et al*. 1979). A social learning approach to crime suggests that observational learning takes place primarily in three contexts: in the family, in the prevalent subculture, and through cultural symbols such as television and books which form part of the social environment (Bandura 1976). Therefore explanations for crime will be found via the behaviour modelled within families, by peer groups, and on television, the cinema, and so forth. Reinforcement for crime comes from both internal and external sources: Bandura (1973b) suggests a range of reinforcing outcomes for crime such as tangible reward, social reward, and seeing other people suffer.

One of the developments from social learning theory was the formulation of a sophisticated model in which the acquisition of social behaviour is explained in terms analogous to the learning of motor skills (Argyle and Kendon 1967). In this light Jeffery's comment, that 'Young adults are more criminalistic than older adults for the reason that they lack responses necessary to produce reinforcement' (1965: 297), can be seen as allied to the view that delinquency is caused by a deficit in socially skilled behaviour. This is a proposition which has been advanced several times subsequently (McFall 1976; Sarason 1968), and a number of empirical studies have shown that delinquents are less socially skilled than non-delinquents (Gaffney and McFall 1981; Spence 1981), although not all studies have found this difference (N. Hunter and Kelley 1986). However, the correlation between social skills level and delinquency does not establish a direct causal link between the two; there is as yet no evidence which points to a *functional* relationship between social skills and delinquency (M. Henderson and Hollin 1983; 1986). Indeed, Furnham (1984) found no significant relationship between self-reported offending and level of social skills in a sample of adolescents.

Thus Sutherland's initial inclusion of learning as a means of understanding crime has been considerably refined and modified by advances in learning theory; both operant and social learning theorists have suggested means by which criminal behaviour can be acquired and then maintained. In summary, learning theories suggest that to understand criminal behaviour it is necessary to conduct a behavioural analysis (Ciminero *et al.* 1986) to elucidate the various consequences of the specific criminal act for the individual concerned. This approach does not seek to prescribe general rules such as 'thieves all steal to obtain money', rather it emphasizes the uniqueness of each individual — a uniqueness which can be understood in terms of patterns of reinforcement and punishment.

There are a number of criticisms of behavioural views of crime. Nietzel suggests that 'behavioural theories do not explain why people who commit the same acts, who perform the same violations of law are treated differently' (1979: 111) and suggests that social labelling theory might provide a better answer to issues of this type. However, taking this a step further, the question becomes 'if social labelling occurs, then by what processes does it function?' A behavioural answer might be formulated by analysing the consequences of labelling for those people — lawmakers, magistrates, schoolteachers, etc. — who apply the labels and so define some individuals as 'criminal'. Further, a behavioural analysis would direct attention to the various discriminate stimuli, such as the offender's race, sex, and social class, which function as antecedents in the labelling process. There are a wealth of research findings which might go some way towards such an analysis: contrary to Nietzel's view, incorporating this knowledge into a behavioural framework might well go some way towards furthering our understanding of the social processes associated with crime.

Nietzel's second criticism is that 'we are all quite aware of the potentially rewarding consequences of property offences; however, few of us steal' (1979: 110–11). Nietzel makes the same point for exposure to television violence and the relatively low levels of actual personal violence. In response there are two points: the first, as described in the previous chapter, is that 'more than a few of us' appear to be stealing; the self-report studies suggest that for some age groups stealing is the norm rather than the exception. The second point is that behavioural theory does offer a variety of explanations for the suppression of behaviour: vicarious punishment — seeing others suffer the consequences of being caught — is one ready explanation; additionally, as discussed below, some of the control theories present a detailed account of *learning* not to offend.

Rutter and Giller (1983) also make a number of criticisms of behavioural theories. They suggest that such theories avoid problems of sex differences, age changes, and developmental factors. This is simply not the case: Herbert (1987), for example, details the way in which these individual and developmental factors must play an integral part in any behavioural assessment and theory of behaviour. Rutter and Giller also suggest that learning theories lack specificity on the acquisition of antisocial behaviour and on the issue of individual differences. These are curious statements as the theories go into great detail, as described above, to attempt to account for the way *all* behaviour is learned; they are also at great pains to stress that individual differences in behaviour result from both unique biological factors and unique learning histories. Finally, Rutter and Giller suggest that there are unresolved problems with behavioural theories such as 'accounting for the observation that punishment is less effective with antisocial children and may actually *increase* their antisocial behaviours' (1983: 253). On examination, however, there is no problem with such an observation; it is the use of terminology which poses the problem. It will be recalled that the behavioural definition of punishment is a consequence which causes a decrease in behaviour: this use is different from the common use of the word 'punishment' which usually means something unpleasant. In behavioural terms, however, punishment cannot be more or less effective with any particular group, nor can it increase behaviour. What seems likely is that Rutter and Giller are *assuming* that certain consequences will be punishing for all children, but have observed that these unpleasant consequences do not decrease behaviour for some children. This observation is readily accommodated by behavioural theory: experimental evidence has demonstrated that continual exposure to aversive stimuli builds a high tolerance level, so that unpleasant consequences which might be predicted to have a punishing effect actually have no effect at all or might even act as a reinforcer (N.E. Miller 1960). Thus, for most people the thought of imprisonment is aversive and one taste of loss of liberty would deter them forever from a life of crime — in such a case prison would, in behavioural terms, punish (i.e. suppress) the criminal behaviour. However, for other people who have experienced a harsh upbringing, material deprivation, and so on, imprisonment may not be such an aversive event; it is unpleasant but can be tolerated as the gains from crime outweigh the inconvenience. Other individuals claim to find imprisonment rewarding, providing a break from an aversive world 'outside'. In neither case is the experience of imprisonment a punishment in a behavioural sense as it fails to suppress criminal behaviour. Indeed, the recidivism rates following custodial sentences testify that imprisonment has little effect on reducing rates of future offending.

Criticisms of behavioural theories have, I suggest, been pitched at the wrong level: the strategy of setting problems which the theory cannot solve is not a helpful one, as demonstrated above when used correctly the theories are sufficiently powerful and versatile to be applied to any problem. A more realistic approach is to query behavioural theories at a conceptual, philosophical level: is behaviour determined by environmental contingencies, or should we look to free will for a better explanation? These issues are discussed in a number of books, see Ions (1977), Modgil and Modgil (1987), and Zuriff (1985). A second line of criticism, staying within a behavioural model, is the lack of research on the role and function of private events. Recent studies are beginning to pay attention to this however, particularly with regard to the importance of cognition (Lowe and Higson 1981). Indeed, the need for a cognitive social learning approach to offending was expressed a decade ago (Sarason 1978), but it is only more recently that significant advances have been made in the study of the relationship between thought and offending.

Cognition and crime The term 'cognition' is an imprecise one, used in a variety of ways by different authors: in general terms it refers to concepts such as memory, imagery, intelligence, and reasoning; although perhaps its most widely used meaning is as a synonym for thinking. In explanations of offending, cognition is implicit in the theories of a number of writers who suggest that various styles of thinking, such as 'impulsive' or 'concrete', are characteristic of criminal populations (Ausubel 1958; S. Glueck and E. Glueck 1950). The link between cognition and crime is perhaps at its most explicit in the controversial writings of Samuel Yochelson and Stanton Samenow.

In the first volume of *The Criminal Personality*, Yochelson and

Samenow (1976) describe their conclusions drawn from interviews with male offenders referred to their hospital for 'determination of competency'. From these interviews, they claim to have discovered the 'criminal thinking patterns' which characterize all criminals. While cautious social scientists might exercise some restraint in accepting the conclusions of investigators who assert that 'The criminal has revealed the working of his mind to us' (1976: 251), and 'We fractionate the criminal's mind and then synthesize it' (252), it cannot be denied that Yochelson and Samenow present some fascinating and idiosyncratic views. They describe a number of styles and errors of thinking — Ross and Fabiano (1985) have counted fifty-two — which define the criminal mind. These thinking patterns include concrete thinking, fragmentation, failure to empathize with others, a lack of any perspective of time, irresponsible decision-making, and perceiving themselves as victims.

While there is much of interest in this work, there are a number of criticisms and shortcomings, some methodological, others theoretical. The sample used by Yochelson and Samenow is an unusual one in that it consisted of 240 persistent offenders, many of whom had been judged 'Not Guilty by Reason of Insanity'. It is questionable just how far it is possible to generalize from this sample to the remainder of the offender population. Their conclusion that all criminals share the same thinking pattern, (see also Samenow 1983) must therefore be treated with caution. Further, as they failed to include a non-offender control group, it is not established that the thinking patterns they describe are peculiar to criminal populations. The interview method of data-gathering, while a rich source of material, does require a check for reliability and validity which is not given. Similarly, there is no indication of any attempt at standardization across interviews. At a theoretical level two principal issues arise: the first is with the concept of 'mind' and the associated assumption that thinking caused behaviour. There are a number of theoretical variations on both mind and the primacy of cognition over behaviour, none of which is fully explored. The second issue lies in their assertion that, by processes which are not well explained, criminals are like a different breed of person (see also Samenow 1984). Indeed, comments of this latter type have led to charges of 'neo-Lombrosian' being levelled against this work.

In summarizing the cognitive approach of Yochelson and Samenow, Ross and Fabiano (1985) express regret at the shortcomings of this work, which has led to a great deal of controversy rather than establishing a valuable contribution to clinical criminology. However, the approach of Yochelson and Samenow is not that of other cognitive models of criminal behaviour. More recent studies have looked for more explicit cognitive variations between offenders and non-offenders. Although the distinction may not be exact, Ross and Fabiano distinguish between *im*personal cognition and *inter*personal cognition. The former is that aspect of cognition which 'deals with the physical world'; the latter is concerned with 'understanding people and their actions', sometimes called social cognition. While impersonal cognition may be a factor in the development of criminal behaviour — for example the research which points to intellectual imbalances in offender samples (Andrew 1977) — Ross and Fabiano argue that interpersonal cognition may well be more important in understanding crime. In reviewing studies of social cognition with criminal populations, Ross and Fabiano described a variety of types or styles of cognition which characterize offenders.

A failure in *self-control*, leading to *impulsivity*, figures repeatedly in explanations of crime (Ahlstrom and Havinghurst 1971; S. Glueck and E. Glueck 1950). Ross and Fabiano suggest that impulsivity may be seen 'as a failure to insert between impulse and action a stage of reflection, a cognitive analysis of the situation' (1985: 37). This failure, they further suggest, may be due to one of a number of factors: a failure to learn to stop and think; a failure to learn 'effective thinking'; a failure to generate alternative responses; or a reflection of hopelessness. The empirical evidence is mixed. Some studies suggest that offenders are more impulsive than non-offenders (Rotenberg and Nachshon 1979), others that offenders are unable to delay reward (Stumphauzer 1972). However, other studies have not found such differences (J.T. Saunders *et al.* 1973). The difference between studies may be due to differing definitions and measures of impulsivity, and the heterogeneity of the offender population.

The concept of *locus of control* refers to the degree to which individuals perceive their behaviour to be under their own *internal* control, as opposed to being controlled by *external* agents such as luck or authority figures (Rotter 1966). A number of studies have shown that offenders tend to external control, that is they explain their behaviour as being controlled by influences beyond their personal control (Beck and Ollendick 1976; Kumchy and Sayer 1980). However, other studies have failed to show any difference in locus of control between offender and non-offender samples (Drasgow *et al.* 1974; Groh and Goldenberg 1976); while Lefcourt and Ladwig (1965) found offenders to be more *internally* controlled than non-offenders. The varied findings are probably due to two unfounded assumptions: that locus of control is a unitary concept, and that offenders form a homogeneous population. With regard to the former point, a number of studies have shown that there are several dimensions to locus of control, such as belief in control over one's immediate environment as opposed to belief in control over political events (Mirels 1970). In terms of the latter point, locus of control within an offender population may be a function of race (Griffith *et al*. 1981); type of offence, for example, violent offenders tend to external control (Hollin and Wheeler 1982); or time spent in prison (Kiessel 1966). If locus of control does have some relationship with offending, it will require rather more sophisticated research than is presently available to discover its exact role.

As social perception develops so the ability to 'see things from the other person's point of view' matures and influences our own behaviour. A long-standing finding with offenders is that they see situations only from their own perspective, not appreciating the view of the other person. This is reflected in low scores on measures of empathy and role-taking ability (Chandler 1973; Kaplan and Arbuthnot 1985): although variations have been reported according to length of criminal career (Deardroff *et al*. 1977) and type of offence (P.L. Ellis 1982).

If social perception is the ability to discriminate social cues and understand their significance, then the next step requires using these perceptions to decide upon suitable social behaviour. This requires a range of cognitive skills such as the ability to generate a range of solutions to a social problem, considering the various consequences of the different solutions, and planning the steps to achieve the different outcomes (Spivack *et al*. 1976). These cognitive skills have become more widely known as 'cognitive problem-solving' over the past few years. Several studies have found that offenders show poorer social problem solving than non-offenders (Freedman *et al*. 1978; Higgins and Thies 1981; J.J. Platt *et al*. 1973). Although some doubt has been expressed about the validity of one of the measures used in some of these studies, and also about the functional relationship of these cognitive skills with offending (M. Henderson and Hollin 1983; 1986; N. Hunter and Kelley 1986).

In total the evidence does indicate some differences in social cognition between offenders and non-offenders. However, two points require clarification: the relationship between impersonal and interpersonal cognitive abilities, particularly with regard to offender populations; secondly, and perhaps more importantly, the process by which the cognition results in offending. It seems likely that the answer to this latter point will come from studies, not yet attempted, of social *decision-making* in offenders.

While social decision-making in offenders has not been researched, decision-making regarding the commission of crime has received a growing amount of attention. This line of enquiry portrays the offender as a rational decision-maker, a 'reasoning criminal'. The beginnings of this cognitive view of crime are, somewhat ironically, to be found in studies which focused on environmental rather than individual factors in explaining the crime. Simply, this view suggests that for a crime to be committed, the opportunity must be afforded for the offence to occur; the criminal is one who decides to take advantage of this opportunity. L.E. Cohen and Felson (1979) elaborated on this view of 'crime as opportunity', suggesting that for example the increase in burglaries over the past decade can be explained in terms of increased opportunity as more family members go out to work, so leaving houses empty for longer periods. Studies have similarly investigated the effects of opportunity on car theft (Mayhew *et al.* 1976), violence (Poyner 1981), robbery and theft (Mayhew *et al.* 1979), and vandalism (Mayhew *et al.* 1976). The cognitive component involves the decision-making process when the opportunity to offend arises. A crime is seen therefore as the result of the offender's consideration of the risks and costs of offending; indeed previous studies have addressed the relationship between risk perception and likelihood of offending (Stewart and Hemsley 1979). Cornish and Clarke summarize this view of crime:

> Its starting point was the assumption that offenders seek to benefit themselves by their criminal behaviour; that this involves the making of decisions and choices, however rudimentary on occasion these processes might be; and that these processes exhibit a measure of rationality, albeit constrained by limits of time and ability and the availability of relevant information. (Cornish and Clarke 1986a:1)

Cornish and Clarke also make the distinction between criminal *involvement* and criminal *events*. The former is the process by which individuals choose to become involved in crime, while the latter refers to the short-term, immediate decisions in a given set of circumstances. Thus the approach is an interactional one, in which the offender reacts in a reasoned manner to environmental opportunities. While this represents a move away from 'dispositional' theories which focus exclusively on the offender, it does not dismiss the importance of personal variables, but rather attempts to place such variables in a wider context.

As an example Cornish and Clarke work through the process of an individual's initial involvement in the crime of burglary, followed by the event decision for a specific burglary, and finally the process underlying the individual committing more and more such offences. The initial involvement includes factors such as type of upbringing and other social variables; the event decision considers the influence of factors such as the presence of a dog or a burglar alarm on the decision to enter a particular house; while the increase in frequency is related to a growing sense of 'professionalism' in committing the crime, and accompanying changes in self-evaluation, life-style, and peer group. As well as burglary the rational choice model has been applied to shoplifting (J. Carroll and Weaver 1986), robbery (Feeney 1986), and drug use (T. Bennett 1986). The rational choice model can also be applied to the decision to give up crime (Cusson and Pinsonneault 1986).

In total, the traditional learning theories have concentrated upon the acquisition of criminal behaviour through reinforcement and modelling. The cognitive theories have followed this trend, but have recently considered the alternative of explaining why offending does *not* occur even when the opportunity arises. This notion of not offending is central to another group of theories which see crime as a failure to learn control behaviour.

Control theories

The thesis underlying control theories is that everyone has the potential to behave in a criminal manner: the issue therefore becomes not one of explaining why some people commit crimes, but rather asking why is it that not everyone commits crimes? In other words, what are the forces which *control* the common propensity to crime?

There are a number of control theories with a sociological bias such as social bond theory (Hirschi 1969) and containment theory (Reckless 1967). While these sociologically orientated theories do not ignore psychological variables, there are a group of theories which stress the psychological aspects of control. It is this latter group of theories which will be of concern here.

Moral development and crime The process of socialization is linked with moral development in the theories of both Piaget (1932) and Kohlberg (1964; 1978). There are various accounts of Piaget's theories on moral development (Scaplehorn 1974), and Aronfreed (1968) compares the views of Piaget and Kohlberg. However, Kohlberg has used his theory to develop an explanation for offending and therefore this particular theory is of interest here.

Kohlberg, like Piaget, argues that moral reasoning develops in a sequential manner as the individual attains maturity. Kohlberg describes three levels of moral development, with two stages at each level. As shown in Table 2.3, at the lower stages moral reasoning is concrete in orientation, becoming more abstract at the higher stages and involving concepts such as 'justice', 'rights', and 'principles'. Offending, Kohlberg argues, is associated with a delay in the development of moral reasoning so that given the opportunity for offending the individual does not have the internal mechanisms to control and resist the temptation. A number of recent reviews have both elaborated this basic premise and discussed the empirical evidence (Blasi 1980; Jennings et al. 1983; Jurkovic 1980).

Table 2.3 Levels and stages of moral judgement in Kohlberg's Theory

Level 1: Pre-morality
    Stage 1 Punishment and obedience: moral behaviour is concerned with deferring to authority and avoiding punishment.
    Stage 2 Hedonism: the concern is with one's own needs irrespective of others' concerns.

Level 2: Conventional conformity
    Stage 3 Interpersonal concordance: moral reasoning concerned with general conformity and gaining social approval.
    Stage 4 Law and order: commitment to social order for its own sake and hence deference to social and religious authorities.

Level 3: Autonomous principles
    Stage 5 Social contract: acknowledgement of individual rights and the role of the democratic process in deriving laws.
    Stage 6 Universal ethical principles: moral judgement determined by justice, respect, and trust and may transcend legal dictates.

The main body of experimental evidence compares the moral judgements of delinquents and non-delinquents. The results are mixed with some studies finding that young offenders use less mature reasoning than non-offenders (Campagna and Harter 1975; Fodor 1972); others failing to show any distinction between the two groups (Alterman et al. 1978; C.K. Miller et al. 1974). There are two procedural explanations for these varied results: the first is the failure to control for behavioural and personality correlates of moral development; the second is the possibility of variations according to the type of offence within the offender population. Indeed, Thornton and Reid (1982) reported that convicted criminals who had offended for no financial gain (assault, murder, sex offences) showed more mature moral judgement than those who offended for money (robbery, burglary, theft, fraud). Thus, as Jurkovic notes: 'Not only do they (delinquents) vary from one another in stage of moral judgement, but they also fluctuate in their own reasoning level on different moral problems' (1980: 724).

As both Ross and Fabiano (1985) and Arbuthnot and Gordon (1986) point out, the concept of moral development is not a simple one and a number of important distinctions require clarification within the overall framework. While research has focused on the *content* of the offender's moral code, that is the offender's beliefs and attitudes, this contextual aspect can be contrasted with the *process* of moral reasoning. It is an assumption that process is related to content: while delayed development may be the cause of an antisocial moral code, it is also possible that as Ross and Fabiano suggest: 'One can argue eloquently and convincingly about social/moral issues yet have a personal set of values which are entirely self-serving, hedonistic or anti-social' (1985: 169). Further, the assumption of a relationship between moral reasoning, moral values, and behaviour must also be queried: several well-known experiments have shown that people will behave in ways which they believe or know to be wrong (Asch 1952; Milgram 1963).

In summary, there are a number of doubts about the general applicability of moral development theory to crime. A direct causal link between moral functioning and criminal behavour remains to be established. Further, tests of moral development which assess answers to hypothetical moral and social issues have also been criticized as having little relevance to the type of thinking an offender engages in when deciding whether to commit a crime (Jurkovic 1980). Indeed, studies of thinking prior to offending show that the criminal is not concerned with moral issues, but rather with the likelihood of being successful (J. Carroll and Weaver 1986). Cognitive, social, and moral development are the subjects of much recent research (Gilligan 1982; Morash 1983) and it may be that these advances will be applied to delinquent populations in the future to respond to some of the doubts expressed above.

Eysenck's theory of crime Eysenck's theory, which is also a control theory, incorporates biological, social, and individual factors. The basis of the theory is that through genetic endowment some individuals are born with cortical and autonomic nervous systems which affect their ability to learn from, or more properly to *condition* to, environmental stimuli. An individual's behaviour, influenced by both biological and social factors, defines that person's *personality*. H.J. Eysenck (1959) defined two dimensions of personality, *extraversion* (E) and *neuroticism* (N); later work (H.J. Eysenck and S.B.G. Eysenck 1968) described a third dimension, *psychoticism* (P). Each of these dimensions is conceived as a continuum with most people falling in the middle range and, it follows, with comparatively few people at the extremes of each scale. Extraversion runs from high (extravert) to low (introvert); similarly neuroticism runs from high (neurotic) to low (stable); as also does psychoticism.

The extravert is considered as cortically *under*aroused and therefore is continually seeking stimulation to maintain cortical arousal at an optimal level: thus the extravert is impulsive and seeks excitement. The introvert is cortically *over*aroused and therefore tries to avoid stimulation to keep arousal levels down to a comfortable, optimal level: introverts are therefore characterized by a quiet, reserved demeanour. In terms of conditioning, that is learning by Pavlovian conditioning or association rather than operant conditioning — see Bartol (1980) for a full account — the theory maintains that extraverts condition less efficiently than introverts. Neuroticism, sometimes called emotionality, is argued to be related to the functioning of the autonomic nervous system (ANS). Individuals at the high extreme of this continuum are characterized by a very labile ANS, which causes strong reactions to any unpleasant or painful stimuli: High N individuals display moody, anxious behaviour. Low N individuals have a very stable ANS and so display calm, even-tempered behaviour even when under stress. As with E, N is also linked with conditionability: High N leads to poor conditioning because of the vitiating effects of anxiety; Low N leads to efficient conditioning. As assessed by standard psychometric tests, each individual scores on both E and N; therefore their position on these two dimensions of personality can be plotted as shown in Figure 2.1.

As conditionability is related to levels of E and N it is further suggested that stable introverts (Low N-Low E) will condition best; stable extraverts (Low N-High E) and neurotic introverts (High N-Low E) will be at some mid-point; while neurotic extraverts (High N-High E) will condition least well.

The third personality dimension, psychoticism (P), is not so well formulated as E and N: while maintaining a genetic basis for P, its biological basis has not been described in detail (H.J. Eysenck and S.B.G. Eysenck 1968; 1976). Indeed, various descriptions of P have been offered: initially intended to distinguish the personality underlying psychosis, as opposed

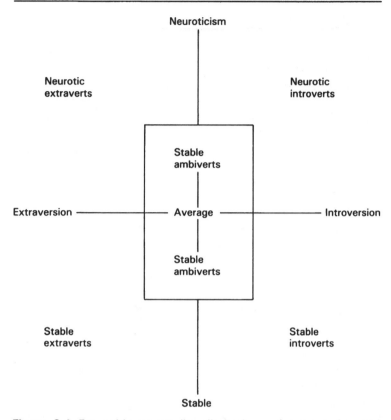

Figure 2.1 Eysenck's personality dimensions of extraversion and neuroticism

to neurosis, the suggestion was later made that P might better denote psychopathy than psychoticism (S.B.G. Eysenck and H.J. Eysenck 1972). The P scale assesses attributes such as a preference for solitude, a lack of feeling for others, sensation-seeking, tough-mindedness, and aggression. Although recently revised (S.B.G. Eysenck *et al.* 1985), there is still some doubt about what exactly the P scale is measuring (Howarth 1986).

The relationship between personality and crime has been described and refined by H.J. Eysenck, (1964; 1970; 1977) and recent summaries are available (H.J. Eysenck 1984; 1987). The principal assumption is that children learn to control antisocial behaviour through the development of a 'conscience': this conscience, Eysenck maintains, is a set of conditioned emotional responses to environmental events associated with the antisocial behaviour. For example the child who misbehaves incurs parental wrath; the fear and pain this brings is associated with the antisocial act, and through this conditioning process the child becomes socialized. The speed and efficiency of social conditioning will mainly depend upon the individual's personality in terms of E and N. As the High E-High N combination leads to poor conditionablity then such individuals will be least likely to learn social control and therefore, it is predicted, will be over-represented in offender populations. Conversely Low E-Low N would lead to effective socialization, so that these individuals would be predicted to be under-represented in offender groups. The remaining two combinations, High E-Low N and Low E-High N, fall at some intermediate level and so would be expected in both offender and non-offender groups. The third personality dimension, P, is also argued to be strongly related to offending, particularly with crimes which involve hostility towards other people. H.J. Eysenck suggests that 'In general terms, we would expect persons with strong antisocial inclinations to have high P, high E, and high N scores' (1977: 58). It is important to note the use of the term *antisocial*: as H.J. Eysenck (1977; 1984) is at pains to point out, not all crimes are antisocial in the general sense of that term. There are politically motivated crimes, impulsive crimes, crimes committed by the intellectually disadvantaged, and so on. In other words, some allowance has to be made for the heterogeneity of the offender population.

Eysenck's theory of crime has generated a great deal of empirical research and there are several reviews of the findings up to 1980 (Bartol 1980; H.J. Eysenck 1977; Feldman 1977; Powell 1977). The broad position is that there is unanimous support for the contention that offenders will score highly on P, and the majority of studies show that offender samples score highly on N. The evidence is mixed for E: some studies reported high E scores as predicted in offender samples, others found no difference between offender and non-offender samples, and a small number of studies reported *lower* scores in offender groups. The general pattern for P, E, and N is similar with both young and adult offender groups. In seeking to account for the discrepant findings for E, S.B.G. Eysenck and H.J. Eysenck (1971) suggested that E might be split into two subscales, Sociability and Impulsiveness, with only the latter related to offending. A study by S.B.G. Eysenck and McGurk (1980) confirmed that an offender sample scored higher than a non-offender sample on Impulsiveness, with no difference between the two samples on a measure of Sociability.

There are two important points to note with regard to these early investigations: the majority of studies have examined the personality traits singly rather than in combination; and few studies have attempted to control for the type of crime. It will be recalled that Eysenck's theory is specifically concerned with the combined effects of different personality traits and with antisocial crimes. A small number of studies have attended to these specific aspects of the theory.

Two studies by Allsopp and Feldman (1975; 1976) suggested that P, E, and N in combination provided support for Eysenck's theory. The most compelling evidence is presented in a more recent study by McGurk and McDougall (1981). McGurk and McDougall report the results of a cluster analysis of the P, E, and N scores of 100 delinquents and 100 non-delinquent college pupils. As shown in Table 2.4, the analysis showed four personality clusters in each group: both groups contained Low E-High N and High E-Low N clusters, but the clusters predicted to be related to criminal behaviour — High E-High N and High P-High E-High N — were, indeed, found only in the delinquent sample. The Low E-Low N group, which the theory would predict to be highly socialized, was found only in the non-delinquent group. McEwan (1983) attempted a similar analysis with a delinquent population and also found four personality clusters. With a more rigorous definition for 'high' and 'low', McEwan's analysis gave rather different clusters to McGurk and McDougall (see Table 2.4). While the High E-High N combination figures prominently, the other groups show varying degrees of dissimilarity with those reported in the previous study. Another study by McEwan and Knowles (1984) also produced four clusters, once again with similarities and differences to the other studies (see Table 2.4).

With regard to type of offence, Hindelang and Weis (1972) found mixed support for the predicted relationship between personality type and nature of offence. Their findings indicated that the High E-High N cluster was significantly associated with general deviancy (behaviour such as petty theft and vandalism) but not with major theft and aggression. S.B.G. Eysenck et al. (1977) compared the P, E, and N scores of groups of offenders: 'conmen' showed lower P scores than the other groups, while property and violent offender groups had lower N scores. The groups did not differ on the E scale. McEwan and Knowles (1984) failed to show any significant variation in the types of offences committed by the personality clusters in their study (see Table 2.4). In terms of numbers of offences, McEwan (1983) compared the criminal records of the

Table 2.4 Eysenck's Theory: summary of cluster analysis studies

	Delinquents		Non-delinquents	
McGurk and McDougall (1981)	Low E-High N	(32%)	Low E-High N	(17%)
(n = 100 in each group)	High E-Low N	(26%)	High E-Low N	(36%)
	High E-High N	(30%)	Low E-Low N	(13%)
	High P-High E-High N	(12%)	High P	(34%)
McEwan (1983)	Low E	(32%)		
(n = 186)	High P-High E	(12%)	(No non-delinquent	
	High E-High N	(36%)	group)	
	Low P-High E-Low N	(20%)		
McEwan and Knowles (1984)	Low P	(35%)		
(n = 102)	High E-Low N	(25%)	(No non-delinquent	
	Low E-High N	(14%)	group)	
	High P-High E-High N	(26%)		

Note: Percentage of group in each cluster shown in parentheses.

subgroups defined in the first part of his study (see Table 2.4). The subgroup with the high P score proved to have significantly more previous convictions than the other subgroups.

The weight of empirical evidence lends support to Eysenck's thesis that there is a relationship between personality (as he defines it) and crime. Indeed, a self-report study of a range of predictors of delinquency showed that P was by far the strongest predictor (Furnham 1984). Following a detailed exposition of the theory Feldman concludes that the 'Eysenckian personality dimensions are likely to make a useful contribution to the explanation of criminal behaviour' (1977: 161).

While this may prove to be the case, a number of reservations, as Eysenck acknowledges, need to be made. The theory does not explain all crime and, with its concentration on extremes of the scale, is not applicable to all offenders. Further, one of the theoretical bases of the theory, the link between classical conditioning and socialization, remains to be established satisfactorily (Raine and Venables 1981). On a broader front the Eysenckian personality traits are not the only personality traits to have been described; studies have pointed to other personality dimensions which may be associated with criminal behaviour (Fraas and Price 1972; McGurk *et al.* 1981; McGurk and McGurk 1979). Still further, the theory demands acceptance of a trait theory of personality which is only one of a number of ways of conceptualizing 'personality' (Phares 1984), and one which has come under fierce attack (Mischel 1968).

In summary, Eysenck's theory is important, emphasizing the inter-action between biological, environmental, and psychological factors. Integration of the theory into mainstream criminology, bearing in mind the various shortcomings, would be one way of bringing individual factors into more sociologically oriented views of crime.

Perspective

A great deal of psychological research and theory on criminal behaviour has played what Toch (1979) calls the 'cause-and-effect game'. The aim of this approach to understanding crime is to isolate the variables (i.e. 'causes') which produce criminal behaviour. As discussed above, these 'causes' have included biological factors such as genes, or psychological factors such as personality or intelligence. Similarly some sociological theories of crime play the same game: in this case the crucial variable becomes social in nature rather than biological or psychological: thus it is poverty, class structure, or family relationships which cause criminal behaviour. Other theories attempt complex, interactional explanations of crime, in which a mixture of biological, psychological, and environmental variables causes the criminal behaviour. This search for a cause of crime is clearly within a positivist tradition in that it seeks to account for criminal behaviour by recourse to factors outside the individual's control. The methodology typically used in this research is 'scientific' in orientation: that is the research seeks to use agreed principles and methods to control, measure, and determine relation-ships between variables in a manner which should give results later work can replicate. Studies which have adopted this positivist style of scientific determinism have considerably advanced the general level of understanding of criminal behaviour; although there are practical and theoretical limitations to this approach to understanding crime. However, before discussing these limitations, it is worthwhile taking a small detour to look closely at the recent interest in cognition and crime.

There is perhaps a tendency to see cognition as at last providing the missing link in explaining the cause of crime — *pace* Yochelson and Samenow. Is this a realistic position? The answer lies in the status accorded to cognition with two views of particular importance here: cognition may be portrayed as 'free will', an independent, autonomous force, controlling and guiding behaviour; or it may be viewed as an integrated part of human functioning, an attribute which plays a part in our interaction with the environment. Ross and Fabiano expand the latter view: 'Social cognitive skills are *learned* skills; their acquisition is very strongly influenced by environmental factors. . . . The effects of poverty, lack of stimulation, or lack of novelty in one's environment can severely restrict the individual's cognitive development' (1985: 143).

With research which stressed the defects, deficits, and developmental delays in cognition or, indeed, morality, a positivist position was evident: the deficit distinguished the offender from the rest of the normal, non-criminal population thereby providing the cause of the criminal behaviour. Although some contemporary commentators such as Ross and Fabiano dissociate themselves from this view by making it clear that 'We do not suggest that cognitive deficits are a *cause* of crime' (1985: 11). However, when the view is advanced, as in 'rational-choice' theory, that the criminal reasons and makes decisions in the same rational manner as the rest of the population, then classical theories seem not too distant. The criminal may be depicted as acting of his or her own free will in deciding to commit a criminal act. Cornish and Clarke seem aware of this possibility in posing a 'disquieting question': 'If most criminal behaviour is portrayed as rational, normal, and commonplace, what will be the effect upon everyday thinking and moralizing about crime?' (1986a: 15). The answer is probably self-evident and underpins, in part at least, the swing to a 'justice model' in seeking to prevent crime (see Chapter 7).

There is no simple answer but a response could be formulated, in a positivist tradition, that although the *process* of decision-making is sound, the *content* of the cognition is flawed. As the content is learned then so we return to familiar grounds. While this may be tenable, it remains within a consensus view of crime, that is the criminal is different from the rest of the population. An alternative to this view might stress the normality of crime, cognition included, but within an interactionist or radical framework. The emergence of cognitive theories of crime, while providing a more complete picture of the criminal, do not in my opinion provide any answers to questions of the causes of crime.

This general failure to discover the 'cause' of crime is also associated with the limitations of scientific determinism in the field of criminology. As noted previously, there are two aspects to this limitation: practical difficulties and theoretical shortcomings. The practical difficulties lie in the number of variables thought to be important in crime: for example Cyril Burt (1925) enumerated some 170 variables involved in understanding delinquency. Even if it were possible to measure accurately these variables, control of such vast numbers of variables in an individual study is impossible. It follows that this leads to sampling variations between studies so that results are produced which continually prove difficult to replicate: hence the continual reference to the 'heterogeneity of the offender population'. (This point is characteristic not only of research into crime, but also of psychological research generally.) There is no ready answer to this, other than carefully designed and documented studies which acknowledge the limitations of the data.

At a theoretical level, psychological research continues to elucidate variables which are associated with crime, but then attempts to explain crime by recourse to psychological rather than criminological theories. Thus criminal behaviour becomes a defence mechanism, or the result of failed maternal attachment, or an extreme of personality development, rather than a phenomenon deserving explanation in its own right. Further, as the psychological theory called on to explain criminal behaviour is typically one which is used to account for psychological abnormality, it is not difficult to appreciate why comments of the type below appear in the literature.

Psychological theories are useful as explanations of the behavior of deeply disturbed, impulsive, or destructive people. However, they are limited as general explanations of criminality. For one thing, the phenomenon of crime and delinquency is so widespread that to claim that all criminals are psychologically disturbed is to make that claim against the vast majority of people. (Siegal 1986: 175–6)

Does this mean that there is but a limited role for psychology in explaining crime? I believe the answer is 'yes' if research continues in the tradition to date. A great number of studies have provided important findings about criminal behaviour but, by drawing solely on theories from mainstream psychology, severely limit the criminological sense of the data. This strategy may go some way toward refining psychological theory, but contributes much less towards explaining crime. Alternatively the role of psychology in explaining crime can, I believe, be an important one if the emphasis is switched to establishing *functional relationships* between relevant psychological, biological, and environmental variables and crime. In order to achieve this aim two points are paramount. The findings of psychological research on criminal behaviour should be discussed with reference to criminological theories (which may, of course, include elements of psychological theory). Also, as well as elaborating on the function of psychological factors, there should also be a contribution from psychology in considering the role of environmental influences, such as the courts and public opinion about crime, in producing and maintaining criminal behaviour. Given this, psychological enquiry may well contribute substantially to understanding crime.

Chapter three

Psychological approaches to understanding serious crime

As crime surveys have shown, most crimes which involve an identifiable person as the victim of the act are relatively trivial in that they involve minor damage to property or thefts of small sums of money. While some victims of such minor crimes do experience adverse reactions following the crime, most victims regain their equilibrium. However, there are crimes against the person which are much more likely to produce adverse long-term effects for the victim, and may either endanger or take life. These two considerations of potentially highly damaging long-term consequences and a threat to life are used here to define serious crime. Such crimes can be seen to fall into two, not necessarily exclusive, broad categories — *violent offences* and *sexual offences*. This chapter will discuss the contribution psychology has made to the understanding of these two types of crime.

Violent crime

Psychological theories of aggression and violence

It should be noted that there is a variability in terminology in the literature: three terms are in common, sometimes interchangeable, use, *aggression*, *violence*, and *criminal violence*. Megargee (1982) and Siann (1985) discuss the issue of definition and have informed the meaning of the terms as used here: aggression refers to the intention to hurt or gain advantage over other people, without necessarily involving physical injury; violence involves the use of strong physical force against another person, sometimes impelled by aggressive motivation; criminal violence involves directly injurious behaviour which is forbidden by law. While concern here is with psychological theories, there are theories from other disciplines, such as anthropology and biology. A number of texts cover the full range of theories (Baron 1977; Siann 1985; Zillman 1979), while Mednick *et al.* (1982) review biological factors, Merikangas (1981) discusses neurological theories, and Riches (1986) details the anthropology of violence. In turning to psychological theories it is plain that there is considerable overlap with other theories. This is true of the first class of theories to be discussed, those theories which postulate some instinctual drive towards aggressive and violent behaviour.

Instinct theories A number of theorists have used the notion of an instinct, an innate impulse, to account for aggression and violence. Within Freud's writings, for example, there is the view that human behaviour is driven by two basic instincts, the life instinct (Eros) and the death force (Thanatos). In the conflict between the instincts of life and death the destructive energy is displaced to the external world. Aggression can be likened to a safety valve as it reduces the energy levels within the system to acceptable levels. If the aggressive behaviour can take the form of non-destructive and socially acceptable acts, then the probability of violence is correspondingly reduced. Such cathartic release might take the form of anger or participating in acceptable aggression such as sport. This 'neutralizing' of the aggressive instinct can go astray so that the aggression becomes 'internalized', potentially culminating in violence, murder, or suicide (Kutash 1978).

Lorenz (1966) approached the study of aggression from an ethological perspective. Following observation and study of animals, Lorenz proposed that aggression stems directly from an innate 'fighting instinct'. This instinct, it is suggested, has evolved over generations owing to its benefits for the survival of the species — *homo sapiens* included. As with Freud's explanation, aggressive energy is seen as continually mounting within the individual and so has, at some point, to be vented. This venting can occur in two ways: a specific environmental aggression-releasing stimulus triggers an aggressive act; or, if the build-up of energy is not released in 'safe' amounts, a violent eruption relieves the tension.

Storr (1970) sought to fuse the psychoanalytic and ethological theories of aggression. Storr agreed that aggressive behaviour stems from an instinctive impulse, biologically determined, which seeks discharge before reaching critical levels. Storr extended the argument by suggesting that the way in which an individual manifests aggression in later life results from unconscious motivations derived from childhood emotional experiences. Further, should negative events occur in the period when the individual seeks to deal with the aggressive drive, then the psychopathological aspects of aggression — typified by depression, schizoid behaviour, and paranoia — may result from the unresolved drive. Fromm (1977), while primarily working within a psychoanalytic tradition, argued that it is necessary to go beyond individual factors and consider the role of social, economic, and political influences in precipitating aggression and violence.

The criticisms of instinct theories centre on conceptual ambiguities and a lack of empirical verification. There is little hard evidence to demonstrate an instinctual biological drive, nor do there appear to be environmental releasers of aggression in humans. Critics suggest that in the balance between innate and learned behaviour, instinct theories inadvisedly prefer biological to social forces — although Storr, for example, has attempted to meet this point.

Drive theory An alternative to explanations based on an innate aggressive instinct followed the development of the concept of a reactive drive. A 'drive' which motivates a particular behaviour, including violence, was seen as being acquired through experience rather than being innate. As the level of the drive increased so the individual is motivated to find conditions in which behaviours can take place which reduce the drive. This amalgam of ideas from psychoanalytic and early behavioural psychology as a means of explaining aggression was advanced by Dollard *et al.* (1939). The theory proposed that if a goal was blocked and expected rewards were not forthcoming, this produces a state of frustration; the frustration instigates aggression leading to aggressive or violent behaviour. The aggressive or violent behaviour may be directed at either the source of the frustration, or displaced to other targets which have some relationship with the primary source of the frustration. Later work pointed to the distinction between 'hostile aggression' and 'instrumental aggression': the former being where the aggression is intended to injure the victim, the latter where the aggression is simply a means to an end as in, for example, armed robbery (Buss 1961).

Dollard *et al.*'s (1939) thesis generated a body of research work which led to a number of reformulations of aspects of the initial theory (N.E. Miller 1941). Berkowitz (1965; 1974) proposed one such modification which has gained prominence. In contrast to the original drive theory, Berkowitz (1965) suggested that frustration produces a state of emotional arousal, or 'anger', which creates a potential for aggression. In order for this potential to be realized, an 'anger-eliciting cue' must be present: this cue, or stimulus, takes the form of something the individual associates with aggression, such as another person's behaviour or the presence of a weapon. This view was taken a stage further with the suggestion that a strong environmental stimuli could produce aggression or violence in the absence of the prior angry state (Berkowitz 1974).

One of the strengths of drive theory was that it offered hypotheses which could be tested experimentally. As a body of research duly amassed, it became apparent that the theory lacked full explanatory power and so attention turned to a search for new theories. As Bornstein *et al.* note: 'As a result of the deteriorating empirical status of instinct and drive theories of aggression, the social learning perspective . . . has grown rapidly in popularity and support in the past decade' (1981: 316).

Social learning theory Bandura (1973a; 1973b) suggested that there are three crucial aspects to an understanding of aggression: the *acquisition* of the aggressive behaviour; the process of *instigation* of the aggression; and the conditions which *maintain* the aggression. As noted in Chapter 2, social learning theory argues that acquisition of behaviour occurs through the process of learning, either through direct experience or by observation. There is empirical evidence to suggest that aggressive behaviour can be acquired through direct reinforcement (Hayes *et al.* 1980), and via observation (Bandura *et al.* 1963). With regard to instigation, Bandura (1973b) noted that the anticipated outcome, in turn the product of previous learning, was vitally important. The anticipation, signalled by environmental cues previously associated with aggression, not only made aggression more likely, but also pointed to the potential victims of the aggression.

Alongside anticipated outcome, Bandura also suggested that aversive environmental conditions such as high temperatures, air pollution, and crowding can act to raise emotional arousal and so facilitate the instigation of aggression. A suggestion supported by recent research findings (Anderson 1987; Rotton and Frey 1985); while it has also been shown that verbal and physical provocation can have a similar effect (Dengerink *et al.* 1978). The effects of provocation have been explained both in terms of the anticipated consequences, such as loss of self-esteem, of failing to respond; and also in terms of the cognitive appraisal of the provocation. An act *perceived* as provocative and antagonistic is liable to increase 'angry' arousal and aggression (Novaco 1976; 1978). Although as Novaco (1978) notes, there may be a reciprocal relationship between cognition and anger such that particular cognitions induce anger, while experiencing anger can lead the individual to think in an aggressive manner. Similar reciprocal relationships, as shown in Figure 3.1, may function between cognition and behaviour, and between anger and behaviour. Finally, from a social learning theory perspective, the maintenance of aggression is through the three types of reinforcement: external reinforcement, vicarious reinforcement, and self-reinforcement.

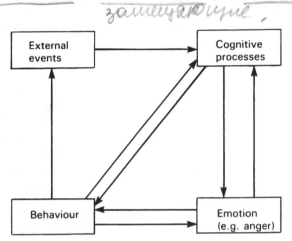

Figure 3.1 Schematic representation of the relationship between cognition, emotion, and behaviour (based on Novaco 1978)

Siann (1985) makes a number of criticisms of psychological theories of aggression as detailed thus far: as a result of laboratory-based research they show a too narrow approach to aggression; they are limited by positivist methodology; and they show a poor conception of human motivation. Siann suggests that aggression might best be considered as a *social* phenomenon; a phenomenon best studied 'in the real world of perceived and actual inequalities, environmental stress and political conflict' (1985: 165).

Social accounts Toch (1969) presents the details of a series of interviews with violent men in an attempt to place violence within a social context and so move towards a 'phenomenology of violence'. Toch's work views violence from the offender's perspective, being concerned with the meaning or sense of the act for that person within the social context in which the act occurred. Toch describes different uses of violence such as alleviating tension in awkward social situations or for defending personal reputations. Typically violence occurs when another person is seen as a threat and some action is taken to respond to the threat; the other person reacts, the instigator responds again, and the *interaction* escalates towards violence. A tradition of social research has followed this style of investigation, with recent work examining the 'rules of disorder' (Marsh and Campbell 1982; Marsh *et al.* 1978). This research has shown that some violence, such as between football fans, is rule-bound to the extent that it is agreed that fights should take place between equal numbers and that certain forms of fighting are not allowed.

Other accounts, mainly from sociologists rather than psychologists, have concentrated even further on the social setting. Wolfgang and Ferracuti (1967) argued that there are subcultures, usually involving young men, in which violence is the legitimate norm: the function of the violence is to provide excitement and a means of achieving status. This argument is supported by the various studies which have shown that violence is prevalent in parts of large cities, and involves a disproportionate number of young males (N.A. Weiner and Wolfgang 1985). In accounting for these violent subcultures it has been suggested that they are the result of the anger and frustration caused by social and economic inequalities (J. Blau and P. Blau 1982; Block 1979; L. Carroll and Jackson 1983), or the product of conflict between opposed cultures (W. Miller 1976). Box (1983) follows a radical criminology approach, arguing that 'violence' is defined by the powerful social classes for the purposes of social control. Thus deaths resulting from the failure to test a drug properly, or inadequate health and safety precautions in a work-place, are not seen as 'murder', but are described as 'accidents' or 'regrettable incidents'. This strategy serves two basic functions: it deflects culpability from the privileged classes; and it locates 'real' crimes in the lower classes.

As with most social accounts two problems arise: the difficulty of including the full range of social factors; and the tendency to exclude individual factors. It is difficult to resist the conclusion that an interactive theory is required, one which seeks to place individual behaviour within a social and political context. Psychological research has contributed to both strands: in the following sections research is discussed which has examined both the situations in which violent crime occurs, and the characteristics of the violent person.

Analysis of the violent situation

The situational approach to understanding violence is firmly established in the psychological literature as one which seeks to analyse the environmental factors associated with violent acts (Monahan and Klassen 1982). In this section the focus is on research which has analysed the contexts in which the crimes of serious assault, robbery and murder occur.

Serious assault Serious assault may be defined as an attack which inflicts severe wounding and physical assault on the victim. (The term, as used here, excludes sexual assaults.) M. Henderson (1986) reported an exhaustive analysis of violent incidents following lengthy interviews with forty-four prison inmates serving sentences for wounding, attempted murder, grievous bodily harm, and actual bodily harm. The transcripts of the interviews were coded across a range of categories such as victim age and sex, place of incident, and time of day. A cluster analysis of the 246 violent incidents described by the interviewees revealed eight distinct types of incident as shown in Table 3.1.

Table 3.1 Typology of violent incidents (after M. Henderson 1986)

Type of violence	Victim	Most frequent means of assault	Location
Crime-related[a] (individual)	Known[b]	Kicking	Domestic
Crime-related (group)	Unknown	Gun/bottle	Domestic
Prison	Peer	Punching	Prison
Prison	Staff	Strangling	Prison
'Social'	Unknown	Punching	Pub/club
Family	Relative	Gun/knife	Domestic
Gang	Unknown	Knife/kicking	Street
'Bullying'	Young person	Slapping/bottle	Street

Notes: [a]violence during the commission of another crime such as burglary.
[b]known/unknown to the offender prior to the crime.

The immediate impact of these findings is the variety of settings, the different types of violence, and range of victims involved in the violent act. The majority of offenders reported being involved in more than one of the types of incident, with 'bullying' the most common and 'crime-related with the offender alone' least common. Within this analysis four broad categories are apparent: violence in conjunction with another crime; family violence; 'public violence'; and institutional violence. The first of these is discussed in the next section, the others deserve mention.

Family violence has rapidly become one of the social problems of the 1980s (which is not to say that it has not always existed) and a number of reviews are available (Borkowski *et al.* 1983; Gelles 1982).

Henderson's analysis shows that family violence, particularly towards women, takes place at night without the presence of other people. There is usually a history of violence between offender and victim, with the incident following an argument in which the victim has retaliated verbally but not physically. Child abuse has attracted a great deal of public and specialist interest (Frude 1980; Kempe and Helfer 1980; Maher 1987). The physical abuse of the child typically takes the form of maltreatment such as burning or beatings with hand, feet, or weapons; alternatively the abuse may take the form of extreme neglect leading to starvation, illness, and so on. In either case the effects are severe and can be fatal.

The dynamics of family violence between husband and wife were described in a study by Dobash and Dobash (1984) of over 100 battered wives. From both personal interviews and official records Dobash and Dobash constructed a pattern of violence, most often taking place in the family home, which began with a verbal confrontation, often construed by the man as a challenge to his authority. As the pattern unfolds the woman typically attempts to avert the forthcoming violence using strategies such as attempting to withdraw from the situation, or trying to reason or debate with the man. As the attack begins, involving slapping, punching, butting, hitting with sticks and other weapons, the woman continues to try to negotiate a way out of the violence. The woman hits back physically in only a very few instances, then out of anger or frustration; the general effect of this was to increase the level of violence. During the majority of assaults there were bystanders present, most often children. The bystanders mainly tried to support the woman, either by begging the man to stop or by running for help. After the attack, which resulted in a range of physical injury inflicted on the woman, the men were reported as acting as if nothing had happened, with few expressing remorse or regret. The injured women sought contact with friends, social and medical agencies, or voluntary bodies for both solace and help. Dobash and Dobash suggest that the quality of the response to this search for contact is vital: an outright condemnation of the violence is entirely more supportive than an implicit blaming of the woman by looking for ways in which she might have caused the violence to take place.

M. Henderson's (1986) analysis showed that 'public violence' is of two types — either involving gangs or taking place in pubs or clubs. Henderson describes two types of gang violence. In the first a group attacks a victim at night, usually after drinking hours; the victim is not known to the attackers but is also liable to have been drinking; weapons are used, as well as kicking, which can result in death. The second type of gang violence Henderson describes as 'bullying', in which younger victims are slapped and pushed, resulting in serious injury. Violence associated with pubs tends to be between individuals, with the offender's associates as onlookers rather than fellow attackers. The offender and victim have both been drinking and violence follows an argument instigated by the victim. In the fight both offender and victim sustain injuries.

Finally Henderson describes two types of institutional violence: violence towards either fellow inmates or towards authority figures. In Henderson's study the violence was towards other prisoners and police and prison staff, although violence can occur in other institutions. W. Davies (1982) discusses prison violence in detail, including hostage-taking; and Drinkwater (1982) reviews violence in psychiatric hospitals.

Robbery Robbery is the theft, or attempted theft, of property or money directly from another person; the theft is accompanied by the use of physical force or the threat of physical harm. In some cases the robber is armed, although most armed robbers use their weapons to intimidate rather than to inflict injury (Dinitz *et al.* 1975). This is not to say that, given the circumstances, the weapons would not be used. McClintock and Gibson (1961) carried out a study of robbery in London and described five situations in which the offence occurred. The first takes place in a bank or jewellers, involving the offender and the staff of the shop or bank. In the second, the offence takes place on the street, including crimes such as 'mugging' and handbag-snatching. The third, robbery on private premises, is unusual in that it involves breaking into a house to commit the offence. When the robbery takes place indoors it is more commonly between two people who know each other: thus in the fourth and fifth types of robbery, the offence takes place either between people who have only a short acquaintance, say at a party, or between people who have known each other for longer periods. McClintock and Gibson found overall that stranger-to-stranger robberies are much more common, accounting for over three-quarters of all robberies.

M. Henderson (1986) described two situations in which violence occurred during the course of stealing. In one the violence was directed towards a stranger, often older than the group of offenders, within the victim's home during daylight hours. Weapons are used causing serious injury and the offenders report a lack of emotion in committing the offence. In the second type the offender is alone at night in the victim's house. The violence, typically involving women or elderly people, takes the form of kicking and can be fatal. The offender reports being drunk at the time of the offence, feeling anxious, losing control, and afterwards saying that the victim did not deserve their injuries. These two types of robberies can be described in terms of the distinction referred to previously between 'instrumental' and 'hostile' aggression (Buss 1961). In the first instance the violence is simply instrumental in achieving the goal of obtaining money. The second instance bears the hallmarks of a 'burglary gone wrong': upon discovery the offender panics, loses control, perhaps because of the effects of drink, and hits out at the householder; the simple burglary escalates to robbery or even murder.

Murder Murder is the *intentional* taking of the life of another person. The emphasis on intent is crucial: if a life is taken without premeditated intent to kill then the act is termed manslaughter. It is, of course, often a matter for the courts to decide whether an act was premeditated and therefore one of murder not manslaughter. Murder is not a common crime: in England and Wales, for example, the 1985 Criminal Statistics show that there were 173 convictions for murder, with a further 35 convictions for attempted murder (Home Office 1985). Similarly, Siegal (1986) notes that in 1984 the murder rate in the USA was 7.9 offences per 100,000 inhabitants. As discussed in Chapter 1, official figures do not necessarily reflect the real levels of a particular crime. This is true of murder: some murders go undetected, in other cases the murderer commits suicide after killing; nevertheless it is probably the case that, in relation to the total number of crimes committed, murder is an uncommon act.

Wolfgang (1958) presents an analysis of the situations in which 588 murders took place in Philadelphia between 1948 and 1952. In a substantial number of cases (37 per cent) the killing followed a relatively trivial event such as an argument, threat, or insult; in the majority of cases the offender and victim knew each other (87 per cent); the offender and victim were almost always of the same race (94 per cent). The majority of murderers were male (82 per cent), usually less than 35 years of age; most victims were also male (76 per cent); and stabbing was the most common means of causing death. The offender, victim, or both had usually been drinking (66 per cent), and offenders typically had previous arrest records, usually for violent crime (66 per cent). The murders most frequently occurred in a domestic setting during the summer months, most often between the hours of 8 pm Saturday and 2 am Sunday. The incidents which were the most violent in character occurred between husband and wife.

Most subsequent surveys broadly agree with Wolfgang's findings, although there are several exceptions. An English study found that the majority (60 per cent) of victims are female (Gibson and Kline 1961); a study in Chicago found that offender and victim were related in fewer instances (58 per cent), and that firearms were more frequently used (Block 1977). Goldstein (1986) presents an analysis of the motives for murder from the 1983 American figures and suggests that about 20 per cent of murders were related to another crime such as robbery, while 44 per cent were associated with arguments. In total, the general picture is of a crime which commonly takes place between people who are at least acquainted and have argued, perhaps following drinking.

While the surveys paint an overall picture, a study by Luckenbill (1977) vividly illuminates the fine detail. Luckenbill analysed the interactions between offender and victim in the time immediately before the act of murder. From this analysis he described six stages in 'transactions resulting in murder'. In stage one the opening move comes from the victim in the form of a verbal comment, or refusal to comply with a request (mostly in child murder), or some physical act such as flirtation. In some instances an insult was clearly intended, in others the offender interpreted the victim's behaviour as offensive. In stage two the offender seeks confirmation of the insult, either by verbally checking with the victim, or with anyone else who might be present; the victim's continuation of the behaviour can also act as confirmation of the insult. In some instances the 'confirmation' is inferred: for example a child's continued screaming confirms refusal to comply with the instruction to be quiet. At stage three the offender opts not to retreat but to stand his or her ground and retaliate. In most cases the retaliation at this stage is verbal, although in a minority of instances it is physical and the murder results. At stage four the victim replies to the retaliation; as Luckenbill notes, 'The victim's move appeared as an agreement that violence was suitable to the transaction' (1977: 183). The victim's move is a continuation of the offensive behaviour, a verbal counter-challenge, or physical attack. This move was often supported by onlookers or others present. With stage five battle commences, usually with a weapon to hand: the act is generally brief, Luckenbill reports that in over half the murders the offender 'dropped the victim in a single shot, stab, or rally of blows' (1977: 185). In the sixth and final stage the murderer acts in one of three ways: he or she voluntarily waits for the police; is held by others present; or flees the scene.

Luckenbill portrays a crime which is not simply perpetrated by one person: 'Rather, murder is the outcome of a dynamic interchange between an offender, victim, and, in many cases, bystanders' (1977: 185). This view of the victim as playing a role, perhaps even a causative role, in determining their fate has been a source of some controversy. Dobash and Dobash (1984), for example, concluded their study of battered wives discussed previously with the note that their research failed to support any interpretation which shifted the blame for the attack from the aggressor to the victim. While not discounting the possibility that Luckenbill's analysis may have some relevance in understanding violence between males, Dobash and Dobash argue that gender and its associated roles and meanings must be considered when male violence is directed at female victims. However, at a general theoretical level, Dobash and Dobash are unhappy with the notion of victim-precipitated violence: 'We would argue that many violent episodes should be understood as often constructed intentionally by the aggressor' (1984: 286).

While an analysis of social exchanges may be efficacious in explaining some murders, particularly domestic murders, there are other types of murder which seem to demand a different level of explanation. *Mass murderers* kill a number of people simultaneously: two American mass murderers, Charles Whitman and James Huberty, killed fourteen and twenty-one people respectively in sustained violent acts, and during the time of writing this book there was in Britain the massacre at Hungerford. The *serial killer* is a mass murderer who kills over a period of time rather than in one outburst. The victims of the serial killer are typically tortured or sexually assaulted before being murdered. In some instances the serial killer may terrorize a city, such as the 'Yorkshire Ripper' in Leeds, or Kenneth Bianchi in Los Angeles: in other instances the serial killer travels the country, taking life as they move from location to location. Levin and Fox (1985) have estimated that about thirty-five mass murderers, including serial killers, are active in America at present.

Before moving on to look at the research findings from studies of the violent individual, it should be noted that there are violent crimes other than those discussed above. Assault and murder, for example, can occur through means other than direct physical violence, such as firesetting, although in some instances this may be violence towards property rather than people (R.W. Hill *et al.* 1982), and poisoning or leaving bombs in public places (MacDonald 1977; Prins 1986).

Analysis of the violent offender

Taxonomies This approach seeks to classify types of violent offender according to one or more variables (Megargee 1966). Conklin (1972) for example suggested that there are four 'specialist' types of robber. The *professional robber* views robbery as a highly effective means of earning a living: robberies, perhaps three or four a year, are carefully planned by organized teams with the victim generally a commercial institution. The *opportunist robber* steals only small amounts as and when a vulnerable target, such as a young or old person, presents itself; the act is not planned in advance. The *addict robber* and the *alcoholic robber* steal to obtain money to purchase more drugs or drink: these robberies are not likely to be planned or organized, and are generally aimed at 'easy' victims. While this general approach can be helpful in illustrating that different people commit violent crimes for different reasons and under different conditions, it does not say a great deal about the *person* involved. A body of work which has attempted to investigate the psychology of the violent offender is concerned with the link between personality and violence.

Personality The model which prompted the main line of research in personality and violence was proposed by Megargee (1966). The basis of the model is that violence occurs when the instigation to violence, mediated by anger, exceeds the individual's level of control of aggressive feelings or impulses. The *undercontrolled* person has very low inhibitors and therefore frequently acts in a violent manner when provocation is perceived. The *overcontrolled* person has extremely strong inhibitors and violence will occur only if the provocation is intense or has been endured for a very long period of time. Megargee predicted that an over-controlled personality would be found in those who have committed acts of extreme violence, but would not be found among those with histories of frequent minor assaults. Blackburn (1968) compared the personality profiles of a group of 'extreme' violent offenders, convicted of murder, manslaughter, or attempted murder, with a group of 'moderate' violent offenders who had committed acts of assault. In keeping with the prediction, the extreme group were significantly more introverted, conforming, overcontrolled, and less hostile than the moderate group; although Crawford (1977) failed to replicate this finding. Quinsey *et al.* (1983) and M. Henderson (1983a) reported that the overcontrolled violent offender showed deficiencies in assertive behaviour. Henderson (1983a) also found that violent offenders who scored low on a psychometric measure of control reported significantly more difficulty in controlling their temper and avoiding fights. While the weight of this research lends support to a distinction based on an overcontrolled–undercontrolled dichotomy, the most significant advances have come from an approach which searches for types, or clusters, of offenders based on their scores on personality measures.

Blackburn (1971) carried out a cluster analysis on the MMPI scores of fifty-six male murderers detained in a secure psychiatric hospital. The Minnesota Multiphasic Personality Inventory (MMPI) is a collection of psychometric measures, including scales such as 'psychoticism', 'dominance', 'hostility', and so on. Initially devised over forty-five years ago (Hathaway and McKinley 1940), the MMPI is a widely used device in psychological research (Graham 1977). Blackburn's analysis of MMPI scores showed four clusters of violent offenders: as shown in Table 3.2, two of these clusters were classed as overcontrolled, and two as under-controlled. The *psychopathic* group is characterized by poor impulse control, high extraversion, outward-directed hostility, low anxiety, and few psychiatric symptoms. The *paranoid-aggressive* group also displays high impulsivity and aggression, but also high levels of psychiatric disorder, particularly psychotic symptoms. These two groups are sometimes referred to as *primary psychopaths* and *secondary psychopaths*. The overcontrolled classification contains a *controlled-repressor* group which exhibits a high degree of impulse control and of defensiveness, and low levels of hostility, anxiety, and psychiatric symptoms. The second overcontrolled group is labelled *depressed-inhibited* and is characterized by low levels of impulsivity and extraversion, inward-directed hostility, and high levels of depression.

Table 3.2 Typology of violent offenders (after Blackburn 1971)

Undercontrolled	Overcontrolled
Psychopathic	Controlled-repressor
Paranoid-aggressive	Depressed-inhibited

Blackburn (1975a) replicated this finding, as did McGurk (1978) with a sample of 'normal' murderers from a prison, rather than hospital, population. M. Henderson (1982) found essentially the same four types in a sample of violent offenders from the prison population. McGurk's (1978) study also pointed to the existence of a fifth group; while Blackburn (1986) found the same four groups, a fifth similar to McGurk's additional group, and a new sixth group. However, McGurk and Blackburn are agreed that these 'extra' groups are variants of the four principal groups rather than distinct types: one is a less aggressive and withdrawn secondary psychopath; the other a more introverted variant of the controlled-repressor group with high levels of mental illness. The evidence therefore supports the fourfold classification of violent offenders. However, before beginning to explain *violent* crime, the prevalence of the four groups in other types of offenders has to be considered.

In two studies with non-violent prisoners, Holland and Holt (1975) and Widom (1978) found four personality clusters: in both studies three of the clusters corresponded to the original clusters with the exception that the depressed-inhibited group was not found. McGurk and McGurk (1979) similarly found three clusters with non-violent prisoners, once again the groups corresponded to the original groups with no depressed-inhibited group appearing in the analysis. M. Henderson (1983b) also found four clusters in an MMPI analysis of non-violent offenders, and this time the clusters matched the original analysis; that is a depressed-inhibited group was found in a non-violent population. M. Henderson (1983b) then compared the non-violent depressed-inhibited group with the same group from the violent population in her earlier study: 'Although the defining characteristics of the two are similar, the violent offender of this [inhibited] group, tends to be more disturbed, introverted, anxious and hostile than his non-violent counterpart' (M. Henderson 1982: 676). It appears, on balance, that the four personality clusters are to be found in the offender population generally, rather appearing exclusively in the violent offender population. The depressed-inhibited profile seems the most characteristic of violent offender populations and may therefore give some clues towards explaining at least some violent acts.

The theoretical position is a matter of debate. Bartol (1980) suggests that the low inhibition of the undercontrolled offender corresponds with Eysenck's proposition that anti-social behaviour is the result of a failure to condition impulse control. While in interpersonal terms, M. Henderson (1982) found that violent inhibited offenders reported difficulty in making friends and functioning as part of a social group. This strikes at the heart of the debate: violence can be seen as resulting from the effects of a stable personality trait; or it can be understood in social learning terms, with the emphasis on a person-situation interaction. Blackburn offers a succinct summary of the position to date.

In the case of the primary and secondary psychopaths, the probability of a violent outcome seems likely to be increased as a result of their typically coercive or hostile approaches to interpersonal problem-solving. For controlled and inhibited individuals, on the other hand, violence may represent a last resort when attempts to resolve a situation through compliance or avoidance break down. In these terms, this broad classification may provide a first stab at understanding a violent act in the individual case. (Blackburn 1986: 268)

While empirical research has supported and refined Megargee's original proposition of undercontrolled and overcontrolled offenders, it seems unlikely that this approach will provide an explanation for violent crime in itself. This is not surprising in that theories of aggression and violence which have relied heavily on individual factors — the instinct and drive theories — have been less than satisfactory. What is required is a marriage of the situational and individual approaches: the social detail of studies like those of Luckenbill, and Dobash and Dobash, together with the intricate psychometric profiles of Blackburn or Henderson alongside the cognitive aspect as described by Novaco. The question which remains to be answered is why some people, in some situations, commit violent acts. The 'people' part of the equation may contain elements from personality theory, or perhaps other factors such as intelligence or preference for personal space (Eastwood 1985), styles of attribution (M. Henderson and Hewstone 1984), or imitative behaviour (Bandura 1973a). The 'situation' may contain the deliberate actions of another person, comments from onlookers, or prolonged stress such as a child who will not stop screaming. Distillation of the vital explosive elements awaits further investigation.

Sexual crimes

Prins (1986) notes that the number of sexual offences in England and Wales is consistently about 10,000 per year, less than 1 one per cent of all recorded crime: a figure which, as Prins suggests, is generally accepted as substantially less than the real percentage. Amir (1971), for example, estimated that fewer than 30 per cent of rapes were reported to the police. A number of factors can lead to non-reporting of a sexual attack. The victim may not wish to face the discomfort of official questioning about the details of the crime; the victim may not want to draw public attention to the fact that she has been involved in a sex offence; the victim may fear reprisals or further attacks should she report the crime; or parents may wish to spare child victims. In some instances the victims may not perceive the forced sexual act as an assault or as rape, perhaps blaming themselves for what happened and so not reporting (Klemmack and Klemmack 1976).

There are a number of offences with sexual content: these range from acts such as exhibitionism and voyeurism, to 'victimless' crimes such as prostitution and some homosexual acts, to crimes involving attacks on women and children. In terms of serious crimes, the focus of this chapter, two aspects of sexual offending have been selected for discussion — rape and sexual offences involving children. This is not to suggest that other sexual offences are not serious, indeed they are: rather that these two offences have attracted by far the greatest amount of psychological research and so illustrate the role of psychology in understanding this particular type of serious crime. Accounts of the other sexual offences not covered here can be found in Howells (1984a) and West (1987).

Rape

A man commits rape if he has sexual intercourse with a woman who does not consent to the act. While, as mentioned above, the prevalence of rape is not known (see L.S. Williams 1984), there are grounds for thinking that there are cross-cultural variations in the prevalence of rape. Sanday (1981) surveyed 156 societies and found almost half to be rape free. Further research has highlighted three social factors which characterize 'rape cultures': the sexes are clearly separated; there is a general subscription to male dominance; male violence is sanctioned for solving personal problems. Thus if the culture is patriarchal, giving men dominance in work, family, and sex, then men can assert their dominance in a number of ways, including rape, to maintain the submissive role of women. A number of texts are available on the cultural and political aspects of rape (Brownmiller 1975; Russell 1975; 1982; Tomaselli and Porter 1986; Toner 1982) which provide the context for research which has focused on the rape itself and the psychology of the rapist.

Offence analysis With the caveat that any empirical research is limited to those cases in which the victim is willing to talk, a number of studies have analysed the situations in which rape occurs. Two American surveys found that in large cities rape is most likely to take place in the victim's home, while in small cities rape is most commonly committed in motor vehicles (Chappell *et al.* 1977; Chappell and Singer 1977). This difference reflects the victimization of hitch-hikers, who are more likely to accept lifts in country areas than in large cities. These surveys also reveal that rape most frequently takes place in the hours between 8pm and 2am, and almost always in total darkness. The obvious reason for darkness is the avoidance of detection, but there may be other reasons. Bartol (1980) and Howells (1984b) suggest that in the dark the offender may feel 'deindividualized', able to set aside any feelings of guilt and remorse, and view the victim as an object rather than a person. It is also possible that as alcohol and drugs are most frequently used in the evening and early hours of the morning that they may be involved in some way.

Ploughman and Stensrud (1986) carried out a detailed study of rape victimization in Buffalo, New York. Their starting-point, influenced by the notion of 'social ecology' (Byrne and Sampson 1986), is that: 'The circumstances under which crimes occur, including rape, appear to be neither random nor trivial but rather are socially structured phenomena that depend heavily upon the spatial and temporal organization of human activities' (Ploughman and Stensrud 1986: 306). In keeping with previous studies of city rape, Ploughman and Stensrud found that most offences took place in either the victim's home or the offender's home. The initial contact between victim and rapist most commonly happened on the street, typically a street in the offender's neighbourhood, often adjacent to the victim's neighbourhood. Most offences were committed between 8pm and 8am, with Saturday the most usual day; while May and November saw the greatest frequency of rapes.

The demographic characteristics of the rape victim have been described in a number of studies. The general consensus of these studies, mostly American, is that victims are young (16 to 25 years) — with elderly victims (over 65 years) very infrequent — single, have a low income, and that black women are over-represented in the victim population (Amir 1971; Chappell et al. 1977; Chappell and Singer 1977; Deming and Eppy 1981; Ploughman and Stensrud 1986). With the additional finding that victims were most often students, with housewives and the employed at much less risk, Ploughman and Stensrud suggested that 'Unmarried women are more likely to be victimized than married women because of their greater exposure to potential rape situations (travelling alone, living alone, living in lower income areas, etc.)' (1986: 320). It should be emphasized that these are American studies and the findings, especially regarding race, may not generalize to other countries. However, an English study did find that most victims were in the younger age range and came from a variety of occupational groups (Wright 1980).

The demographic characteristics of the rapist have also been described in a number of studies. The rapist is typically young, generally 16 to 30 years, although it has been suggested that adolescent sex offenders may be more common than generally acknowledged (Davis and Leitenberg 1987). Rapists tend to come from a lower socioeconomic class, and American studies have shown an over-representation of black males convicted for rape (Amir 1971; Chappell et al. 1977; Klaus and DeBerry 1985; Ploughman and Stensrud 1986). Alder (1984) found that almost half of a large sample of convicted rapists were or had been married, and almost 60 per cent had one or more children. It is unlikely that all rapists are psychiatrically disturbed in terms of a formal diagnosis, and therefore are not as a group psychologically 'sick' or 'psychotic' in a clinical sense (Henn et al. 1976). About one-quarter of arrested rapists have raped previously, with approximately one-third having a history of arrest for violent offences (Chappell et al. 1977). It also seems likely that convicted rapists will continue to offend when released from custody: Romero and Williams (1985) found a 10 per cent recidivism rate for sexual offences in a sample of convicted sexual assaulters, although this particular sample committed as many non-violent as violent offences on return to the community. In considering this 10 per cent recidivism as measured by arrest rate, note should be taken of the finding of Groth et al. (1982b) who, using a self-report methodology, discovered that rapists admitted to an average of over five undetected offences, with a range up to 250 undetected rapes.

The surveys also show that in about one-third of cases the victim and offender are acquainted prior to the rape (Chappell et al. 1977; M.J. Walker and Brodsky 1976); although this may be an underestimation as victims related to their attacker may be less willing to report. Ploughman and Stensrud (1986) found that when the victim knew the attacker, it was most often an acquaintance previously encountered in either the victim's or offender's home or place of work. In other cases, in decreasing order of frequency, the relationship was with a friend, neighbour, ex-husband or boyfriend, family friend, relative, and fellow employee. Does this pattern bear similarities with the notion of 'violent transactions' in which murder victims are seen as precipitative agents in their eventual death? West is blunt and to the point: noting that while in some instances rape may be 'preceded by some social interaction between the woman and the offender . . . this in no way justifies the man in forcing himself upon an unwilling companion' (1984:10). In any case, it is highly improbable that every rape follows a withdrawn sexual invitation. The associated view that men have sexual impulses which, once aroused, cannot be controlled, is not one which meets with general agreement among contemporary theorists. Indeed, the fact that the majority of rapes are planned in advance contradicts the view of rape as an uncontrollable, impulsive act. What may be of more importance in understanding the nature of these social encounters is the rapist's perception of the interaction in tandem with their general beliefs and attitudes towards women: these points are addressed below in considering the psychology of the rapist.

In a minority of cases, between 10 per cent and 15 per cent, the rapes involve more than one attacker; while in about one-quarter of rapes the attacker demands other sexual acts, usually oral sex and less often anal intercourse (Amir 1971; Chappell *et al*. 1977; Chappell and Singer 1977). In more than half the reported cases weapons are used, typically guns and knives. Given these findings, it is not surprising that along with the physical injury resulting from the forced sexual act, other serious physical injury occurs which often requires medical treatment or hospitalization. In some cases the viciousness of the attack results in severe internal injury, while in a minority of cases the rape is sadistic in the extreme, culminating in sexual murder (Schlesinger and Revitch 1983).

Offender taxonomies Attempts to classify rapists have used a range of strategies such as specific aspects of the offence, characteristics of the victim, and psychiatric or legal sub-groupings (Amir 1971; Gebhard *et al*. 1965; Gibbens *et al*. 1977; Henn *et al*. 1976; Rada 1978). Another approach seeks to classify the act according to the motives of the offender: thus Guttmacher (1951) described three types of rapist: the '*true sex offender*' who has a sexual motive in committing the rape; the *sadistic sex offender* for whom physical violence is of primary importance; and finally the *aggressive offender* for whom the rape is simply part of a general criminal, antisocial life-style. However, with the exception of two more recent studies, Prentky *et al*. conclude a review of these taxonomies with the comment that 'past attempts to classify sex offenders have, by and large, failed to examine comprehensively the motives of men who assault women' (1985:40). The two recommended taxonomies are those suggested by M.L. Cohen *et al*. (1971) and by Groth (1979); Prentky *et al*. (1985) also offer a taxonomy of their own devising.

As shown in Table 3.3, M.L. Cohen *et al*. (1971) defined four types of rapists. The *displaced-aggression* rapist uses the rape to express anger and aggression, with the aim of physically injuring the victim who is typically a wife or girlfriend. The *compensatory* offender uses the rape to satisfy the need for a sexual goal, the aggression being a step towards fulfilling that aim: the rape is therefore a way of compensating for inadequacy in achieving sexual goals by conventional methods. For the *sex-aggression-diffusion* rapist the rape is a sadistic act in which the sexual and violent components of the act become fused, so that it is the victim's pain which excites sexual arousal. Finally, the *impulsive* rapist acts without planning, raping when the opportunity presents itself, as perhaps during the course of a burglary.

Table 3.3 Types of rapist (after M.L. Cohen *et al.* 1971)

Type	Motivation	Characteristics
Displaced aggression	Aggression	Anger, rage; physical injury
Compensatory	Sexual	Rape fantasies being acted out
Sex-aggression- diffusion	Aggression and sexual	Sadistic sexual assault and severe physical injury
Impulse	'Opportunity'	Impulsive reaction to chance opportunity

From clinical observation of 500 rapists Groth (1979) described three types of rape according to the varying degrees of hostility and control associated with the act (see also Groth and Hobson 1983). The *anger rape* typically follows arguments, sexual jealousies, and social rejection: the offender reports experiencing anger and rage, together with a sense of being wrongly treated, prior to the attack. In committing the sexual act the rapist uses far more force than is necessary to ensure compliance; the aim appears to be to inflict physical injury with the rape almost an afterthought, an additional way of inflicting pain. Groth estimated that 40 per cent of the sample could be classified as anger rapists. The *power rape* is different in that sexual conquest is the goal; physical force is used only to the degree necessary to force compliance. Groth suggests that it is, however, not sexual gratification which is the goal, rather the experience of power which alleviates personal insecurities and asserts manhood and heterosexuality. Groth suggested that 55 per cent of the sample were power rapists. Finally, with *sadistic rape* sexuality and aggression are bound in a reciprocal fashion. The victim is made to suffer, typically by being tied, tormented, and often tortured; the victim's humiliation and suffering is sexually exciting, rape fuels the experience yet further. This was the least common type of rape, accounting for 5 per cent of Groth's sample.

Following a study of 108 offenders, Prentky *et al.* (1985) described eight types of rapist. These eight types are defined by combinations of levels of three variables: the meaning of aggression, the meaning of sexuality, and the offender's level of impulsivity. They define two types of aggression: *instrumental* in which the aggression is used to force compliance; *expressive* in which the act is principally violent. There are four levels of meaning of sexuality: *compensatory* in which the behaviour is used to act out some sexual fantasy; *exploitative* in which the rape is an impulsive, predatory act; *displaced anger* where the sexual act is an expression of rage; *sadistic* in which the rape is an enactment of sexual-aggressive fantasies. Impulsivity is dichotomized as *high* or *low*: while differing slightly in definition according to the level of the other two variables, the low levels are associated with offender characteristics such as shyness, introversion, and susceptibility to cues such as perceived threat; high levels are characterized by 'acting out' behaviours, low social competence, and character disorders.

It is informative to compare these taxonomies with the way in which offenders view rape. Scully and Marolla (1985) interviewed 114 convicted rapists, examining the rapists' 'own perceptions of the crime and themselves'. Following the interviews Scully and Marolla described five types of rape. In the first, the rapists said that revenge and punishment were their motives: following some perceived indiscretion from their partner, the man raped another woman to get even with their wives or girlfriends. These rapists reported extreme anger, even rage, at the time of committing the act and physically assaulted their victims. A second group saw the rape as an 'added bonus' to another crime: 'The decision to rape was made subsequent to the original intent which was burglary or robbery . . . after they realized they were in control of the situation' (1985: 257). A third group claimed they were sexually motivated in committing the rape, the rape serving to obtain what was not available or not offered. The 'date rape' frequently figured here, typical of a situation in which the man believed that the woman was sexually available — other women included in this 'available' category were those met in bars or hitch-hiking — and when his sexual advances were turned down the man took what he saw as rightfully his. Scully and Marolla described the fourth group as rapists who enjoy impersonal sex and power: the act of rape provides an experience of control and dominance which also avoids the emotions generally associated with intimacy and tenderness. Finally, a fifth group raped for recreation and adventure, typically in gangs where the rape is seen simply as another form of criminal activity. The payoffs for the rape for these offenders are very much in terms of social rewards from the gang for participating in the illegal group activity. Victims of this type of rape were typically hitch-hikers, women abducted by force from the street at night, or women who believed they had a date with one of the gang members only to be taken to a predetermined location and raped by each of the gang. Scully and Marolla reported that the rapists admitted to little or no compassion for their victims. The majority said that after the rape they 'felt good', 'relieved', or 'nothing'; with only 8 per cent saying they felt 'guilty' or 'bad', and fewer than 1 per cent expressing any concern for their victim.

These various reasons for raping contain elements of revenge, power, and opportunity similar to the taxonomies described above, strongly supporting the argument that rape is not simply a matter of sex. Different men rape to gain different rewards. However, while taxonomies are helpful in furthering understanding of the complexities of the act and the motivation of different rapists, they say little about the question of individual differences between rapists and non-rapists. Unless the position is taken that all men are potential rapists, some distinction between rapists and non-rapists should exist. In looking for this difference psychological research has focused principally on three areas: the cues which are sexually arousing for the rapist; the attitudes towards women held by men who rape; and the level of social behaviour displayed by rapists.

Psychology of the rapist In studying sexual arousal in sex offenders penile plethysmography is the most widely used technique: simply, the methodology relies on measuring changes in penile volume and diameter in response to stimuli such as slides, audiotapes, videotapes, and self-imagery (Abel *et al.* 1981b; Crawford 1980; Laws 1984). Measurement of sexual arousal is technically sophisticated (Earls and Marshall 1983) with associated technical and practical issues such as validation of the test stimuli (Earls and Quinsey 1985), the subject's voluntary control of erectile response (Malcolm *et al.* 1985), and the relationship between physiological and psychological arousal (Balder and Marshall 1984). Given these considerations, a considerable body of research has accumulated on the reactions of rapists to stimuli of varying sexual content.

The first studies of this type clearly showed that rapists were aroused by stimuli which depicted acts of non-consenting sex (Barbaree *et al.* 1979). Recent research has been consistent with this pattern: greater arousal to rape stimuli in rapists than in non-rapists, and greater arousal to consenting sexual scenes in non-rapists compared with rapists (Quinsey *et al.* 1984). These findings led to the hypothesis that rapists have a preference for aggressive sex because they find this the most arousing form of sexual behaviour.

Other studies have suggested a rather different picture from that of a difference in arousal patterns between rapists and non-rapists. Abel *et al.* (1977) found that rapists were more aroused by rape scenes than non-rapists, but that the rapists were equally aroused by mutually consenting sex: if consenting and non-consenting scenes are equally arousing for rapists then this plainly argues against a preference hypothesis. Barbaree *et al.* (1983) reported similar results to Abel *et al.* (1977) and suggested an explanation in terms of inhibition rather than preference. Both rapists and non-rapists are similarly aroused by the sexual cues present in all sexual scenes: while cues of violence or non-consent act to inhibit arousal in non-rapists, the rapist's arousal is not inhibited by such depictions. The lack of inhibition may be due to a failure to acquire inhibitory control, or alternatively a failure of inhibitory processes due, for example, to drug or alcohol use or high emotionality. Quinsey *et al.* (1981) found differences between rapists and controls in their responses to a rape scene, but also found that if non-rapists were told that arousal to deviant material was commonplace in males then high arousal levels were obtained. A series of studies by Malamuth and colleagues (Malamuth 1981; Malamuth and Check 1980; Malamuth *et al.* 1980) led Malamuth and Donnerstein (1982) to suggest two caveats to the view that normal males do not experience the same arousal as rapists to rape scenes. The first concerns the context of the rape: if the victim is shown as becoming involuntarily sexually aroused by the rape then 'normal' males become as, if not more, aroused than rapists: it is only when the victim continues to suffer that arousal remains low in normal subjects. The second point concerns individual differences: while it is tempting to dichotomize between rapists and non-rapists, the evidence suggests that while some men do not rape they report that given the right conditions — not being apprehended and punished — they would be capable of rape (Check and Malamuth 1983; Malamuth 1981). Malamuth and Donnerstein (1982) note that the arousal patterns of this third group of men, classed as 'high likelihood of raping', are very similar to that found in rapists. In keeping with the inhibition hypothesis studies have demonstrated that alcohol intoxication (Barbaree *et al.* 1983) and anger (Yates *et al.* 1984) can act to disinhibit arousal in non-rapists.

A recent study by Baxter *et al.* has added a new twist to the debate in finding that 'Both the rapists and the nonrapists . . . responded significantly less to the rape episodes than to the consent episodes' (1986: 518). As Baxter et al. note, this is not consistent with the sexual preference hypothesis, nor does it fully accord with an inhibition hypothesis. They suggest that this novel finding may be a function of a larger sample size than in previous studies, or due to differences in rapist samples across studies. A line for research to follow which suggests itself from the present position is to test for differences in sexual arousal across one or more of the above taxonomies. Howells summarizes the position: 'The complexity and ambiguity of the relationship between deviant arousal and deviant behaviour should be appreciated. Rapists may be discernible from non-rapists . . . but many apparently normal males may show significant arousal to deviant material' (1984b: 121). The relationship between stimuli and arousal respose is not a simple one; however, if there is some cognitive mediation perhaps this might be evident in studies of rapists' attitudes towards women and rape.

Field (1978) found a relationship between attitudes towards women and perception of rape, such that men who saw women in more 'traditional roles' were more likely to say that rape was the fault of the woman. Segal and Stermac (1984), amending some shortcomings in Field's design, compared the attitudes towards women of rapist, non-sex offender, and non-offender groups. Segal and Stermac conclude that their results 'failed to demonstrate that rapists as a group are exclusively conservative or negative in their attitudes towards women' (1984: 440). Overholser and Beck (1986) compared rapists with other offender and non-offender groups using the Attitudes Towards Sex and Violence Scales and the Rape Myth Acceptance Scale (M. Burt 1980). The rapists did not differ from the other groups on either measure. Stermac and Quinsey (1986) similarly found no difference between rapists and non-rapists on a measure of attitudes towards women. Thus it appears that rapists do not hold attitudes towards women that are any different from those held by men who do not rape. Indeed, Check and Malamuth (1985) suggest that the type of attitudes commonly held by men support the feminist perspective on the general pervasiveness of rape myths and the 'normality of rape'.

Moving from attitudes to behaviour, Howells made the point that 'Social competence with females is generally a necessary condition for consenting sexual behaviour with an adult and it is not difficult to see that impaired social skills might make a partner inaccessible and that, in some cases, offenders might resort to . . . rape as an alternative sexual outlet' (1986: 191). The evidence exploring this suggestion has provided mixed results. Segal and Marshall (1985a) assessed a range of social skills in rapist and control groups and found no differences between groups. (Interestingly the rapists were judged the least physically attractive of all the men in the study.) Stermac and Quinsey (1986) failed to find any significant difference between rapists and other offender controls on various measures of social behaviour, with the one exception that rapists were less assertive. However, Segal and Marshall (1985b) found no difference in assertiveness between rapists and matched control groups. Overholser and Beck (1986) did find skill differences: the rapists in their sample showed significantly less skilled social behaviour, particularly in the area of conversation skills. The rapists also showed significantly more anxiety, measured physiologically using GSR, during the role-plays which formed part of the study. An explanation for some of the variation in findings is that the samples in the Segal and Marshall studies were not matched for age which might have influenced some of their measures.

While social skills include overt behaviour, the skill model also emphasizes the importance of social perception, both of one's own and others' behaviour (Hollin and Trower 1986). Segal and Marshall (1986) assessed rapists' perception of a heterosexual interaction and found that the rapists did not differ significantly from controls in their level of social skill, their prediction of their own ability, or on a measure of the discrepancy between the two. It appears that the rapists are accurate in perceiving their own performance. D.N. Lipton et al. (1987) looked specifically at the ability of rapists to process interpersonal cues from women, particularly negative cues. This study used a newly developed measure of heterosocial perception, in which videotaped interactions of either a 'first date' or an 'intimate couple' are viewed then rated for content of affective cues such as 'romantic' and 'bad mood'. The results showed that when compared to both offender and non-offender control groups, 'Rapists displayed a significant deficit when reading women's cues in first-date interactions . . . comparison with violent nonrapists supported the view that the rapists' deficits are related to sexual aggression in particular rather than to aggressive behaviour in general' (1987: 20). The rapists' misperceptions involved a low degree of sensitivity to negative and bad mood cues: however, it is not clear why the effect was found only for the 'first date' and not the 'intimate' scene. While these results are interesting in that they point to an aspect of heterosexual interaction in which rapists may be deficient, clearly this in itself is not an explanation for rape. As Lipton *et al.* suggest, the cognitive decision-making process following the (mis) perception is a candidate for future research, to which might be added the need to understand the development of such perceptions in both an individual and cultural sense.

Sex offences involving children

As with sex offences involving adults, the gap between reported offences involving children and the real number of offences is unknown. Both Finkelhor (1986) and Alter-Reid *et al.* (1986) review the prevalence studies and suggest that a number of factors, such as the method of data collection and the operational definition of abuse, can influence the figures. It is generally agreed that the official figures are an underestimation: in a typical study Mrazek (1984) estimates that 10 per cent to 15 per cent of children and adolescents experience at least one incident of sexual victimization, with girls twice as likely as boys to be victims. The offence behaviour includes genital fondling, oral sex, and sexual intercourse. The majority of offenders are male, about three-quarters of whom select female victims; the remainder chose male victims, with only a very small proportion victimizing both male and female children (Langevin 1983).

Offence analysis From interviews with individuals who had been victims of abuse as children, Finkelhor (1984; 1986) presents a picture of the act of child sexual abuse. Genital fondling was the most common type of assault for both female and male victims: this included the adult's contact with the child's genitals, using either hand or mouth, or the child's contact with the adult's genitals. Sexual intercourse was not often reported, although other activities such as masturbation and exhibitionism were frequently experienced. The low incidence of penetration may be due to physiological restrictions: the relative size of the male sexual organ and the child's vagina or anus means that the child experiences severe pain and injury if penetration is attempted. Another explanation for the low incidence of penetration is that the majority of child abusers are not seeking adult-style relations but rather an escape to more child-like sexuality (Gebhard *et al.* 1965). Finkelhor (1986) also found that the majority of sexual abuse (60 per cent) took the form of a single, unpleasant experience: the child is able afterwards to avoid the adult or tell a parent who then takes preventive action. In the other cases the contact becomes episodic, sometimes on a regular basis: Finkelhor reports an average duration of thirty-one weeks for female victims. Although

89

typically lasting for months rather than years, some abuse spans a great deal of time — Finkelhor recorded one case which lasted for eleven years.

At one time the occurrence of child sexual abuse was either denied or attributed to childhood sexual fantasy, then following recognition of the reality of abuse, the blame was attributed to the child (see A. Miller 1984). The child was seen as either actively encouraging the sexual contact (Burton 1968), or corroborating by failing to take self-protective steps (De Francis 1969). As Finkelhor suggests, this image of the child as a sexual agent is easily traced to the psychoanalytic view of the child's sexual impulses. In discussing the proposal that the child may be an active and willing partner, Finkelhor is unequivocal in his view, which perhaps represents the present consensus, that children are the recipients of sexual actions, not the initiators. He strongly maintains that any movement away from depicting the child as anything other than a victim of force and coercion is not only not helpful, but also positively destructive. It is the fear and anxiety produced by the act and threats of retribution by the offender, not compliance or corroboration, which prevent the child from telling an adult about the abuse. The recent availability in Britain of a confidential telephone service for children to report abuse (both physical and sexual) has resulted in a massive response — although it is impossible to tell what percentage of calls are genuine.

The 'high risk studies' have highlighted a number of facts about the victims of child sexual abuse (see Finkelhor 1986). Females are more likely to be victimized than males, approximately at a 2.5:1 ratio. Children are victimized at all ages from birth to 18 years (after which the term 'child' is not used, although abuse still occurs), with peaks of vulnerability at 6–7 years and particularly during the pre-pubescent ages of 10–12 years. However, it is possible that older children are more likely to report abuse, so the lower figures with younger children are not a source of even scant comfort. While there may be some association between social class and physical abuse of children (Straus et al. 1980), this does not appear to be the case with child sexual abuse (Finkelhor 1986). Further, there do not seem to be any ethnic differences in rates of sexual abuse, nor does the incidence appear to differ between rural and urban communities (Finkelhor 1986).

In terms of social network, girls with few friends report more abuse, but it is unclear whether this is an antecedent or consequence of the abuse. Several family factors have been consistently associated with sexual abuse: these include living without the biological father; a mother who is disabled or ill; a mother employed outside the home; the presence of a stepfather (Finkelhor 1984; 1986; Gruber and Jones 1983; Russell 1986). With regard to aspects of family relationships as predictors of abuse, two findings are outstanding: the sexually abused child is likely to report a poor relationship with his or her parents, and the presence of a poor parental relationship, characterized by conflict and little mutual affection. In almost half the cases with female victims the abuser was a member of the family, and a further third of abusers were acquaintances. Male victims showed a different pattern, with less than one-fifth of abusers being relatives but over half acquaintances. In the remainder of cases the abuse occurred with a stranger. Given the predictive power of family functioning, it is convenient to blame the parents for the abuse. While this may be true in some cases — incest being the obvious example — it should also be recognized that parental absences and conflicts can be the result of social and economic factors. The fault, if blame is to be apportioned, may lie as much in a social structure which fails to provide adequate child care when parents are necessarily working as in the parents themselves.

Offender taxonomies A number of approaches to classifying child sexual abusers have been reported, focusing on either the nature of the offence or some characteristic of the offender. Groth *et al.* (1982a) made the distinction between *child rape* and *child molestation*. The former offences involve violence and are seen as similar to adult rape; the latter are offences in which the child is coerced by non-violent means, and the harm to the child is psychological rather than physical. Howells (1981) made the distinction between *preference molesters* and *situational molesters*. The former have a stable primary sexual orientation towards children and are uninterested in emotional and sexual relationship with adult partners. Preference molesters, sometimes termed *pedophiles*, defend their behaviour as an acceptable form of sexual activity. The situational molesters are normal with respect to forming heterosexual adult relationships: the offence with the child is impulsive and seen by the offender as abnormal. Lanyon (1986) suggests that the preference–situational distinction might be better seen as a dimension of offender behaviour rather than a strict dichotomy between different offender groups.

While the three groups — child rapists, preference molesters, and situational molesters — seem reasonably well defined, other dimensions are also important. There are homosexual as well as heterosexual offenders, although it is unclear whether such offenders have adult homosexual preferences (Freund and Langevin 1976). Another often-made distinction is between *incestuous* and *non-incestuous offenders*: the implication being that some offenders abuse children only within their own family, while others victimize children who are not relatives (deChesnay 1985; Herman 1981; Meiselman 1978). However, recent research by Abel, Mittleman, Becker, Cunningham-Rather, and Lucas (cited in Conte 1985) casts doubt on some of the distinctions between incestuous and non-incestuous offenders. With a sample of 142 men who sexually abused their daughters, Abel *et al*. discovered that 44 per cent of the men also abused female children outside the family home; 11 per cent had also been abusing male children, while 18 per cent admitted raping mature women. As Conte (1985) suggests, while it is clear that incestuous offenders are sexually aroused by children, other assumptions about this offence remain unsubstantiated.

Another approach to taxonomy, similar to that used with violent offenders, attempts to generate 'profiles' of the offender using standard psychometric measures such as the MMPI (Langevin *et al*. 1985; Quinsey 1983). Despite a number of attempts, Conte is accurate in his comment that 'There is no currently verified profile of the typical adult who sexually abuses children' (1985: 345).

Psychology of the child sex offender Conte (1985) suggests five dimensions which might usefully guide the study of the psychology of the child sex offender. The first of these is the offender's *denial* of any problem: the denial may be due to a fear of lack of confidentiality; difficulty in admitting the offence in an interview setting; or the offender's interpretation of the abuse as something other than harmful. The role of denial would seem to warrant attention as it would seem likely that differences would exist between offenders who deny for reasons of shame or guilt, and those who deny any problem at all. The second dimension Conte suggests is *sexual arousal*. The research with child sex offenders has used identical methods to measure arousal as in the previously discussed studies with rapists. The weight of evidence with child offenders suggests that there are individuals who are sexually aroused by children (Freund 1967; Freund and Langevin 1976). Quinsey *et al*. (1975) and Abel *et al*. (1981a) found that despite claims to be normally aroused by adults, child offenders showed greatest arousal to stimuli depicting children. Abel *et al*. also found that incest offenders were aroused by pedophilic stimuli which were *not* descriptions of sexual acts with their daughters or stepdaughters. Avery-Clarke and Laws (1984) were able to identify correctly aggressive child offenders on the basis of their responses to imagined scenes of violence against children.

Sexual fantasy is the next dimension: Conte (1985) suggests that sexual fantasy involving children paired with arousal via masturbation may be an antecedent in child sexual abuse. However, as Conte notes, there are considerable problems in gaining access to fantasies, verifying the content of fantasies, and pinpointing the aetiological role of fantasy. The same points also apply to the next factor, *cognitive distortions*, although, if reliable, the content of such distortions is illuminating. Abel *et al.* (1984) identified seven distorted attitudes and beliefs commonly expressed by child molesters (see Table 3.4). Such cognitions may serve a number of functions: they may be a strategy for coping with guilt and remorse; a means of rationalization for future acts; or a means of denial of any abnormality.

Table 3.4 Cognitive distortions in child molesters (after Abel *et al.* 1984)

1 Genital fondling is not really sex so no harm is done
2 Children don't tell because they enjoy the sex
3 Sex enhances a relationship with a child
4 Society will eventually see that sex with children is acceptable
5 A child enquiring about sex means he or she wants to experience sex
6 Physical sex is a good means of teaching children about sex
7 A lack of physical resistance means that the child wants sex

Moving from cognition to overt behaviour, *social skills* are the next factor in Conte's scheme. As with rapists, the suggestion of a link between social skills and offending rests on the assumption that a skills deficit leads to child abuse as an alternative means of achieving sexual goals. Segal and Marshall (1985a; 1985b) found that the social skills of child molesters were significantly poorer than those of rapists who, as discussed above, did not differ from control groups. Overholser and Beck (1986) also reported that child molesters were less skilled than controls. The skill deficits extended to social perception and levels of social anxiety, leading Segal and Marshall to note that 'Child molesters presented a clearer picture of heterosocial inadequacy than did rapists' (1985a: 55).

Finally, Conte suggests that a variety of variables might be collected under the general label 'other problems'. These other problems include 'alcohol or drug abuse, depression, poor self-concepts, relationship problems, impulse problems such as abuse of credit cards, and difficulty controlling or expressing anger' (1985: 352). To this list might be added fear of negative evaluation and highly stereotyped views of sex role behaviour (Overholser and Beck 1986).

Theories of sexual offences

The first point to be made is one of distinction: do sex offences require a different theory from violent offences? Current opinion, based on the empirical evidence discussed above, holds that rape is a violent offence. Romero and Williams tentatively make the point that

> All forms of bodily assault committed by sex offenders, particularly sexual assaulters, should be carefully examined as parallels may exist between the two types of offence. If this is the case, then the distinction between sex offenders and violent nonsex offenders may be conceptually weak where sexual assaulters are concerned. (Romero and Williams 1985: 63)

Following an empirical study of almost 1,000 serious offenders, Alder is less reserved in concluding that

> Contrary to the prior understanding of rape as the sexually motivated behaviour of a sexually maladjusted male who is likely to repeat the offense, present evidence suggests that rape may be more appropriately conceived of as one violent action in a repertoire of other nonsexual criminal behavior. (Alder 1984: 158)

Therefore, with the caveat that some explanation is required as to why the rapist rapes — i.e. why he is sexually aggressive rather than physically aggressive in a non-sexual manner — rape is probably best understood in terms of theories of violence.

If there is general agreement that rape is a violent crime, then there is also general agreement that child sex offenders, with the possible exception of child rapists, require a different level of explanation. Finkelhor (1984; 1986) reviews theories which focus on the offender, the victim, the family, and social and cultural factors. While these theories offer some degree of illumination, they fall prey to the criticism of attempting to fit the act to an existing theoretical perspective, rather than generating an explanatory model from data concerning the phenomenon itself. Finkelhor (1986) has, however, begun to formulate the necessary model which seeks to integrate the diverse views and empirical data. This model, summarized in Table 3.5, consists of four complementary processes which may act in varying combinations in individual cases to create sexual interest in children. Finkelhor is at pains to stress that the four levels include individual, physiological, and sociocultural variables and concepts.

Table 3.5 Finkelhor's (1986) model of child molesting

I *Emotional congruence*	Children attractive because of their low dominance and male socialization to dominance; offender immature, low self-esteem, aggressive.
II *Sexual arousal*	Children sexually arousing due to offender's socialization through personal experience, models, or child pornography; possibility of physiological explanation e.g. hormonal levels.
III *Blockage*	Problems in forming adult relationships with women; related to sexual anxiety, poor heterosocial skills, attitudes towards sex.
IV *Disinhibition*	Offender able to overcome inhibitions through drugs, alcohol, cognitive distortion; or situational stress disrupts inhibitors.

Emotional congruence seeks to address the issue of why an individual finds children a source of emotional gratification. The suggested reasons include the child's lack of dominance, and the offender's low self-esteem and immaturity. *Sexual arousal* to children, clearly shown in a number of studies, may be due for example to learning experiences (including sexual abuse) in childhood or to the use of child pornography: although Langevin and Lang (1985) cast doubts over both these factors. The offender's *blockage* in seeking adult partners may result from social anxiety or poor social skills — both of which the data support. Finally, *disinhibition* may have a role to play, perhaps via alcohol or situational stress, in enabling the offender to overcome the conventional social and moral restraints against such behaviour. (Frude 1988 has offered a rather similar model to explain physical abuse of children.) The key, as Finkelhor (1986) sees it, is the manner of male sexual socialization: he contends that men are raised to 'sexualize their emotions' so that sex is the way to achieve emotional needs. Men are taught to be attracted to younger, smaller, less dominant partners — children are simply the logical extension of this continuum, while the general lack of socially sanctioned involvement of men in childcare serves to distance them from a full understanding of children.

There are two important points with regard to this model. The first is that it clearly defines areas with which future research should be concerned: that is the model is testable and open to verification, refinement, or refutation. Second, the approach does not seek to exclude or impose any particular theoretical perspective in the interpretation of the data. However, it would be anticipated that if the model is followed empirically one of the principal theoretical approaches — psychodynamic, social learning, etc. — would eventually prove able to accommodate the refined model with the greatest ease.

Perspective

The search for greater understanding of violence is not simply a theoretical quest; it is a matter of considerable professional and public concern. In dealing with violent offenders the legal system is faced with the decision of first whether imprisonment is necessary or, for the imprisoned offender, whether it is safe to release a given offender back into the community on parole. In other words, someone is faced with the task of predicting the *dangerousness* of the person who has previously committed violent acts. The acid test of any research lies in its predictive power — on the basis of what is known about violent crime is it possible to say that this person will commit more violent crimes while this other person will not?

While a great deal has been written on the topic of dangerousness (Hinton 1983; Monahan 1981; Peay 1982; Prins 1986; Sepejak *et al.* 1983) some of the most recent commentators are forthright in noting that prediction is not good: Howells, for example, suggests that 'Psychiatric and psychological predictions of violence . . . have consistently shown to be poor and inaccurate' (1987a: 658). Howells goes on to suggest that an important reason for this is 'the failure of clinicians to incorporate information about situational, rather than personal variables' (1987a: 659). This statement can be traced to a preference for theories depending on internal dispositions to violence, rather than socially oriented explanations. While the 'person' should not be ignored, a more complete understanding of violence would appear to be required before predictions of dangerousness can be made with any degree of confidence. Not all psychologists agree with this view: Litwack and

Schlesinger have the confidence to suggest that 'mental health professionals can play a legitimate — and even indispensable — role in assessing the dangerousness of previously or potentially violent individuals' (1987: 249). It may be that the guidelines offered by Litwack and Schlesinger will prove their worth in due course: it would certainly be gratifying to see accurate predictions being made.

Research into sexual crimes has reached the consensus that such offences are best conceptualized in terms of violent rather than sexual motivation. However, the taxonomies indicate that there is a subgroup of offenders who appear to be sexually motivated, the act of rape being perhaps compensation for an absence of normal, consenting sex. Therefore while understanding of rape as a violent act may profit from the type of research suggested above, it may be expedient to acknowledge the heterogeneity of rapists: it needs to be explained why some men use rape as an act of violence, while for other men it is a sexual act. W.L. Marshall and Barbaree (1984) have presented a behavioural view of rape which may well direct research towards addressing this very point. Marshall and Barbaree's theory is similar to the social learning perspective on violence in that it seeks to accommodate biological, situational, and early learning experiences alongside what is known of patterns of sexual arousal and cognitive functioning in rapists. These person variables are then considered in interaction with both the immediate situation and the political and economic climate. Child sex abusers appear to be a distinctive group from a psychological viewpoint: research has elucidated a number of distinguishing cognitive and behavioural features of child offender populations. As with other serious offences a unifying theory is required, although Finkelhor (1986) has made significant steps in this direction.

While the focus of much research is on offenders, it should not be forgotten that crimes have victims, and that with serious crimes the victims are liable to suffer in the extreme. Gilmartin-Zena (1985), for example, found that rape victims reported immediate difficulties in a number of areas: behavioural changes, such as going out alone less frequently, were common; physical symptoms such as difficulty in sleeping were often reported; and emotional disturbance, as evinced by bouts of crying, were experienced. A two-month follow-up revealed that while these initial disturbances declined slightly, the rape victims reported a *rise* in interpersonal difficulties such as within their relationships with partners or friends. The provision of services to assist the post-rape adjustment of victims is clearly a matter of concern to victims, family, and professionals (see Osborne 1982). The reactions of children to sexual abuse are similarly varied, often extending into adult life (Finkelhor 1986).

In conclusion, the hope can be expressed that research leading to a greater understanding of the serious offender has potential beyond simply increasing knowledge of criminal behaviour. Increased understanding will lead to more effective strategies for preventing violence, both in terms of predicting future offending, and also in enabling more effective strategies to be devised for changing the offender's criminal behaviour.

Chapter four

Mental disorder and crime

While the term 'mental disorder' has been used in the chapter title, there would be grounds for choosing 'mental abnormality' instead: the two terms are used interchangeably in the literature to refer to the same group of offenders (Craft and Craft 1984; Gunn 1977). This different terminology for the same topic provides a starting-point for the discussion of some of the conceptual issues relevant to the relationship between mental state and criminal behaviour.

The term 'abnormal' can be used in two ways: it can mean unusual in a statistical sense, or it can be used to imply 'bad' or 'wrong' in a moral sense. It might be said that child sexual abuse is abnormal: meaning that most people do not sexually assault children, or alternatively that child sexual abuse is wrong. (It is also possible to combine the two, meaning that child sexual abuse is both statistically unusual and also wrong.) In most instances however the term has negative connotations, the word 'abnormal' is not used when we wish to express admiration or approval. For example, people who score very highly on IQ tests are statistically abnormal, but we prefer terms such as 'gifted' or 'genius', reserving 'abnormal' for those at the other end of the IQ distribution. Thus the notion of a 'mentally abnormal offender' lends itself to the image of a criminal who is mentally corrupt, a 'bad' person. 'Disorder' on the other hand has quite different associations: it implies a system thrown into disarray, confused and upset at present but perhaps capable of being put back into working order. To call a person disordered does not therefore generally impute qualities of good or bad, but rather makes distinctions such as between confused and competent or disorganized and capable. Thus the term 'mentally disordered offender' suggests an individual who is mentally disturbed, someone who might well be called 'mad'.

In Chapter 2 various explanations for criminal behaviour were discussed which included the view of the criminal as a person who freely chooses to behave in a way which is judged unacceptable by the rest of society. The criminal exercises free will and decides to act in an anti-social manner and can therefore be seen as a 'bad' person. The distinction between 'bad' and 'mad' becomes clear when we consider another way of explaining human behaviour, the so-called 'medical model'. When applied to physical conditions, the medical model might more properly be called an 'organic' or 'physiological' model. If a person presents with behaviours such as sneezing or a sore throat the physician will attempt to determine a physical cause, and so may discover the presence of a cold virus, or an allergy, and so forth. In other words the *symptoms* lead to the *diagnosis* of a *disease* which has some physical, organic basis, a virus, a genetic predisposition, a physical insult or trauma. (Of course the exact physical cause of some diseases are unknown; in such instances the term 'disorder', rather than disease, is favoured.) While not perfect, the model works reasonably well within physical medicine.

The notion of madness arises when the presenting behaviours are not physical in nature; when the person reports hearing voices, or believes people are plotting against him or her, or has a morbid fear of contamination by germs. If we follow a medical model then these behaviours are seen as symptoms of some underlying disease (or more properly, disorder, as the nature of the disease is not well described). This non-physical disease is 'madness' or, using the preferred terminology, mental disorder. The exact cause of the disorder can be debated: depression, for example, may be reduced to a physiological basis such as a biochemical disorder, perhaps with some genetic basis; or it may be seen to be caused by a dysfunction of another system, the mind. The concept of 'mind' is, of course, one which has exercised philosophers for centuries, as is the question of whether mind will eventually be able to be explained purely in physiological terms. At its most unsophisticated, the medical model might substitute mentalistic notions for physiological processes, or perhaps equate the two, arriving at the position that mental disorder is analogous to physical disorder. The person who reports hearing voices would therefore be said to be *mentally disordered*, which might well in this case be diagnosed as schizophrenia. Such a diagnosis requires an individual with specialist knowledge, a doctor of the mind, to decide who is mentally disordered, who is mad and who is sane: in contemporary society that specialist knowledge and attendant power lies in the hands of psychiatry (P. Miller and Rose 1986).

Now, while diagnosis of physical disease is far from an exact science and not totally dependent upon known physical causes, in many instances a physical cause for a physical disorder can be described. The same cannot be said of mental disorder: 'mind' has no physical location, it cannot be X-rayed, dissected, or seen under a microscope. It is therefore an inferential leap to suppose that disordered behaviour is a product, a symptom of mental disorder; with the point still holding if 'physical' is substituted for 'mental'. It should be clear therefore that diagnosis of mental disorder is a subjective judgement, albeit with complex systems such as DSM III (American Psychiatric Association 1980) to guide decision-making. These difficulties with mental disorder at both conceptual and diagnostic levels are a topic of continual debate both within and outside psychiatry (Clare 1976; Ullmann and Krasner 1975). Indeed, the 'anti-psychiatry' movement, led by figures such as David Cooper, Ronald Laing, and Thomas Szasz, not only questioned orthodox psychiatric practice but also moved the whole debate into the realms of politics and social control (D. Cooper 1967; Laing 1967; Szasz 1961; 1970).

These concerns of psychiatry are important at two levels for understanding criminal behaviour. The first position which might be taken is that criminal, antisocial behaviour is a symptom of mental disorder; seeking thereby to apply a crude medical model to crime, so that criminal behaviour is seen as a symptom of mental disorder. Siegal makes the point that 'the phenomenon of crime and delinquency is so widespread that to claim all criminals are psychologically disturbed is to make that claim against a vast majority of people' (1986: 176). While it is not too difficult to make a case for widespread psychological disturbance (just play with the definition of disturbance), I think that the majority of psychologists and criminologists would agree with the spirit of Siegal's statement. However, it should not be thought that the medical model has been set aside completely; Washbrook makes the following observations:

> There is very little difference between the longitudinal patterns of physical illness, mental illness, and the clinical, criminological pattern of a large number of delinquents. The older criminologists were prepared to consider this but the so-called 'new criminology' has tended to oust this formula. . . . The medical model must be readopted, though the new criminology should not be swept aside but relegated to the place where I believe it belongs. . . . More and more the psychiatric hospital must move towards the hospital for physical illnesses and likewise there must be a tendency to push prisons towards the psychiatric hospital model. (Washbrook 1981: 127-8)

Rather than criminal behaviour being evidence of mental disorder, the alternative position can be adopted that the relationship between mental disorder and crime is one where the two phenomena co-exist. Within this broad position two options are available: while co-existing mental disorder and crime are independent of each other; alternatively that when it is present, mental disorder can be a cause of crime — which, of course, is not the same as saying crime is evidence of mental disorder. In order to consider the nature of the relationship between mental disorder and crime the starting-point will be the extent of mental disorder in offender populations.

Mental disorder in offender populations

One strategy for investigating the relationship between mental disorder and crime is to estimate the prevalence of psychiatric disturbance in known offender populations. In a typical study Gunn *et al.* (1978) assessed the psychiatric morbidity and need for treatment in the population of two English prisons. A combination of questionnaire and interview led to the conclusion that over 34 per cent of the sample of 149 prisoners could be diagnosed as showing a moderate, marked, or severe level of psychiatric distrubance. In almost half the cases the symptoms were of depression, and in a further third anxiety states were evident. While drug and alcohol problems were also common, psychoses were seldom evident. Further data from a wider prison population led Gunn *et al.* to estimate that 31 per cent of convicted prisoners can be regarded as psychiatric cases; this compares with a figure of about 14 per cent in the general population who consult their doctor for psychiatric reasons.

Prins (1980) presents an overview of about twenty studies (see Table 4.1) which have looked at the prevalence of various types of disorders in offender populations.

Table 4.1 The prevalence of mental disorder in penal populations (from Prins 1980)

Disorder	Number of studies	Highest percentage	Lowest percentage	Mean percentage
Psychosis[a]	11	26.0	0.5	8.4
Mental subnormality	7	28.0	2.4	10.2
Psychopathy	8	70.0	5.6	26.9
Neurosis	4	7.9	2.0	5.0

Note: [a]principally schizophrenia and depression

The most striking aspect of the figure in Table 4.1 is the wide variation between different studies. This variation is a function of three factors: the time-span covered by the studies — the earliest being reported by B. Glueck (1918), the most recent by Guze (1976) — which will have seen a number of legal changes regarding the disposal of mentally disordered offenders; the differing populations, from murderers to Approved School boys; the varying diagnostic standards between studies which probably not only reflects changes over time, but also variations between countries. Given this, it is generally accepted that psychiatric problems are common in penal populations (Bukstel and Kilman 1980; Howells 1982; Porporino and Zamble 1984; P.J. Taylor and Gunn 1984), although level of major psychoses may not differ greatly from the general population (Coid 1984; Gunn et al. 1978). This latter point regarding the major psychoses may not, however, be the case for all prisoner groups. P.J. Taylor reported the findings from a survey of psychiatric disorder in London's life-sentenced prisoners which concluded: 'Over two-thirds of London's life-sentenced men and women appeared to have some form of psychiatric disorder. As many as 10 per cent. of the sample were psychotic, almost certainly schizophrenic' (1986: 73). Taylor reports that depression and personality disorder were the principal disorders in the sample.

However, a greater percentage of mental disorder in offender populations than in the rest of the population does not establish a causal link between the disorder and the criminal act. Feldman (1977) suggests a number of alternative explanations: the crime may be executed less skilfully by mentally disordered individuals, leading to easier detection; the police may be more likely to charge the mentally disordered, if only as a means to ensure some form of treatment; guilty pleas may be more readily made, again with the aim of securing treatment. Recent American research has added weight to one of Feldman's suggestions. Teplin (1984) found that for similar offences those with mental disorder had a significantly greater chance of being arrested than those without mental disorder. Further, as Feldman also notes, the fact that an individual exhibits a mental disorder in prison does not necessarily mean that the disorder was present when the crime was committed. Prisons are not the most pleasant environments and may precipitate a disorder which did not exist prior to imprisonment (Wormith 1984): although it remains to be established why, given similar conditions, not all inmates manifest the same mental health problems. In summarizing the position, Gunn comments: 'If prison populations are studied they apparently contain a large number of mentally-disordered individuals, but this may be more closely related to their function as institutions than to any special relationship between crime and mental disorder' (1977: 327).

Offending in psychiatric populations

The alternative to looking at mental disorder in offender populations is to reverse the strategy and examine offending in psychiatric populations. Prins (1980) and Howells (1982) have reviewed the evidence and point to a number of important findings. Howells notes that there are marked discrepancies between early and recent studies. The early studies typically reported that psychiatric hospital populations had similar levels of criminal behaviour to the general population (L.H. Cohen and Freeman 1945). Later studies differed, finding that psychiatric patients are more likely to commit offences (Rappeport et al. 1967). However, the term 'offence' requires clarification: for some offences, generally non-violent, the rates are similar in psychiatric populations and the general population; while for robbery and possibly rape the incidence is higher in psychiatric populations (Rappeport and Lassen 1967). It should also be noted that the majority of studies are American; a German study found very much lower rates of serious crime in a sample of mentally disordered offenders (Häfner and Böker 1982). This variation may relate to the point made by Rabkin (1979) that the crime rate can rise in psychiatric in-patient populations if social policy dictates the use of hospital facilities for individuals who exhibit socially deviant, criminal, behaviour. The higher incidence of offending in psychiatric populations may not then be a function of a generally high level of offending, rather a result of an exceptionally high frequency of offending by a small proportion of the psychiatric population. Following this, it is probably also the case that in-patient populations are a biased sample of the general mentally disordered population. Therefore there is a confound between three factors, mental disorder, crime, and institutionalization; any relationships between the three may be causal or correlational; at present it is impossible to say.

On the basis of studies of both mental disorder in offender populations and offending in psychiatric populations it must therefore be concluded that the relationship between mental disorder and crime remains equivocal.

Type of mental disorder and crime

Thus far the term 'mental disorder' has been used without qualification, although it is apparent that it covers a range of types of behaviour and diagnostic categories. While, as discussed previously, there are difficulties with the term 'mental disorder' clearly it is necessary to have a definition, for legal purposes if nothing else. The Mental Health Act, 1983, in England and Wales divided 'mental disorder' into four categories: 'Mental illness, arrested or incomplete development of the mind, psychopathic disorder and any other disorder or disability of mind' [s. 1(2)]. In practice it is the first three categories which assume the greatest importance and so these will be discussed in turn; examining both the nature of the specific disorder and its relationship with offending.

Mental illness and crime

In truth, the term 'mental illness' causes more problems than it solves: Ashworth and Gostin note that mental illness is not defined in the Mental Health Act and therefore 'much will depend upon medical opinion' (1985: 212). In practice the term is used for a wide range of diagnostic categories including psychoses, affective disorders, anxiety states, hysteria, and so on (see Prins 1980). Inspection of admissions to Special Hospitals (see Chapter 7) shows that by far the greatest number of mentally ill serious offenders are diagnosed as schizophrenic, with depression the next most frequent diagnosis (Craft 1984; J.R. Hamilton 1985). Does any special relationship exist between these two particular disorders and crime?

Schizophrenia The most important indicators of schizophrenia, which would *not* all be found in one person, include disturbances of thought, perception, affect, and motor behaviour (Cutting 1985; Neale and Oltmanns 1980). Thought disorder refers to a disturbance of the process of making associations between thoughts. Perceptual disturbances are evinced by hallucinations, which may be visual or tactile but are most commonly auditory, typically as voices commenting or giving instructions. Affect can be flat and expressionless or alternatively it can be inappropriate such as anger without provocation, or laughter at misfortune. Finally, motor disturbances can take the form of bizarre facial grimaces, repeated gesturing, or excited agitation of the body; alternatively unusual postures can be adopted and held, in a state of immobility, for long periods. As noted, not all these behaviours would be found in the same person, although some pattern does emerge: disorganized or hebephrenic schizophrenia is characterized by hallucinations, delusions, and inappropriate affect; catatonic schizophrenia by motor disturbances; and paranoid schizophrenia by delusions of persecution, incorporating 'ideas of reference' in which personal significance is continually perceived in the actions of other people. Given this range, it may well be expedient to think of schizophrenia as a group of disorders rather than a single disorder which always manifests itself in the same fashion. While of uncertain aetiology, contemporary theories favour a complex interaction between genetic, neurochemical, and social factors as an explanation for schizophrenia. It is generally accepted that the incidence of schizophrenia is close to 1 per cent in the general population: this sets a baseline against which to compare the rates of schizophrenia in offender populations.

Spry (1984) reviews the evidence on the incidence of schizophrenia and crime and notes a division in research findings: with studies of non-disordered offender groups the incidence of schizophrenia is around the 1 per cent mark (although P.J. Taylor's 1986 figures for life-sentenced offenders were substantially higher); with selected samples of offenders referred for psychiatric treatment, typically having committed serious offences, the incidence is much higher. For example, Green (1981) reports that 74 per cent of a sample of fifty-eight men admitted to a Special Hospital having committed matricide were schizophrenic. Does this suggest that schizophrenia is related to serious offences? As Spry notes, many people associate schizophrenia with crime, particularly violent crime. Indeed, there are indications that a relationship may exist between paranoid ideas and violence, and that the victims of violent attacks are often those who figured in the schizophrenic's delusions (Häfner and Böker 1982; Planansky and Johnston 1977). Crimes of this type catch the public imagination: Prins (1986) notes the case of Ian Ball, in which delusional thought processes were manifest in a plot to kidnap a member of the royal family: Prins (1983; 1986) discusses the crimes of Peter Sutcliffe, the 'Yorkshire Ripper', in which there was some controversy as to the role of his paranoid schizophrenia in the murders he committed. It should be stressed, however, that the publicity generated by these cases is in inverse proportion to their frequency; the deluded and paranoid people who commit such crimes are rare.

While these extreme cases are infrequent, the finding remains that schizophrenics are slightly more likely to commit violent offences than other disordered groups or the general population (Sosowsky 1978). While schizophrenia may be directly related to violence, with delusional and paranoid beliefs of apparent importance, a simple relationship between the disorder and the crime is unlikely to exist. P.J. Taylor suggests that: 'It is not unusual to find that the violent act of a schizophrenic cannot be directly explained by the current psychopathology. This does not, however, negate the relevance of the illness . . . social and illness variables must be considered together' (1982: 280). The point Taylor makes is an important one: as well as considering a causal relationship between schizophrenia and violence, attention should also be paid to the similarities in social, environmental, and organic antecedents common to both violence and schizophrenia. More recent findings by the same researcher reinforce this point. From a survey of 121 psychotic offenders, Taylor concluded that '20% of the actively psychotic were directly driven to offend by their psychotic symptoms, and a further 26% probably so' (1985: 497). When social factors such as homelessness were considered along with the nature of the crime, so that 'the direct and indirect consequences of psychosis are considered together, then over 80% of the offences of the psychotic were probably attributable to their illness' (1985: 497).

Depression Clinically two types of depression are distinguished: *major* (or *unipolar*) *depression* and *bipolar disorder*. Major depression is characterized by profoundly sad mood, overwhelming feelings of self-blame, guilt, and worthlessness, appetite disturbances, fatigue and long periods of sleep, lethargy, and recurrent thoughts of death and suicide. Bipolar disorder is typified by bouts of mania as well as periods of depression: during the manic phase the individual shows elated or irritable mood, high levels of furious physical activity, goes long periods without sleep, and displays a general air of self-importance and inflated self-esteem (Davison and Neale 1986). Of the two, major depression is by far the most common, with estimates suggesting that 8 per cent to 11 per cent of men and 18 per cent to 23 per cent of women will be clinically depressed at least once in their life; bipolar disorder is less frequent, appearing in about 1 per cent of the population (Weissman and Myers 1978). Theories of depression incorporate a wide range of biological, cognitive, behavioural, and social factors (Gilbert 1984).

As with schizophrenia — or, indeed, any mental illness — there are difficulties in establishing the relationship between depression and crime. A range of possibilities exists: the crime may have been committed because the offender was depressed; the offender may become depressed after the crime, either because of guilt or imprisonment; the offender may have been depressed when committing the crime, but the depression was not instrumental in causing the crime. In terms of a direct causal link, one of the more familiar and tragic associations between depression and crime occurs when an individual becomes convinced that life is hopeless and before committing suicide kills his or her children and other members of the family. West (1965) studied seventy-eight cases of murder followed by suicide and estimated that twenty-eight of the offenders were depressed at the time of the offence. (Although this does not prove that the depression caused the offence.) Lawson suggests that a general pattern in certain murders by depressives lies in the 'social circumstances and pathological features of the domestic killing' (1984: 146). The social circumstances involve a negative life event such as an upset in a long-term relationship, while the act itself shows no sign of planning or even malice.

As well as murder, depression has been associated with other crimes including shoplifting (Lawson 1984) and violence (Häfner and Böker 1982). With regard to violence, Häfner and Böker (1982) found that the violence was principally directed at relatives, suggesting similarities with the 'extended suicides' discussed above. As Howells (1982) notes, depressed in-patients are not a violent population, suggesting that the relationship between depression and crime (when it is causal) is closely tied to social, particularly interpersonal, factors.

Although most studies do not indicate which type of depression is present, it is reasonable to assume that major depression is involved. However, McCulloch and Prins (1978) do describe a case involving a manic episode, a car salesman, and violence towards property. While Blumberg (1981) suggested that, after schizophrenia, manic depressive episodes were the disorder most commonly found in arsonists; Gunderson (1974) similarly suggested that firesetting during a manic state may be more common than is generally acknowledged.

The broad picture which emerges for mental illness and crime does not really take us much further than the general evidence for 'mental disorder' and crime. Mental illness, particularly schizophrenia and depression, are found in criminal populations but the exact nature of the relationship between the two remains unclear. P.J. Taylor's (1985) work is however beginning to show how psychosis and crime may be seen as complex psychosocial phenomena, rather than in a simple relationship in which one factor has a linear causal effect on the other.

Mental handicap and crime — intellectual functioning

The Mental Health Act seeks to define a group of offenders characterized by 'arrested or incomplete development of mind which includes . . . impairment of intelligence and social functioning' [s. 1(2)]. The Act distinguishes between 'severe' and 'significant' mental impairment although the difference between the two is not clarified (Ashworth and Gostin 1985). The group the Act refers to are those generally referred to as mentally handicapped, although other terms such as mentally retarded and mentally subnormal are sometimes used. It should of course be emphasized that mental *handicap* is not the same as mental *illness*. The former refers to the person's enduring level of intellectual and social ability; the latter is an episodic disturbance which does not necessarily affect intellectual functioning. The assessment of mental handicap relies on a combination of results from tests of intellectual and social ability. While there is no legal level of IQ score by which to define impairment, in clinical assessment it is generally taken that an IQ in the region of 70 points (on tests with a 'normal' score of 100) is taken as 'borderline'. Thus a score of 70 or below, in conjunction with a low level of social functioning (Sparrow *et al.* 1984), may be indicative of some degree of handicap (having eliminated any other explanations such as memory loss, trauma, and so on). IQ scores below 50 usually indicate a substantial degree of impairment.

The 'two group theory' suggests a division between two types of mental impairment (Schonebaum and Zinober 1977). The first is a 'normal impairment', as defined by those individuals who are at the lower end of the IQ distribution. This may be because of family factors, including genetic endowment, or because of poor schooling or other environmental factors. While low in terms of IQ points, such individuals are usually well adapted socially. The second group are those who score very low on IQ tests (below 50) and show poor social adaptation. Unlike the first group, there is usually an identifiable cause for the impairment: this may be a genetic or chromosomal abnormality such as Down's syndrome; a biological disturbance such as phenylketonuria (PKU); damage or infection *in utero*, as with rubella; birth complications such as anoxia; childhood disease like meningitis; head injury resulting in brain damage; or poisoning such as by lead, radiation, or toxic chemicals.

In examining the relationship between mental handicap and crime two approaches have been used: the study of the intellectual functioning of offenders generally, and investigation of the specific offences of mentally handicapped offenders. Before looking at the evidence it is as well to make a number of points about measuring intelligence. Most research comparing offender and non-offender groups has used IQ tests to measure intellectual ability. However, the possibility must be considered that this means of measurement introduces unwanted variance into the results: in other words, are the tests biased against offender groups? The important point is whether the standardization of the test included offenders. Standardization can be thought of as the estimation of test norms, that is, the levels or standards present in the general population. A properly standardized IQ test should in theory always yield the same average score in a random sample from the general population. It should not, for example, be possible to score higher on an IQ test simply because, say, of age: the average score on a properly standardized test should be the same for any age level; if not, then the test is biased against some age groups. Thus if the population sample on which the test was standardized did not include offenders, then the possibility cannot be discounted that any difference in IQ between offender and non-offender groups may be due to test bias. Of course it is also the case that any differences may be due to social class, cultural, and educational differences between offender and non-offender samples. This is not test bias, rather a reflection that intellectual performance is affected by environmental factors. To be sure that real differences in IQ exist between offender and non-offender samples it is necessary to be confident that the particular IQ test employed is not biased against offenders, and that effects due to differences in class, educational background, and so on have been controlled or allowed for in the research. In practice the environmental variables are likely to exert a greater influence on IQ test scores than variations in standardization. Nevertheless, both points should be held in mind when considering the evidence on intelligence and offending.

Intelligence in offender populations Opinion on the nature of the relationship between intelligence and crime has gone through a number of historical phases. As discussed in Chapter 2, Charles Goring, a contemporary of Lombroso, studied 3,000 English convicts and found them to be of generally low intelligence. Goring suggested that crime was therefore the result of a lack of intelligence, in turn determined by genetic factors. As criminology grew in sophistication such simplistic, unitary causes of crime were replaced by complex multidimensional theories, often with a strong sociological content. The inclusion of individual characteristics such as intelligence into such theories gradually passed out of fashion. Indeed, the occasional study suggested that there was little to be gained from such a line of investigation: Woodward (1955) calculated that on average offenders were not more than eight IQ points below the population mean — a small difference, say 92 as compared to 100. However, in the 1960s and 1970s research once again began to suggest an association between IQ and crime. An American study by

Hirschi (1969) found a significant association between IQ and self-reported delinquency, an association which remained even after allowing for the influence of race and social status. A longitudinal study of boys living in London reported by West and Farrington (1973) found a strong correlation between IQ and recidivism, with boys of lower IQ more likely to become recidivists. The correlation remained when the analysis controlled for family size and income. These and other studies led Hirschi and Hindelang (1977) to reintroduce intelligence as an important factor in understanding the development of criminal behaviour. More recent studies have added confirmatory evidence to this line of thought (Moffitt *et al.* 1981).

If the correlation appears reasonably strong, its meaning is less clear. West and Farrington (1973) extended their analysis and discovered that lower IQ was also associated with problem behaviour in early life, suggesting that the link between IQ and delinquency was via this earlier association. Richman *et al.* (1982) similarly showed that the IQ link with behavioural disorders could be found by 3 years of age. It seems likely therefore that IQ and crime are associated via one or more other pathways. Rutter and Giller (1983) suggest two possible routes. The first is that low IQ leads to educational failure, which leads to low self-esteem and emotional disturbance, in turn leading to conduct disorder and criminal behaviour. While there is support for a relationship between learning disability and crime (Keilitz and Dunivant 1986), this does not account for the findings which suggest that the associations are present at pre-school ages (Richman *et al.* 1982; West and Farrington 1973). The second hypothesis is that IQ and conduct disorder share a common aetiology, the exact nature of which is open to speculation: this could be a biological, social, or familial influence; or even another individual factor such as temperament (Offord *et al.* 1978).

Other research has examined the IQs of convicted offender populations. As with all studies of offender populations, it should be remembered that these are a highly selected sample and may be unrepresentative of the general offender population, especially with regard to intelligence. Craft (1984) collated information from fifteen studies of IQ in convicted prisoners carried out between 1931 and 1952. The earlier studies show low mean IQs, ranging from a mean of 71 to a mean of 88: the most recent studies show a marked difference, all finding mean IQs of 92. This may reflect changes in IQ tests, as well as policy changes over the decades regarding the disposal of offenders with low IQs. Although significant fluctuations in prison population IQ levels over a short period of time have been recorded (Barnes *et al.* 1984).

It should be pointed out that most of the studies discussed this far are not concerned with very low IQ scores, but rather more with IQs which tend towards the 'below average' classification. While low IQ is as common among men first convicted in adulthood as among boys first convicted as juveniles (West and Farrington 1977), this does *not* imply that criminals are, by definition, mentally handicapped. Offenders may display a lower IQ on average — but this means that some offenders will have normal or above normal IQs. Further, mental handicap is as much concerned with social functioning as with IQ, but the research has mainly been concerned with intelligence.

A number of studies have been concerned with very low IQ scores in offender populations. Craft (1984) reports that in convicted prisoners the percentage with IQ scores less than 70 varied from a high of 31 per cent in a 1931 study, to about 10 per cent in 1940s studies, to a low of 4.2 per cent in a 1950 study. Prins (1980) presents a similar survey (including different studies), noting a high of 28 per cent of convicted offenders deemed 'subnormal' in a 1918 study, falling to 2.4 per cent in a 1964 study. This probably reflects changes over time in the disposal of mentally handicapped offenders. More recent studies have controlled for variables such as type of test and time of testing and have found about 2.5 per cent of the prison population have IQ scores below 70 (Denkowski and Denkowski 1985; MacEachron 1979). The importance of social functioning is seen in a survey by Denkowski and Denkowski (1985) of the prevalence of mentally handicapped inmates in the prisons of twenty states in the USA. From their figures on individually tested prisoners, it can be calculated that 2.25 per cent of prisoners are classified as retarded in those states which rely on IQ testing and do not use a formal means of assessing adaptive behaviour. In the five states where IQ and adaptive behaviour was assessed (using a standard psychometric test) the percentage of mentally handicapped prisoners is 1.28 per cent. These lower figures — in the region of 2–2.5 per cent — are similar to the incidence of mental handicap in the non-offender population. Therefore mental handicap is unlikely, in itself, to be a strong factor in the aetiology of crime: nevertheless mentally handicapped people do commit crimes — is there anything remarkable about this group?

Offending and mental handicap N. Walker (1965) compared the indictable offences of 305 males ordered over a one-year period to be committed to hospital as mentally handicapped, with the offences of all other male offenders dealt with by the courts in the same year. While there were no differences in the frequency of violent and property offences, the percentage of handicapped offenders sentenced for sexual offences was six times as great as that for the other offenders. Similarly A. Shapiro (1969) found that in a sample of compulsorily detained mentally handicapped offenders, 35 per cent had committed a sexual offence. Tutt (1971), with a sample from a 'subnormality hospital', found that almost 16 per cent had been convicted of a sexual offence prior to admission. These rates are much higher than the expected figure for sex offences in the general offender population, which would be of the order of 3 per cent. Robertson (1981) carried out a follow-up study of the offences of a group of over 300 mentally handicapped offenders who appeared before the courts for a criminal offence and had received a hospital order (under Section 60 of the old 1959 Act) and had subsequently been released into the community. As can be seen from Table 4.2, most of the offences are not unusual, although the rate of sex offences in males is relatively high.

Table 4.2 Principal offences of mentally handicapped offenders (from Robertson 1981)

	Males	Females
Larceny	54	60
Breaking and entering	33	9
Sexual indecency	12	–
Soliciting	–	9
Arson	3	1
GBH/wounding	2	3
Rape	1	–
Manslaughter	1	0
Robbery	1	0

Note: The figure is a percentage of the sample who committed a particular crime; offenders can commit more than one type of crime, therefore the figures do not total 100%.

Robertson (1981) also compared the male mentally handicapped offenders with a sample of male mentally ill offenders. In personal terms, the handicapped offenders were much younger and less likely to have been married. The handicapped group had fewer hospital admissions, with about half having been in-patients prior to the Section 60 order, compared to about 80 per cent of the mentally ill group. With regard to criminal history, the handicapped group were younger when receiving their first conviction and had committed many more offences as juveniles. Despite this, the mentally ill group had more court appearances and had spent longer in prison. While the incidence of theft was similar in the two groups, the mentally ill offenders had been convicted of more (non-sexual) violent offences such as assault and criminal damage, with more sexual offences in the handicapped group. As Robertson comments, apart from the sexual offences, the pattern shown by the handicapped offender of petty juvenile crime developing in later life to various acquisitive offences is similar to that found in the general offender population. This contrasts sharply with the atypical pattern seen in the mentally ill population in which, as Robertson notes, 'juvenile offending is rare and where criminality may be one consequence of a general social deterioration following chronic illness' (1981: 102).

It is, however, important to note several ways in which the mentally handicapped offender is disadvantaged compared to his or her more able contemporaries. The mentally handicapped offender may not have learned the difference between acceptable and unacceptable behaviour, therefore a 'crime' cannot be elevated to the status of a 'right' or 'wrong' act in the sense that the person knowingly transgressed the law. The handicap may mean that the crime itself is carried out less efficiently, leading to easier detection, or the mentally handicapped person may be exploited by more able offenders. In some cases mental handicap is associated with emotional outbursts, particularly following some stressful event, which may in turn precipitate aggressive acts (McCulloch and Prins 1978). A lack of social skills may mean that acts intended to be friendly are seen by others as aggressive or hostile, resulting in unfortunate consequences. A similar point may hold for sexual skills: as Craft and Craft (1978) note, the sexual experimentation of mentally handicapped people may be more visible and hence more upsetting than convention allows. Thus the high sexual offending of this group may reflect a paucity of skills in making acceptable sexual approaches; such social naivety may be seen by the 'victim' as assault and criminal proceedings are likely to follow.

In the discussion of theories of mental handicap, the distinction was made between 'normal' mental handicap and those cases where the handicap results from some known, usually organic, cause. Research into mental handicap and offending has not considered this distinction: a point which may be something for future research to address as the aetiology of mental handicap in the offender may be informative theoretically, and have practical implications in terms of management and the services offered to this type of offender.

Psychopathic disorder

The 1983 Act defines psychopathic disorder as 'a persistent disorder or disability of mind (whether or not including significant impairment of intelligence) which results in abnormally aggressive or seriously irresponsible conduct' [s. 1(2)]. As various commentators have noted, this is a less than perfect definition in that it does not specify what is meant by 'persistent', 'abnormally aggressive', or 'seriously irresponsible' (see Ashworth and Gostin 1985). To complicate matters further, the American system varies the terminology: as Davison and Neale note, 'In current usage the terms *sociopath* and *psychopath* appear interchangeably with antisocial personality' (1986: 233). Given this, what characteristics identify such an ill-defined category of offenders?

Identifying the psychopath Cleckley (1964; 1976) identified the psychopath by listing the characteristics observed in clinical practice: as can be seen from Table 4.3 these identifying characteristics place emphasis on the emotional and social emptiness of the psychopath.

Table 4.3 Cleckley's (1976) characteristics of the psychopath

1 Superficial charm and good intelligence
2 Absence of delusions and other signs of irrational thinking
3 Absence of 'nervousness' or other psychoneurotic manifestations
4 Unreliability
5 Untruthfulness and insincerity
6 Lack of remorse or shame
7 Inadequately motivated antisocial behaviour
8 Poor judgement and failure to learn by experience
9 Pathologic egocentricity and incapacity for love
10 General poverty in major affective reactions
11 Specific loss of insight
12 Unresponsiveness in general interpersonal relations
13 Fantastic and uninviting behaviour with drink and sometimes without
14 Suicide rarely carried out
15 Sex life impersonal, trivial, and poorly integrated
16 Failure to follow any life plan

Hare (1980) conducted a factor analysis of data derived from the Cleckley criteria and found five factors, which offer a succinct description of the psychopath: they show (1) an inability to develop warm, empathic relationships; (2) an unstable life-style; (3) an inability to accept responsibility for their antisocial behaviour; (4) an absence of intellectual and psychiatric problems; (5) weak behavioural control. Blackburn and

Maybury performed a similar analysis on the Cleckley checklist which 'yielded results which are broadly in agreement with those of Hare (1980) in indicating that a unitary dimension describable as lack of empathy or affection pervades most of the criteria' (1985: 383). However, as numerous commentators have noted, many of the terms used by Cleckley are vague and imprecise, causing difficulties for clinicians and researchers alike. Hare (1980) constructed a more precise scale for the assessment of psychopathy in criminal populations: this scale is shown in full in Table 4.4.

Table 4.4 Psychopathy checklist (from Hare 1980)

1 Glibness/superficial charm
2 Previous diagnosis as psychopath (or similar)
3 Egocentricity/grandiose sense of self-worth
4 Proneness to boredom/low frustration tolerance
5 Pathological lying and deception
6 Conning/lack of sincerity
7 Lack of remorse or guilt
8 Lack of affect and emotional depth
9 Callous/lack of empathy
10 Parasitic life-style
11 Short-tempered/poor behavioural controls
12 Promiscuous sexual relations
13 Early behaviour problems
14 Lack of realistic, long-term plans
15 Impulsivity
16 Irresponsible behaviour as a parent
17 Frequent marital relationships
18 Juvenile delinquency
19 Poor probation or parole risk
20 Failure to accept responsibility for own actions
21 Many types of offence
22 Drug or alcohol abuse not direct cause of antisocial behaviour

Factor analysis showed that the new scale also contained five factors, similar to those found in the factor analysis of the original Cleckley checklist. Analysis also showed high agreement between the new scale and Cleckley's original criteria. Hare (1986) has subsequently shortened the list (removing items 2 and 22) to give a *Psychopathy Checklist* for use by clinicians and researchers.

The approach adopted by Cleckley and Hare to identifying the psychopath rests on clinical observation of the defining characteristics; statistical techniques are then used to produce a reliable psychometric instrument based on the observations. A different approach to the same task is to use existing psychometric measures to define a particular 'psychopathic' personality. The work of the British psychologist Ronald Blackburn is of particular significance here.

As discussed in Chapter 3, Blackburn's original psychometric research described four types of violent offender, within which the distinction was made between *primary psychopaths* and *secondary psychopaths*. The primary group is characterized by high levels of hostility, low anxiety levels, and has few psychiatric problems. The secondary psychopaths also show high levels of hostility but with attendant anxiety, guilt, and psychiatric disturbance. Blackburn (1982) has shown that the original four groups can be described in terms of two factors, psychopathy and sociability. Primary psychopaths are high on psychopathy and sociability; secondary psychopaths also score highly on psychopathy but are low on sociability (that is they are withdrawn). Blackburn (1982) presents data which suggest that primary psychopaths are more likely to commit violent acts, while secondary psychopaths are more likely to commit sex offences.

Hare (1985; 1986) compared a variety of assessment procedures including the checklist shown in Table 4.4 and various self-report inventories including the MMPI (although not the measures used by Blackburn). Hare concludes that 'Self-report inventories simply do not sort subjects in the same way that clinical-behavioral procedures do' (1986: 20): Hare recommends the twenty-two-item Psychopathy Checklist as a valid measure of psychopathy as it relates strongly to 'criminal activities, violence, institutional behavior, and outcome on conditional release, including parole' (1986: 21), although, as Hare points out, agreement is not perfect among such clinical assessments. Further, despite its clinical utility, this checklist approach does little towards contributing to the understanding of the aetiology of psychopathy and the development of a theoretical model of the disorder.

A third level of identification is a more informal one, but none the less important for that, the criteria used by practitioners to diagnose psychopathy. W. Davies and Feldman (1981) asked a sample of over thirty 'forensic specialists' to rate the importance of twenty-two signs of psychopathy. The ratings, as shown in Table 4.5 clearly indicate which signs sway the experts.

In summary, what has been identified about the psychopath? It is not a well-defined condition, nor is it universally popular (Howells 1982), yet it is one which is used and cannot be ignored. A publication by the Department of Health and Social Security and the Home Office offers a pragmatic, operational definition:

Table 4.5 The importance of various signs of psychopathy as rated by forensic specialists (from W. Davies and Feldman 1981)

		Mean rating
1	Not profiting from experience	8.25
2	Lacking control over impulses	8.22
3	Chronically or recurrently antisocial	8.16
4	Lacking a sense of responsibility	7.53
5	Behaviour unaffected by punishment	7.50
6	Inability to form meaningful relationships	7.28
7	Emotional immaturity	7.28
8	Inability to experience guilt	7.25
9	Lack of moral sense	6.75
10	Deficiency in goal-directed behaviour	6.31
11	Self-centred	6.25
12	Frequent law-breaking	5.81
13	Frequent lying	5.75
14	Is aggressive	5.63
15	Occupationally unstable	5.45
16	Irresponsible sexual behaviour	4.03
17	Excessive alcohol consumption	3.84
18	Shows pronounced swings in mood	3.13
19	Abnormal EEG	3.00
20	Hyperactivity	1.25
21	More intelligent than average	1.19
22	Homosexuality	1.13

Note: 10 = very important; 0 = not at all important

The consensus view is that psychopathic disorder is not a description of a single clinical disorder but a convenient label to describe a severe personality disorder which may show itself in a variety of attitudinal, emotional and inter-personal behaviour problems. The core problem is impairment in the capacity to relate to others — to take account of their feelings and to act in ways consistent with their safety and convenience. (DHSS and Home Office 1986: 4)

While there is debate about the means of identification of the psychopath, indeed about the utility of the term psychopath, a body of research evidence has accumulated which seeks to examine a range of correlates of psychopathy. The force of this approach is that it may provide an empirical means of differentiating the psychopath from the non-psychopath and, should the distinction be established, so move towards a theory of psychopathy. The research falls into the three areas of background variables, physiological functioning, and cognitive-behavioural factors.

Background variables in psychopathy The most cited aetiological variables in psychopathy are the familiar ones of family functioning, childhood behaviour, and genetic influences. W. McCord and J. McCord (1964) suggested that lack of affection and severe parental rejection were primary aetiological factors, while a longitudinal study by Robins (1966) pointed to a variety of early behavioural problems which were strongly associated with psychopathic behaviour as an adult. These problems included early referral to a child guidance clinic for theft or aggression, a history of truancy, lying, non-compliance, no signs of guilt or remorse, and general irreponsibility regarding school and family routines. As with the McCord and McCord study, family characteristics of little or no discipline were also associated with later psychopathic behaviour, as was antisocial behaviour shown by the father. However, it should be added that this pattern of a wayward childhood is a predictor of many disorders in later life, including criminal behaviour not labelled psychopathic, as well as a range of clinical disorders from neuroses to psychoses. Therefore these findings do not point exactly to the particular antecedents of psychopathy.

Some investigators have suggested that the basis of psychopathy, viewed as an extreme of antisocial behaviour, lies in genetic transmission. The evidence in support of a genetic component to antisocial behaviour was reviewed in Chapter 2, noting findings from adoption and twin studies which support the proposition. Cadoret (1986) extends this argument to psychopathy.

While family, longitudinal, and genetic studies suggest various correlates of psychopathy, they do not provide all the answers: how does the genetic transmission work and what factors mediate poor parenting to produce psychopathic behaviour? An answer may lie in a suggestion made by Cantwell (1975) that adult psychopathy is associated with childhood hyperactivity, the common thread being a similar neurological abnormality of possible genetic origin. Is the key to unlocking psychopathy physiological in nature?

Physiology and psychopathy There is a considerable body of research evidence on physiological and psychophysiological functioning and psychopathy (Blackburn 1983; Raine 1985): for the most part investigators have concentrated on the central nervous system (CNS) and the autonomic nervous system (ANS).

Studies of CNS functioning have relied on the electroencephalogram (EEG), a recording of the electrical activity of the brain. A review by Syndulko (1978) pointed to the methodological difficulties of EEG studies, but nevertheless suggested high frequencies of EEG abnormality in psychopaths; the problem is, however, that not all psychopaths show EEG abnormalities, and in those that do the pattern of abnormality is not consistent. Further, the pattern varies across situations: Hare and Jutai (cited in Davison and Neale 1986) found abnormal EEGs when the psychopaths were resting, but normal EEGs when the psychopaths were in an active state. Blackburn (1975b; 1979) found little evidence to support the notion of a general association between EEG arousal and aggression; but suggested that differences may exist between primary and secondary psychopaths. The primary psychopaths showed the lowest levels of EEG arousal, while the secondary psychopaths appeared more alert even when resting.

Studies of ANS functioning in psychopaths have concentrated upon reactivity and arousal levels as indices of ANS activity. One of the most cited results from this line of research is that when resting, psychopaths have unduly *low* levels of electrodermal reactivity, but in stressful situations there are very *high* levels of cardiac reactivity (Hare 1978; Jutai and Hare 1983). This can be viewed as a fast heart-rate indicating the 'gating out' of sensory input and so lowering cortical arousal, meaning that the psychopath is effectively 'tuning out' unpleasant environmental cues. Skin conductance is therefore low because to all intents and purposes environmental stimuli, especially aversive stimuli, are being ignored.

While of interest, these physiological findings assume greater significance when considered in the context of cognitive-behavioural evidence.

Cognitive-behavioural performance in psychopaths Cleckley suggested that one of the main characteristics of the psychopath was a failure to learn from experience. This poor learning is evident in the psychopath's failure to avoid the negative consequences of antisocial behaviour. A number of studies have experimentally tested this suggestion employing the technique of *passive avoidance learning* in which the subject learns to respond to anticipatory cues in order to avoid some unpleasant outcome (usually electric shock in laboratory studies). The findings indicate that psychopaths perform poorly on passive avoidance learning tasks: a result taken to indicate that psychopaths are in a low state of ANS arousal and are relatively anxiety-free (Chesno and Kilmann 1975; Lykken 1957; Schachter and Latané 1964). The physiological evidence on ANS functioning suggests how this might occur: high cardiac arousal gates out the cues indicating the forthcoming unpleasant event, leading in turn to lower arousal and impaired avoidance learning. However, this picture becomes a little more complicated by evidence which showed an effect of the type of aversive event. When the aversive consequence of poor learning was physical pain or social disapproval the psychopaths performed poorly as compared to non-psychopathic controls; however, if the outcome was financial penalty, the psychopaths learned more efficiently than the controls (Schmauk 1970). The introduction of a cognitive component might account for this difference in responding: for example some 'punishments' may have little or no meaning for psychopaths. Thus a prior cognition 'signals' a stressful event which, in turn, is gated out as indicated by the levels of physiological functioning.

If the experimental learning task is made more complex by including the competing goals of monetary reward for good performance and avoiding monetary loss for poor performance, then psychopaths perform at a lower level than controls (J.P. Newman and Kosson 1986; J.P. Newman *et al.* 1985). As psychopaths are equal to controls with financial loss only, it may be that psychopaths have difficulty attending to competing contingencies once they are trying to gain a reward. Newman *et al.* (1987) employed an experimental task in which money could be gained and lost: they found that while controls were able to adjust their performance to allow for increases in the probability of losing, psychopaths failed to make such adjustments and so lost accordingly. This pattern of behaviour is termed 'response perseveration': the continuation of the same action regardless of the consequences it produces. In other words, a failure to learn from experience. Newman *et al.* (1987) found that if a 5-second delay was forced between one response and the next, so as to interrupt response set and allow increased time to attend to feedback from the last response, then the deficit between psychopaths and controls was reduced. The reason for this effect of delay is uncertain.

These learning difficulties, as demonstrated in experimental tasks, may — perhaps in conjunction with physiological variables — be related to the under-socialization and poor social performance of psychopaths. While psychopaths may commit crimes of aggression and brutality, this type of behaviour does not seem to be specific to particular types of situations: Blackburn (1982) found that even in a hospital ward psychopaths were rated by nurses as more aggressive, more likely to use threatening behaviour to both staff and other patients, and less likely to follow institutional rules than other patients. The pattern of non-conformity to social rules (including offending under this broad heading) and subsequent lack of remorse can be seen as a failure to learn to avoid social censure; alongside response perseveration in that the same behaviour is continually repeated regardless of the situational demands.

Blackburn and Lee-Evans (1985) examined the anticipated reactions of primary and secondary psychopaths to anger-evoking situations. (It should be noted that this study was concerned with *anticipated* reactions — there may be differences between anticipated and actual behaviour.) They found that psychopaths reported stronger anticipated reactions than controls, particularly for situations involving personal attack. The primary psychopaths anticipated less strong reactions than the secondary psychopaths: this is in accord with Blackburn's (1982) earlier suggestion that the aggression of primary psychopaths is more likely to be 'incentive-motivated', while that of secondary psychopaths is 'annoyance-motivated'. Blackburn and Lee-Evans suggest that the cognitive processes associated with the angry reaction may be of particular importance, particularly with regard to the attentional bias in perceiving hostility in social cues. This suggestion is at odds with a view of psychopathy which suggests a lack of sensitivity to social cues in proposing that the psychopath's aggressive behaviour is in fact a maladaptive strategy in interpersonal problem-solving.

In total the psychology of the psychopath is not clearly understood despite contributions such as those discussed above and others from areas as diverse as ego psychology (Dorr and Woodhall 1986), analogies with child development (Kegan 1986), and conceptualizations in terms of an interpersonal circumplex (Blackburn and Maybury 1985). Indeed the psychopath remains something of a puzzle: the most reliable fact is that there are relatively small numbers as reflected in official records. In England and Wales in 1984 there were 410 restricted patients classified as psychopathic detained in hospital. Of this number, 200 had been convicted of homicide or other offences against the person, 90 of arson, and 70 of sexual offences (DHSS and Home Office 1986). The number of unclassified psychopaths is, of course, unknown. When compared to mentally ill and mentally handicapped offenders, psychopaths are much more 'criminal': they have committed more offences, particularly theft and assault; received more prison sentences; and spent more time in prison (Robertson 1981): which all suggests that the prison population may contain substantial numbers of psychopathic offenders.

Thus the difficulties posed by the psychopath are numerous: the term itself is ill defined both legally and empirically; the diagnosis of psychopathy is correspondingly unreliable, but once delivered is a powerful label; and there is disagreement about the concept of psychopathy. Two strategies present themselves for resolving this state of affairs. The first is to remove psychopathy from legal and diagnostic classifications, and there have been recommendations that this should be done, notably by the Butler Report (Home Office and DHSS 1975). The second strategy is to pursue empirical research to refine the concept to a degree which allows reliable and valid classification or admits that this is impossible. To place the debate in context it is as well to remember, as Blackburn and Maybury note, 'psychopathy is a theoretical construct rather than a palpable entity' (1985: 375).

In summary, it can be said that mental disorder and criminal behaviour do, at times, co-exist. The nature of the relationship is altogether less clear. In some cases the relationship appears to be partially causal; however, as Taylor stresses, both disorder and crime must be placed in a social context to gain a full picture of the offence. Anticipating future research, it is unlikely that hard and fast rules will be generated regarding mental disorder and crime. It is more likely that each case will have to be considered on its individual merits to determine, in that particular instance, the nature of the relationship between the disorder and the crime. This is a point of some significance in a legal context when the court must decide on issues of responsibility in order to determine whether the offender can be held accountable and therefore punishable for their actions.

Perspective

The mentally disordered offender poses special problems for a legal system, such as that in this country, which incorporates the notion of *mens rea*: that is it must be shown that the individual acted with criminal intent, exercising free will, and can therefore be held fully responsible for the crime they committed. (While there are considerable philosophical and psychological difficulties with the concept of *mens rea* (Crombag 1984), the discussion here will be limited to the mentally disordered offender.) The question therefore becomes 'Can mentally disordered offenders be held responsible for their crimes?' The responses to this question are many and varied and full exploraiton of an extensive, specialized literature is beyond the scope of the present work. However, a brief overview gives a flavour of the important issues involved.

While the status of the mentally disordered offender has a long history in English law (see N. Walker 1968), the famous case of Daniel

M'Naghten in 1843 is generally seen as the beginning of contemporary legislation. M'Naghten attempted to kill the prime minister of the time, Sir Robert Peel, but erroneously shot and killed the prime minister's secretary. In his defence it was pleaded that M'Naghten suffered from paranoid delusions, one of which was that Peel was persecuting him: the defence maintained that at the time of the offence M'Naghten had lost control and had been unable to resist his delusions. M'Naghten was found 'not guilty by reason of insanity': a decision which gave rise to the so-called 'M'Naghten Rules' for a defence on the grounds of mental disorder. These rules incorporate two principles: the defence must show that at the time of the offence the accused did not know the nature and quality of his or her actions, or alternatively that the accused did not know that his or her actions were wrong. These rules seek to establish a dichotomy between those who can be seen as 'responsible' (i.e. bad) and those who are 'not responsible' (i.e. mad). The Homicide Act, 1957, changed this state of affairs with the introduction of the notion of 'diminished responsibility'. As the Act notes, a defence (for murder) can be made on the basis of proof of 'substantially impaired mental responsibility'.

The important element in these developments — which posed considerable practical problems in their implementation (see J. Hamilton 1981; Samuels 1975) — is that it is necessary to show a causal relationship between mental state and the crime. This position changed again with the Mental Health Act, 1959. Feldman notes that the Act allows that: '*Any* offender committed by a higher court may be detained in hospital or made subject to a guardianship order. It makes no *requirement* for a causal link between the abnormality and the offence' (1977: 163). Thus if an offender is shown to be mentally disordered, as defined by the Act, then he or she passes into the world of hospitals rather than prisons. (Although, as the Butler Report (Home Office and DHSS 1975) pointed out, psychopaths do go to prison on the grounds of being untreatable.) The 1959 Act gave the court a range of sentencing options, from a hospital order which might entail out-patient treatment, to enforced detention in a Special Hospital. The more serious crimes were, of course, more likely to lead to compulsory detention in a closed, secure hospital. Further, as offenders were being sent for treatment, not punishment, no time limits were set for the length of detention. As several authors have pointed out, there were a variety of shortcomings in the 1959 Act (Gostin 1975; 1977) and following the deliberations of the Butler Committee (Home Office and DHSS 1975) a revised Mental Health Act was introduced in 1983. The 1983 Act made a number of changes including amendments to some definitions of mental disorder, changes in the rules for compulsory admission to hospital, a review of the individual's rights regarding consent to treatment, and an overhaul of discharge procedures (see Shapland and Williams 1983). This legislation is at present in force in England and Wales, with variations in Scotland and Ireland. The American system is discussed by Beran and Toomey (1979) and Monahan and Steadman (1983).

As Bean (1980) has suggested, the 1959 Act marked a significant change in power as it diminished judicial control over mental disorder, handing over that power to the medical, particularly psychiatric, profession. The mentally disordered criminal became, so to speak, the province of the medical rather than the legal system. A number of recent criminal trials have illustrated the difficulties this has created. For example in the trial of Peter Sutcliffe, the 'Yorkshire Ripper', the jury were required to decide on the accuracy of the diagnosis of four psychiatrists who stated that Sutcliffe was mentally ill. History now shows that the jury decided that Sutcliffe was not mentally ill, at least to a degree which would impair his mental responsibility for the crime he had committed. He was tried, found guilty of murder, and sentenced to life imprisonment, three years later he was transferred to a special hospital because of his mental illness (see Prins 1986; Spencer 1984). While there were a number of reasons for these manoeuvres, not least in terms of a struggle for the final word between the professions involved, a contributing factor is the reliance of both law and psychiatry on notions such as *mental* responsibility, *mental* disorder, and state of *mind*. As discussed previously, 'mind' does not exist in a material sense, it is an inferred, theoretical construct: there are no definitive tests of normality of mind, no measures of the quality of mind. Therefore the decision as to 'mental responsibility' will always be a subjective one, open to argument and discussion, as evidenced by the volumes written on the subject. It is rather hard to resist the view that, in the cold light of day, it is faintly ludicrous to have to debate at great length the normality of an individual who *behaves* towards other people in the way which Sutcliffe did. The question of outcome, that is, treatment or punishment, for such offenders remains nevertheless a fundamental moral issue. Whether it is lawyers or psychiatrists who are best placed to decide on that issue remains a question for debate.

Chapter five

Psychology and the police

In the preceding chapters the focus has been centred on the contribution psychology can make to understanding why a person commits a crime. However, the study of crime encompasses more than just the criminal: a crime may be the beginning of a chain of events which starts with the police, moves through the courts, and ends with a sentence of one type or another. In this and the following two chapters each of these three areas — the police, the courts, and the management of sentenced offenders — will be looked at from a psychological perspective.

In this chapter the topic is psychology and the police: a topic which includes both psychological studies of the police and psychology as applied to police work. It should be added that there is a vast literature on the police: at a macro-level the most extensive and informative studies have emanated from criminology, law, politics, sociology, and the police themselves (Benyon and Bourn 1986; Holdaway 1979; D.M Peterson 1979; Pope and Weiner 1981). Psychologists have had very little, if anything, to say at this broad, social level. However, at the micro-level of the individual police officer, psychology has had rather more to contribute. While there is a tradition of police psychology in the USA (Reiser 1972; 1973; 1982) which has spread to other parts of the globe (Bull 1986a; Horncastle 1985; Yuille 1986), it is only more recently that texts and reviews have been published in Britain (Ainsworth and Pease 1987; Bull 1984; Bull et al. 1983).

There are two strands which appear in the literature on psychology and the police: psychological studies of the police, and psychological concepts and methods as applied to police work. Within these two strands there is a considerable range of interest, from police officers' daily reception of briefing information (Bull and Reid 1975), to involvement in the evaluation of organizational systems such as community policing

tch 1984). For present purposes I have selected topics from
hology which have been studied in some depth in this country,
strate the scope and style of police psychology, or that appear
at are set for expansion. Maintaining the distinction drawn
above, the material is discussed under the broad headings of 'The police
officer' and 'Psychology for the police'. I have particularly noted the
country of origin of the research: this may be important as there are
obvious differences between British, American, and European police
forces in terms of social role and accountability, organization, and powers
(Roach and Thomaneck 1985; N.L. Weiner 1981). Whether these broad
social and organizational differences extend to psychological differences
between police officers in different countries remains a matter of
conjecture.

The police officer

A police personality?

Who wants to become a police officer? Is a particular type of person
attracted to police work? The popular belief is that the police have a
distinct type of personality which sets them apart from the rest of the
population. Siegal gives an American perspective: 'The typical police
personality is thought to include authoritarianism, suspicion, racism,
hostility, insecurity, conservatism, and cynicism' (1986: 500). Potter
(cited in Adlam 1981), commenting on the British police, suggests that:
'It is commonly accepted that police officers tend to be authoritarian,
dogmatic, and conservative'. Arguments for and against these views can
be found at an anecdotal level (see Adlam 1981), and there is much
speculation from within police ranks on the 'police personality' (Kirkham
1981; Mark 1978).

The evidence from the few British studies is far from conclusive,
although it does nevertheless address several important issues. A
psychometric study by Clucas (cited by Colman and Gorman 1982) found
a sample of policemen from northern Britain to be extraverted, tough-
minded, and conservative compared to the population norms of the tests
used. (The term *conservative* as used in this context is understood as
a steadfast resistance to change and a preference for safe, traditional,
and conventional behaviour.) Similarly Potter (cited in Colman and
Gorman 1982) in another psychometric study carried out in 1977 found
police recruits to be more conservative than the general norm: however,

following training there was a slight reduction in conservatism. Cook (1977) found conservatism scores similar to those reported by Potter, and that officers with twelve months' service tended to be less conservative than the recruits — although still more conservative than the general population. Cochrane and Butler (1980) compared the values held by police officers, recruits to the police force, and civilians. Using the Rokeach Value Survey (Rokeach 1973), it was found that overall the police placed significantly more value than civilians on *a comfortable life, mature love*, and *self-respect*, and significantly less value on *a world at peace*. Recruits differed from civilians only in placing less importance on 'a world at peace', and officers from recruits only in placing more value on 'self-respect'.

A more recent study by Colman and Gorman (1982) collected data using four psychometric tests and an open response format to three questions on the 'death penalty', 'coloured immigration', and 'mixed marriage'. Two groups of police officers were used: recruits from an initial training course, and probationer constables with an average of twenty months' service: a non-police control was also included in the study. A comparison of the characteristics of the three groups revealed that they differed significantly on age, and that the control group had a higher level of educational attainment. Analysis of the psychometric data showed that the controls were significantly less conservative and less authoritarian than the two police groups; there was no difference between groups on the measure of dogmatism. (The term *authoritarian* as used here indicates a belief in the rightness of those with authority and power at the expense of individual freedom and the rights of minority and unconventional groups within society.) The responses to the open format items were rated by independent judges on a scale labelled 'liberal/tolerant — illiberal/intolerant'. More illiberal responses came from the police groups on the topics of the death penalty and coloured immigration. The initial training group were retested at the end of their nine-week programme and it was found that the recruits had become slightly less conservative and authoritarian — although the means remained higher than the controls. Colman and Gorman argue that the differences in age and education do not account for their findings — a point which might have been settled by a more sophisticated statistical analysis — and conclude that 'the police force tends to attract to it people who are more conservative and authoritarian than those of comparable socioeconomic status' (1982: 8). The change in test scores following training reflects, Colman and Gorman suggest, the effect of the liberal studies included in the training. However, the high scores by the probationer group suggest that this liberalizing effect is short lived. Colman and Gorman sound two notes of caution: their study was conducted in the Midlands and so requires replication elsewhere; there are perils in assuming that illiberal attitudes will necessarily be translated into illiberal actions. Waddington commented unfavourably on this study, suggesting that an interpretation of the data had been made in 'a selective and distorting fashion, so as to give a false and damaging impression of police officers' attitudes' (1982: 591). Colman's (1983) rejoinder to Waddington's criticisms is scathing, to say the least, in reasserting the points made in the original study.

Brown and Willis (1985) studied authoritarianism in British police recruits, using samples of recruits from the north and south of the country; a group of recruits to the fire service served as a non-police control. The three groups in the study — two police, one fire service — completed a psychometric measure of authoritarianism during the first week of training, again at the end of the 12–13-week training period, and finally after three months of work experience. At the first test there was no significant difference between the three groups; that is the police and fire service recruits held similar levels of authoritarian values upon entering their chosen career. At the end of the training period both police groups showed significantly *less* authoritarianism than the fire service group. However, at the final point of testing, some six months after joining, there was no significant difference in authoritarianism between the fire service personnel and the police officers from the northern force, while the police officers from the southern force were less authoritarian than both the other groups. Thus if the changes are charted for the two police groups, they began training with similar authoritarian values; they both showed a decline in authoritarianism after the training period. After three months 'on the beat' the police from the northern force had reverted to their pre-training level, while the police officers from the southern force show a significant overall decline in authoritarianism over the period of the study. Brown and Willis suggest that these findings show that the police are no more or less authoritarian than 'their working-class similars who join the fire service' (1985: 104). The liberalizing effect of training replicates the findings of Colman and Gorman (1982), although the reasons for this effect are unclear. Brown and Willis favour an explanation in terms of the influence of the instructor conducting training rather than anything contained in the training itself. A final point concerns the difference which developed between the recruits from the north and south who entered the police with similar levels of authoritarianism but six months later were significantly different. Brown and Willis suggest two factors which may have been of influence: the higher base-rate of crime in the north; or differences in police style with a chief constable in the north who preferred a 'law and order' approach to policing as opposed to a southern ethos of community policing.

Gudjonsson and Adlam (1983a) looked at a different set of personality variables using two psychometric tests. The Eysenck Personality Questionnaire (EPQ) contains scales labelled Psychoticism (P), Neuroticism (N), and Extraversion (E); P can be thought of as 'tough-mindedness', N as emotionality, and E as sociability. The I5 test is composed of three subscales, Impulsiveness (Imp), Venturesomeness (Vent), and Empathy (Emp); Imp can be understood as a tendency to act quickly, Vent as a liking for adventure, and Emp as sympathy with the feelings of others.

The personality measures were administered to four groups of police officers: a group of recruits, a group of probationary constables with eighteen months' mean length of service, a group of constables with mean length of service of almost twenty years, and a group of senior police officers also with a mean of twenty years' service. The scores for each group were compared with normative data to reveal that compared to the general population: 'The recruits were found to be high on E, Imp and Vent, but low on P. The probationary constables, on the other hand, were introverted and had low Emp' (1983a: 509). An identical comparison of experienced police and senior officers with general population norms revealed that 'both [police] groups scored very low on Imp, Vent, Emp and P' (1983a: 509). Gudjonsson and Adlam suggest that the personality profiles of the recruits reflect the attraction of the popular image of the police as an exciting and varied occupation. They further suggest that the differences between the recruits and the experienced officers may be due to the sobering effects of police work, although it may also reflect which recruits graduate through training to enter the force. In total two conclusions are drawn: the variety of personality profiles argues against strict stereotyping of the police officer; however, the low scores on the Empathy scale do lend some credence to the image of the police officer as a 'controlled somewhat unfeeling individual' (1983a: 512). As Gudjonsson and Adlam are quick to point out, this does not necessarily mean that the police are unconcerned about the public; it may well be that 'not being inclined to become emotionally involved may be an effective adaptive mechanism that helps police officers cope more successfully with stressful situations' (1983a: 512).

A central point in the debate about the 'police personality' is illustrated by the contrary views of Colman and Gorman (1982) and L. Brown and Willis (1985). Colman and Gorman argued for a 'predispositional model' in which the personality traits or social attitudes exist prior to joining the police; indeed, it is these particular personal qualities which make police work attractive to such individuals. Brown and Willis differed in favouring a 'socialization model' in which personality and values are formed as a consequence of the prevailing values in the police culture. While this debate was concerned with the British police, the same argument is evident in the American literature with advocates of both the predispositional model (Rokeach et al. 1971) and the socialization model (Genz and Lester 1976). An American study by Austin et al. (1987) attempted to test these two models by monitoring the authoritarianism of police officers who had been made redundant. They argued that if the socialization model was correct then when officers leave the police environment changes in values should be found. If the predispositional model holds, that is that the values are stable characteristics not dependent upon reinforcement from the police culture, then leaving the police should not cause any change in values. Austin et al. found that while the level of authoritarianism varied significantly according to age and race — with older and black officers showing the highest levels — there was no change after leaving the police culture. Indeed, a comparison of two groups of ex-officers who had been out of the force for one and two years respectively showed no effect of time away from the police culture on levels of authoritarianism.

While the findings of Austin et al. say a great deal about the robustness of authoritarian values, the question of acquisition of these values remains unanswered. Were the values present prior to joining the police, or were they the product of socialization within the police culture? The relative merits of the predispositional and socialization models can be considered from another viewpoint: if there is a predisposition what is there about police work which would attract a certain type of person? Alternatively is there any evidence that the police culture nurtures certain types of personality and associated values?

In looking at the attraction of the police service as a career the question becomes one of determining the payoffs for joining the police. Hunt (1971) in an American study found that white candidates for the police force listed, in order of importance, the following reasons for wanting to join the police: pay, security and fringe benefits; opportunity to maintain law and orer; and helping people. In a British study Reiner (1979) found that the most frequently cited attraction of the job of police officer was the way of life it offered — interest, excitement, outdoor activity, a 'man's job — rather than financial consideration. Although, as Reiner suggests, the importance of financial considerations may vary according to economic conditions and the state of the job market. Reiner (1979) also asked a sample of 168 British police officers to rate the most important aspects of their work. As shown in Table 5.1, there was a reasonable match between what was seen as important in a job, and what was experienced once working as a member of the police force. Interest and variety were valued; interest and variety were found in the job. The police officer's lot is clearly not too unhappy: over half the sample said they would rejoin the police if they were to begin their careers again.

Table 5.1 Police ratings of job content and comparative assessment of police work (from Reiner 1979)

Content	Per cent rating most important	Per cent rating police work very good
Interest and variety	53	86
Pay	30	14
Good workmates	1	74
Performing public service	13	58
Pleasant work conditions	2	12
Supervisor not breathing down neck	1	44

However, while there are various payoffs for police work, different individuals will be attracted to different priorities. An American study by Hochstedler (1981) suggested various 'police types' based on different approaches to police work. The *supercop* is concerned with protecting society from serious crime: he or she is prepared to use force in fighting 'real crimes' such as rape and robbery, probably ignoring minor crimes. The *professional* officer perceives him or herself as performing a difficult and complex task which demands a range of skills and abilities. Such officers are generally competent and efficient in their work. The *service-oriented* officer is more akin to a social worker than a crimefighter; his or her aim is to help and rehabilitate within the community rather than to use the power of the law. Hochstedler suggests that these types of officers are the most likely to experience frustration as their goal is long-term change which, in many instances, he or she is unable to achieve. The *avoider*, as the name suggests, tries to do as little as possible; this is not always because of laziness, but may be due to confusion, fear, or 'burn out'. (The sources of fear in police work are discussed later under 'Stress', pp. 139–45.) Hochstedler's research suggests that there may be some empirical basis for this typology, although the categories may not be completely distinct from each other. The idea of a 'supercop' is a familiar one, promulgated in countless television sagas on both sides of the Atlantic such as *Starsky and Hutch* and *The Sweeney*. The recent trend however is towards a much more 'human' professional and service-oriented portrayal of the police: it may be more than coincidence that *Cagney and Lacey* and *Juliet Bravo* both use women police officers for this softer image.

The other side of the coin, that the job produces the person, is to be found in various accounts of police work (Kirkham 1981). The emphasis in such accounts is on initiation into the police culture. Butler and Cochrane (1977), for example, found that British police officers became more self-assertive, more independent, and more dominant with increasing socialization into the police force. In a study of the British police, Adlam suggested a number of stages to this process of socialization. In the first few years of being a police officer there is a general 'broadening of experience', followed by the development of independence and emotional 'hardening'. Eventually the officer becomes 'more confident, more suspicious and cynical, more compassionate and understanding of the plight of others . . . and more calculating and manipulative' (1981: 157). All this in a culture in which 'officers like to pursue robust and traditionally masculine interests during their off-duty time, or as one officer put it: "Beer, sport, and women — preferably all at once" ' (1981: 157). In reading comments such as these it is prudent to remember Colman and Gorman's caution regarding the variance between words and deeds.

Adlam's observation of increasing cynicism with time spent in the police forces is in accord with the views of American commentators such as Niederhoffer (1967) and Westly (1970). Niederhoffer argued that with time the officer becomes increasingly frustrated with him or herself, their department, and the community in which they work. This frustration, in turn, breeds cynicism about police work and also about the public: as Kirkham pragmatically states: 'Chronic suspiciousness is something that a good cop cultivates in the interest of going home to his family each evening' (1981: 81). Regoli *et al.* (1979) studied cynicism in American police and found that while it existed, its level depended on a range of factors such as social class, educational attainment, and size of the police department.

In conclusion it is apparent that there is, as yet, no answer to the question of whether there is a 'police personality'. It is obvious that certain individuals are attracted to police work — or there would be no police force — and a little of the nature of this attraction has been revealed. Does this attraction draw individuals with certain values, prejudices, and personality characteristics? The evidence is unclear on this point, with only a limited number of available studies. The evidence does indicate however that there are police officers who hold, for example, authoritarian values and racially offensive attitudes (see Lea 1986). The question of whether other demographically similar groups, such as members of the fire service, hold similar values has something of the quality of a red herring. Members of the fire service do not have to police the inner cities and work face-to-face with people from racial and other minority groups. It is not surprising that the police culture, as with other work cultures, reinforces certain attitudes, beliefs, and behaviours: the exact definitions of these cultural values remains to be fully researched, as does the question of their relationship with personal values prior to entering the police and with work-related behaviour. As L. Brown and Willis's research suggests, it would be hazardous to accept that this culture is uniform across all forces in all parts of Britain; or, indeed, in police forces in other countries. Further, the evidence strongly suggests that length of service is related to personal change. Lefkowitz (1975) has suggested how the process might operate: certain 'types' are attracted to police work, and are then picked out in the selection process; the powerful effects of the police culture and the experiences of police work then act to shape up attitudes and behaviour. To date there is no evidence on the relationship between perceived payoffs for police work and personality characteristics prior to applying to join the police; no studies of psychological differences between those selected and rejected for the police service (see Burbeck and Furnham 1984 below); and a lack of *longitudinal* data on the psychological effects of a long police career. More information is also needed on police attitudes to the crimes they are likely to encounter, especially for emotive and distressing crimes such as rape (Le Doux and Hazlewood 1985). This whole area is one which, in Britain at least, is in need of a comprehensive long-term research programme to answer the many questions about the psychological characteristics of police officers.

Memory ability

Psychological investigations of the memory of police officers have been specifically concerned with the question of whether the police are better at perceiving and recalling incidents than the general public. Vernis and Walker (1970) conducted an experimental study in which a group of police officers and a matched control group were shown a series of photographs. Some of the photographs contained 'suspicious' details — such as a parked car with an open door and a bag of tools on the back seat — within the scene they depicted. When later asked about the content of the photographs there was no difference between the two groups in their observation of the suspicious details; however, the police were significantly more likely to give a criminal interpretation to the scene. A similar study by Marshall and Hanssen (cited in Clifford and Bull 1978) showed observers a short film in which a man approached a pram, tampered with the protective netting, and then walked away as a woman appeared. The observers were required to make two statements, one immediately and another after a one-week interval. Overall the police observers noted more details at immediate recall, but made more errors than the non-police observers at delayed recall. In keeping with the results of Vernis and Walker, this study also found that the police were more likely to put a criminal construction on witnessed events. This led to a number of errors of commission, that is reporting events which did not happen, such as 'One in five of the policemen said they saw the man put his hand into the pram and take the baby out' (Clifford and Bull 1978: 188). Tickner and Poulton (1975) showed films of street scenes, containing a number of inserted critical events, to police and non-police observers. The observers were instructed to watch for certain people and actions, such as normal exchange of goods and theft. The rate of detection of people and events did not differ between police and civilians, with a low detection rate of fewer than one-third of targets identified: this despite the observers being shown a photograph of the target person. Again in keeping with previous findings, the police reported more thefts than the non-police observers.

Clifford and Richards (1977) changed the methodology to a 'live' encounter in which a person (the 'target') approached a policeman and conversed for either a short (15-second) or long (30-second) period. Thirty seconds after the conversation the experimenter asked the policeman to recall the person he had just spoken with: recall was assessed using a ten-item checklist containing items such as hair colour, presence of facial hair and so on. (It says a lot for the London constabulary that of the twenty-two officers who discovered that they were unwittingly taking part in a psychology experiment only three refused to continue.) The procedure was repeated with a civilian group. The results showed that at short exposure there was no difference in the recall accuracy of police and civilians as measured by number of correct responses. With a longer exposure the police were significantly more accurate, and the civilians were more likely to give a 'no answer' response. These findings led to a revision of Clifford's view that 'The police are no better than the general public at perceiving and remembering events, actions and people' (1976: 177), to 'providing an irreducible minimum time for viewing was not prevented, police had processing skills which could be employed and which eventuated in better recall' (Clifford and Bull 1978: 191). However, it is worth noting the findings of Billig and Milner (1976) which suggest that the race of the target may be important. Billig and Milner found that police observers made more recognition errors, from photographs, of black faces than of white faces. Police officers with experience of working in black neighbourhoods made similar numbers of errors to non-experienced officers. Thus the police do not differ from the general finding across a range of subjects that cross-race face recognition is poor, although the exact reasons for this are not clear (Clifford and Bull 1978).

Bull and Reid (1975) tested police officers' retention of information from their daily briefings. While the effectiveness of briefings was a function of both presentation (with television preferable to face-to-face) and amount of information presented, it was found that the memory capacity of the police officers was similar to that of the general public. There was, however, an indication that the recall of second-year officers was slightly better than first-year officers. Ainsworth (1981) took this a stage further in comparing the performance of experienced officers (averaging over nine years' service), new officers (average service less than a year), and civilian controls. The subjects were shown a film of a street scene in which a number of staged incidents occurred. These incidents were offences such as car theft, 'suspicious circumstances' such as a man loitering outside a bank, and traffic offences such as causing an obstruction. There were two main findings: no difference between the three experimental groups in the number of offences detected; however, for the traffic offences alone, the inexperienced officers showed the highest reporting, the experienced the lowest. Ainsworth concludes that: 'The claim that police officers are specially trained to be vigilant in the perception of offenses and suspicious circumstances was not supported by the data presented here' (1981: 235).

In considering the force of this body of evidence a comment on experimental methodology is appropriate. In studies using photographs and filmed material the police were aware that they were being tested which may have caused bias and selectivity in their performance. In the one study in which police were superior to civilians (Clifford and Richards 1977) a live methodology was used in which performance was assessed under natural rather than artificial conditions: Hollin (1982) has discussed the relative merits of live and staged methodology in applied memory research. However, the one 'live' study was of person recall only and we are left with Clifford's comment that 'The police are very likely to misinterpret events because of their past experience' (1976: 177).

The ability of police officers to recall and interpret events is an area of practical importance when considered in conjunction with the *perceived* expertness of police officers as witnesses in court. While there is information from a Canadian study (Yarmey 1986a) that police are seen as highly reliable witnesses, there is no comparable British study. As Ainsworth comments:

> The fact that police officers are portrayed as having been specially selected and trained in the handling of information for presentation of evidence in court may mean that more credibility is given to the testimony of these 'experts' than to the evidence of other witnesses. If police officers are no more perceptive than members of the public, this credibility may be unwarranted. (Ainsworth 1981: 236)

Police selection

While it is clear that the Home Office is aware of the issues related to police selection (Home Office 1981; 1984) there is a marked absence of published British psychological research in this area. The following section therefore draws on research from the USA where psychologists have been involved in police selection (see Yuille 1986).

As Reiser and Klyver (1987) note, there are two sides to police selection: the 'screening-out' of undesirable candidates and the 'screening-in' of the right candidates. One approach to screening for police selection has been the use of psychometric tests such as the Minnesota Multiphasic Personality Inventory (MMPI), the California Psychological Inventory (CPI), and the 16 Personality Factor Questionnaire (16PF).

Of these tests, N.D. Henderson (1979) suggested that the CPI offers the best option for 'selecting-in'; while the MMPI may be choice for 'screening-out'.

Along with psychometric testing, an interview is often used in police selection. The interview may take the format of the traditional interview board (James *et al.* 1984), or be a 'stress interview' aimed at determining the applicant's responses to personal pressure (Mills 1976). Another American innovation is the use of computer-based testing as a means of screening candidates. There are difficulties with such an approach if it is used in isolation, such as the impersonality of the procedure and the lack of perceptual assessment at the non-verbal level (Kiesler *et al.* 1984).

Police selection is also concerned with the assessment of specific strengths and weaknesses in a candidate. Thus, for example, if police work is particularly stressful (see pp. 139–45) it would be advantageous to select candidates least likely to be affected by stress (Territo and Vetter 1981). This strategy might also be beneficial in selecting officers for high-risk duties such as bomb squads. The other side of this coin is to screen out applicants who may become dishonest: Shealy (1979) suggested that measures of maturity and moral judgement may be of assistance in assessing an applicant's leanings towards corruption or lack of integrity.

In looking to long-term predictors, Spielberger *et al.* (1979a) found four factors predictive of success in police officers: these were high values for achievement, few family moves, less requirement for encouragement at work, and taking part in athletics at school. These qualities were associated with high CPI scores on the scales of capacity for status, sociability, achievement, dominance, and intellectual efficiency. Following this, Spielberger *et al.* (1979b) suggested that there were three categories of predictor variables — physical and demographic variables, psychological attributes, and performance on situational tests. However, different 'performance criteria' are thought to be necessary to predict success at different stages of a police officer's career; while different predictors may be needed for women and minority groups. Reiser and Klyver suggest that further research is required 'to find valid and defensible job-related predictors of success for police officers' (1987: 443).

In one of the few British studies in this area, Burbeck and Furnham (1984) examined personality trait differences in successful and unsuccessful applicants to the Metropolitan police. Over 250 applicants completed the Eysenck Personality Questionnaire (EPQ): it was stressed to applicants that the EPQ was being used in a research context and was not part of the selection process. It was found that the successful candidates were more extraverted and less neurotic than the unsuccessful candidates. In addition, the EPQ scores of the candidates differed markedly from population norms in showing higher extraversion and lower neuroticism and psychoticism. Two hypotheses suggest themselves: either the applicants are from a self-selected sample of highly extraverted and stable individuals; or the applicants are 'faking good' by giving EPQ responses which they consider to be desirable. Burbeck and Furnham favour the latter hypothesis for two reasons: the very high scores on the lie scale indicate faking; and the similarity between the applicants' scores and scores from subjects instructed to 'fake good' (Furnham and Henderson 1982). The findings of this study illustrate the perils of psychometric assessment: as Burbeck and Furnham counsel, the results of personality tests should at best be 'used to assist in selection and not as decision-makers in their own right' (1984: 262).

Two points emerge from the literature on police selection. The first is that given the uncertainty surrounding the notion of a 'police personality' some decisions on appropriate psychometric indices remain to be made. The second point concerns the suggestion that psychometric and interview data can predict success at police work. While this might be the case, the exact predictors of success await definition.

Psychology for the police

Stress

The topic of stress has concerned psychologists working in the diverse fields of clinical, medical, and occupational psychology (Cox 1978; Dohrenwend and Dohrenwend 1974; J. Marshall and Cooper 1981; McLean 1979). In the field of occupational stress the police have been the subject of a great deal of attention: Reiser and Klyver (1987) calculate that in the past 15 years more than 100 articles, several books, and a variety of manuals have been published on police stress. One of the attendant issues in the study of stress is a definition of that term: most authorities arrive at an operational definition in terms of an interaction between situational demands and individual characteristics which manifests itself in either physical, psychological, or interpersonal distress and disruption. With regard to the police there are three principal issues. What is stressful about police work? Which officers are most vulnerable? What effects does it have on police officers?

Studies of police stress In a review of the research literature on police stress Terry (1981) distinguished four types of stressor which he termed *external, internal, task-related*, and *individual*. External stressors include frustration with the workings of the criminal justice system such as perceived light sentences for offenders, unfavourable public opinions of the police, poor media coverage, and a dislike of administrative and political decisions which are seen as interfering with the job of policing. Internal stressors are mainly organizational in nature, including discontent with training, equipment, promotion prospects, career structure, amounts of paperwork, and level of pay. Task-related stressors include fear, danger, exposure to distressing events such as accidents and child abuse, and work overload. Finally, individual stressors include concern about personal competence, success, and safety. As to the effects of stress, Terry deduced that the literature on police stress 'shows the presence of 35 physiological effects of job-related stressors' (1981: 65). These physiological effects include headaches, digestive and circulatory disorders, and cardiovascular problems. Terry further suggests that high divorce and suicide rates in police officers may be associated with stress. However, as Terry points out, disentangling the myriad of variables involved in statistics on divorce and suicide to adduce the exact contribution of stress is a daunting task. Terry's review of the evidence accumulated in the 1970s generally supports the view that police stress can be categorized in the fourfold manner described above (see also M.S. Davidson and Veno 1980). Therefore, rather than repeat what is available elsewhere, I have chosen here to examine more recent research on police stress, particularly stress in the British police.

Cooper et al. (1982) investigated the sources of stress among almost 200 British supervisory officers of rank sergeant, inspector, chief inspector, superintendent, and chief superintendent. The study assessed physical health, mental health, and sources of work stress for all ranks. The first data analysis was a factor analysis, across all ranks, of work stressors: as shown in Table 5.2, nine types of stressor were identified. Work overload accounted for by far the greater percentage of the variance, indicating that the police rate items such as 'too much work to do', 'large amounts of paperwork', and 'shift work' as the principal sources of stress in their occupation. There is a marked similarity between these factors and the categories identified by Terry (1981) from the American studies.

In looking for associations between stressors, rank, and physical health Cooper et al. suggested that supervisory police officers *may* be at a

Table 5.2 Police work stressors (from C.L. Cooper *et al.* 1982)

Stressor	Percentage of variance in factor analysis[a]
1 Work overload	59.6
2 Lack of personal recognition and frustrated ambition	9.8
3 Perceived unnecessary obstacles which inhibit the police function	6.9
4 Autocratic management consequences	6.5
5 The effect of perceived police/public relations	3.9
6 Work function/environment interface	3.5
7 Short-term high-intensity police stressors	3.3
8 Responsibility for a police unit	2.5
9 Complaints against police	2.6

Note: [a]This can be taken as the specific degree of stress attributable to each stressor from the total amount of stress present.

greater risk of coronary heart disease than the general public. With the middle supervisory levels, such as inspector, at greater risk than lower and higher management. The particular sources of stress for the middle levels were Factors 3, 4, and 6 (see Table 5.2). With regard to mental health, it was found that, with the exception of the sergeants, the job-related factors were predictive of overall levels of mental health. The inspectors identified Factor 4 as the major source of mental stress; the chief inspectors nominated Factors 1, 2, 3, and 4 as causes of mental stress; while the superintendents and chief superintendents nominated Factors 1, 3, and 6 as their principal mental stressors. For the sergeants there was not an overall prediction, but Factors 1, 2, and 3 were associated with levels of depression. As Cooper *et al.* note, the overall picture is similar to that found in American studies (Kroes *et al.* 1974).

Gudjonsson and Adlam (1983b) adopted a somewhat different procedure: ninety-three senior British police officers, of rank inspector or above, individually rated a list of forty-five potentially stressful situations on a scale from 0 to 100 (high score equates with high stress). The five situations which the officers rate as potentially the most stressful are shown in Table 5.3. It is an illuminating exercise in cross-cultural differences to compare these responses with the five main 'critical life events' in an American police study reported by Sewell (1983) (see Table 5.3).

The differences in the findings of Cooper *et al.* and Gudjonsson and Adlam can be accounted for by differing experimental procedures. While

Table 5.3 British and American police views of extremely stressful situations

British[a]
1 Being taken hostage by terrorists
2 Confronting a person with a gun
3 Being taken hostage in a crime
4 Negotiating over hostages
5 Dangerous or violent confrontation

American[b]
1 Violent death of a partner in the line of duty
2 Dismissal
3 Taking a life in the line of duty
4 Shooting someone in the line of duty
5 Suicide of an officer who is a close friend

Notes: [a]Gudjonsson and Adlam (1983b); [b]Sewell (1983)

Cooper *et al.* looked at the current situation, Gudjonsson and Adlam asked how stressful a situation would be *if* it took place. It is undoubtedly stressful to be held hostage, but paperwork happens to far more people, police officers included. Therefore in considering stress it is necessary to consider the probability of the stressful event.

Gudjonsson (1983a) investigated life event stressors in over 100 British police officers. The concern here was with events which had been experienced, although the nature of the events was restricted by the measure used — the Life-Events Inventory (LEI), a list of events known to be related to stress. The police officers and a control group of hospital administrators completed both the LEI and the Bodily Sensations Questionnaire, a measure of stress-related physical reactions such as a racing heart and headaches. In terms of stressful events the police reported promotion, trouble with their own children, and trouble with superiors at work as the most frequent stressful life events experienced in the previous year. The level of stress, as assessed by the LEI, was no different from that of the hospital administrators, nor from the normative scores for a range of other occupations. With regard to stress reactions, 60 per cent of the police sample reported experiencing one or more physical reactions with moderate frequency, most often 'sensations from the stomach': this figure compares with 78 per cent of the hospital administrators. These findings suggest that the police, or at least this sample, are no different from other professions in their experience of stress and their reactions to it. However, Gudjonsson suggests two reasons why these results may mask the real extent of police stress: as the sample are senior officers they may have developed effective coping strategies; alternatively the officers may be denying the presence of stress and its effects.

Gudjonsson took this a stage further in examining patterns of fear in police recruits, constables, sergeants, and senior officers. Gudjonsson was concerned with two types of fear — fear of failure and negative evaluation, and fear of tissue damage and bodily harm. The results showed that 'fear of tissue damage and bodily harm were most marked for recruits and least evident among sergeants and senior officers' (1984a: 234); while 'fear of negative evaluation was highest in experienced police officers' (1984a: 235). Acknowledging other possible explanations, Gudjonsson suggests that experience of police work modifies the type of situation which is experienced as stressful. While recruits find it stressful, for example, to deal with car accidents and mutilated bodies, senior officers become able to cope with this type of experience but are increasingly sensitive to the consequences of any administrative or managerial errors they may make.

Gudjonsson and Adlam (1985) expanded their research still further with a study comparing the occupational stressors of probationary constables, station sergeants, and senior officers. Stress was measured using the Stress Situation Inventory, as in the Gudjonsson and Adlam (1983b) study, which requires individual officers to give stress ratings to situations which they have experienced in the past year. It was found that overall the probationary constables and the sergeants reported significantly higher levels of stress. However, in accord with previous findings (Gudjonsson 1984a), there were differences between the groups: the probationers more frequently reported dangerous or violent confrontations and dealing with messy car accidents; the senior officers most frequently cited paperwork and job overload as causing stress.

In summary, the British research suggests that police officers experience a range of stressors which broadly correspond to the four categories identified in American research (Terry 1981). It is also evident that officers of different rank differ both quantitatively and qualitatively in their experience of stress; and that different individuals may respond differently to identical situations (see also Russo et al. 1983). The less senior officers appear to experience the greatest levels of stress, primarily focused on situations which threaten bodily harm. At senior officer level the level of stress appears to be equivalent to other professions — paperwork, job overload, and decision-making are part of a great many occupations. Reiser and Klyver (1987) arrived at similar conclusions following a survey of American research. This is not to say that police stress is not important: extreme consequences can result from an officer's decision made under stressful conditions. It is not surprising therefore that psychologists have been involved in stress management programmes with the police.

Stress management The management of stress can work at a number of levels although individual programmes for the person experiencing stress are the most common. Ainsworth and Pease (1987), for example, offer a section on 'How to recognize stress' which gives guidelines for police officers to assess their own stress-related behaviours. Formal stress management programmes have also been developed for police officers. In a typical stress management programme the sources of stress are identified and some coping strategy, such as self-monitoring or relaxation, is offered. Sarason *et al.* (1979), for example, used cognitive-behavioural techniques to assist officers to cope with the stress-related emotions of anxiety and anger. It should be noted that different officers may respond best to different control strategies (Kirmeyer and Diamond 1985): a point which generalizes to any counselling with the police (Reiser and Klyver 1987). While coping strategies can be borrowed from mainstream clinical and occupational psychology, another approach is to discover what coping strategies are routinely used by police officers themselves. This latter approach was taken in two British studies of senior officers (Gudjonsson and Adlam 1982) and junior officers (Gudjonsson 1983b). The officers were simply required to say what they considered would reduce the stress they experienced in their job. The strategies are shown in Table 5.4. It is interesting to note that very few officers thought that being armed would be helpful; that similar strategies were nominated by senior and junior officers; and that the changes themselves are at an organizational rather than individual level.

Table 5.4 Factors nominated as stress reducing by both junior and senior police officers (from Gudjonsson and Adlam 1982; Gudjonsson 1983b)

1 Better training in how to cope with demanding situations
2 Greater support from senior colleagues
3 Better familiarity with police procedures
4 Improved police–community relations
5 Fewer bureaucratic obstacles

The notion of change at an organizational level to reduce stress is taken up by Ainsworth and Pease (1987) who suggest a number of areas

— including equipment design, communication between departments, and definition of tasks and responsibilities — in which change could be of benefit in reducing stress. In the final balance each case will have to be considered in detail: in some instances, perhaps following experiences which promote feelings of fear, disgust, or anger, some individual work would be appropriate: in other instances change at an organizational level, perhaps to reduce amounts of paperwork or job overload, may be the most effective way to reduce stress and its effects on both individual and organizational performance.

Training

Can psychology contribute to the training and eventual job performance of police officers? If psychology is about understanding, predicting and, when appropriate, changing behaviour, and if police work involves inter-action with people, then it is not unrealistic to suggest that the former might be relevant to the latter. An American text on police crisis intervention (A.P. Goldstein *et al.* 1979) provides a perfect example of how the relationship between psychology and police training might func-tion. This text consists of three related strands: the first is a 'crisis intervention manual for police', composed of a series of stages the officer may identify in a crisis. Thus the first stage is 'calming the situation', moving through various steps such as observing and dealing with threats to personal safety and calming the individual involved. A variety of strategies which may be used to achieve these goals are presented. The second stage is gathering relevant information, the third giving infor-mation, and finally taking appropriate action: as with stage one, various steps and strategies are presented.

The second part of the text gives a detailed account of the nature of five types of crises — family disputes, mental disturbance, drug and alcohol intoxication, rape, and suicide — the police officer is likely to face. The emphasis here is on presenting information, increasing the general level of theoretical understanding and then outlining the associated practical issues: for example, the chapter on mental illness covers the aetiology of mental illness, defines some technical terms, notes the potential dangers, discusses management procedures, and addresses the legal issues involved.

Finally the third part of the text looks at 'training police in crisis intervention skills'. Aimed primarily at trainers, this describes the tech-nique of 'structured learning' — perhaps more familiar as 'skills training' in this country — and how it can be used by police trainers to train the skills discussed elsewhere in the text.

The approach taken by Goldstein *et al.* is, I suggest, a model for good training: it offers a mixture of information, theory, strategies, and skills essential to any training programme. The major limitation is that there is very little empirical evidence that this strategy is effective in practice; or, indeed, that trained policemen actually employ the skills after completing the training programme. However, as Reiser and Klyver (1987) note, in parts of the USA there is evidence that the style of training advocated by Goldstein *et al.* is playing a role in equipping police officers to deal with a wide variety of demands associated with police work. Reiser and Klyver note that in their work at the Los Angeles Police Department:

> Areas of training include leadership style, motivation of employees, listening skills, counseling skills, stress awareness, management for employees, discipline without punishment, communication skills, teaching and training, team building, ethics, planning and organization, time management, goal setting, control and audits, conflict resolution, inner-group relations, decision making, and dealing with minority and women. (Reiser and Klyver 1987: 453)

In Britain the involvement of psychologists in police training has not been as extensive as in the USA but recently there have been significant changes in this state of affairs. As Poole (1986) chronicles, changes in police training have been particularly evident in the London Metropolitan Police. Twenty years ago police training in London was restricted in both scope and content, concerned mainly with teaching the correct procedures in traditional didactic fashion. Poole suggests that the picture was not dissimilar in other forces elsewhere in the country. During the 1970s there was a movement towards an increased emphasis on social studies in training for police recruits: this drew on a number of disciplines, including social and public administration, social psychology, and sociology, in what was called 'Integrated Police Studies'. In 1981, following the recommendations of a working party reviewing training for police recruits and probationers, the concept of 'Human Awareness Training' (HAT) was developed. The aims of HAT were threefold, as Bull notes: 'The Met's human awareness training (HAT) focuses on the three interrelated topics of interpersonal skills (comprising conversational skills and purposive encounter skills); self-awareness (comprising self-knowledge through tests and participation in structured experience);

and community relations (comprising race awareness and cultural awareness)' (1985: 109). These aims were to be achieved by a change in training techniques, moving towards a skills training model as suggested by A.P. Goldstein *et al.* (1979), using role-play, videotaped feedback, practice of skills, and so on.

The first version of HAT was used by the Metropolitan Police in 1982. Since then there have been various modifications which include greater specificity of training objectives, strengthening of assessment methods, improved training for the trainers themselves, and the introduction of racism awareness training. Indeed, the modifications have culminated in a change of name from human awareness training to 'policing skills'.

Evaluation is one of the fundamental components of training and the 1982 HAT was evaluated by two psychologists, Ray Bull and Peter Horncastle, funded by the Metropolitan Police via the Police Foundation. The full details of their evaluation of HAT are available in a number of publications (Bull 1985; 1986b; Bull and Horncastle 1986; 1987): this work is discussed here in some detail to illustrate applied police psychology.

In evaluating HAT Bull and Horncastle used a variety of measures. The *social anxiety questionnaire* assessed levels of anxiety in social situations and avoidance of such situations, along with fear of being judged negatively by others. It was found that social anxiety declined over the twenty-week training period, and was continuing to decline when re-assessed six and twelve months after training. A *self-esteem questionnaire* assessed trainees' perceptions of their own ability under pressure. The level of self-esteem was influenced only marginally by the training. In contrasting the different effects of training as gauged by these two measures, Bull and Horncastle suggest: 'A tentative interpretation is that while HAT taught officers how to cope, it did not strongly affect their underlying image of themselves as social beings' (1986: 5-6).

A second level of evaluation utilized the *interpersonal relations questionnaire*, which assessed how individuals tend to behave towards other people and want others to behave towards them. While the data were not conclusive, Bull and Horncastle suggest that the recruits appeared to become more self-sufficient over time, depending less on other people. However, as changes might be expected as a function of time spent in the police force, it is not clear how much of this change can be attributed to HAT. The *personal profile analysis*, a personality measure of traits such as 'dominance' and 'steadiness', failed to show any influence of training.

At a third level, the *recruit training questionnaire* was developed to give information on changes in trainees' beliefs and attitudes across a range of topics such as views on the importance of good community relations. Bull comments that the results from this measure suggest that: 'Few of the changes in scores between the beginning and end of training reflect well on the HAT aspect of the initial training course. . . . Where changes do occur between the beginning and end of training these are mostly of an anti-HAT nature' (1986b: 110–11). For example, at the end of training there was *more* disagreement than at the beginning with the statement that 'The teaching of social studies and community relations is useful in preparing police officers for their forthcoming role in society'. It is possible that the values of the 'police culture' are antipathetic to the aims of HAT and are able to exert a greater influence on attitudes. As might be predicted from this finding, the general tone of the *probationer feedback questionnaire* was less than enthusiastic about HAT. While skills were valued, the knowledge-based aspects of the training were not well received; indeed 30 per cent of officers reported that training was unsatisfactory or inadequate. However, a comparison of HAT trainees with officers trained just before the introduction of HAT suggested that, despite the negative comments, the HAT trainees were expressing a higher level of satisfaction with training than did their predecessors. Follow-up data also suggested that the HAT officers attracted fewer complaints in their first three years of service than a matched group of non-HAT trained officers. In summary, the general conclusion from the evaluation was that of the three components of HAT 'interpersonal skills' was best trained; 'self-awareness' was of a reasonable standard; 'community relations' was poor. The evaluation, which spanned the period 1982–84, also contained recommendations for improving HAT, leading to many of the modifications noted previously (Bull 1985).

In order to gain a sense of perspective it should be noted that for all its faults HAT appears to be a distinct improvement on what went before, is effective in increasing skills, and would appear to be a long way ahead of training elsewhere in this country and on a par with police training in most other countries. Also, as Butler (1986) argues, there are limitations to what training in the area of community relations can achieve: it may be possible to give the individual officer new skills, but this does not mean that the community will respond in the way that might be wished. Finally, as all trainers will agree, trainees can be more than forthcoming with negative criticism, sometimes taking for granted the advances which have been made.

While the evaluation of the training itself formed Phase I of the project, the real measure of success is contained in Phase II which is concerned with the degree to which officers are using HAT skills in carrying out their job. Bull et al. (1987) report the findings of a follow-up of the officers who had completed the skills training. The follow-up, at up to forty-three months after completion of training, used the same measures as in Phase I, together with observation of patrol duty and reports from citizens who had had dealings with the officers. Bull et al. found that

> There is considerable evidence that concepts and skills imparted to recruits during initial police training in Policing Skills are effectively transferred to the workplace, resulting in probationer constables who are generally well versed in the skills of managing encounters with the public. (Bull et al. 1987: 10)

The HAT programme and its evaluation illustrates the application of the psychologist's skills in both measuring the effectiveness of police training and suggesting modifications to improve training programmes. A further use of the psychologist's skills would be to involve him or her in planning course content. A psychologist familiar with the research literature would be able to point to new areas in which a knowledge base is being accumulated and which would be relevant topics for police training: examples include interviewing mentally handicapped people (Tully and Cahill 1984), resolving hostage incidents (McKenzie 1985), and enhancing eyewitness identification (Buchanan 1985). It is clear, therefore, that the psychologist can have a role to play in police work: the issue which remains to be resolved is the nature of the relationship between the police service and the psychologist.

Perspective

In considering the interaction between psychology and the police various levels of relationship can be defined. At the most impersonal level psychologists may be concerned with research into topics which relate to police work. This may not even demand any formal contact between the psychologist and police personnel, as illustrated by some of the studies on police memory ability. However, while lacking personal contact, such research serves a dual function: it can be used to inform police practice; or it may be the platform from which psychologists are able to comment upon issues related to the police. An example of the latter case is

Lloyd-Bostock and Shapland's (1986) paper on the questions raised for psychologists by the Police and Criminal Evidence Act, 1984. Lloyd-Bostock and Shapland suggest that two particular areas of the Act should be of concern to psychologists: they are able to make this claim on the basis of past research into police interrogation (Irving and Hilgendorf 1980) and police–public relations (Moxon and Jones 1984). Thus psychologists not only are in a position to comment on the substance of the Act, but also are well placed to monitor the effects of the new legislation.

As discussed previously, psychologists are involved in the training of police officers. Horncastle (1985) notes that this involvement can take place in one of two ways: the psychologist carries out or assists in the actual training; or the psychologist designs the training programme without coming into contact with the trainees. Further, the psychologist may advise trainers on training methods and principles; or be responsible for the way in which psychology itself is incorporated into training programmes. In following the latter point, M. Taylor (1983) has suggested a number of ways in which psychology can contribute to professional activity, including police work. Psychology, Taylor argues, can offer a *context* in which to locate professional activity; it can offer *content* to inform and improve practice; it may provide the means by which to *integrate* professional practice and theory; and it offers a set of *methods* to analyse and evaluate practice. With regard to the police, Taylor maintains that it is vital that the issues which are addressed using this psychological framework are seen as relevant by the police themselves. This would have to be achieved by involving police officers in planning and conducting research: a strategy which would demand close working relationships between psychologists and police officers. In a comment on Taylor's suggestions, McKenzie suggested that developments within the Metropolitan Police would lay the foundations 'for a considerable increase in the involvement of psychologists with the British police service' (1984: 146). The evaluation of HAT, as discussed previously, is perhaps evidence for this claim. Unlike some research, this type of work demands close working relationships between psychologists and the police.

The same holds true if the psychologist is asked to advise the police, in terms of either support or reform, at an organizational level. However, a number of police psychologists caution that the pace of this work may slow, and that the psychologist may encounter suspicion, hostility, and the attitude that only 'the police are able to comment legitimately on police matters' (Horncastle 1985; Reiser and Klyver 1987). The psychologist contemplating police work may benefit from considering the relative merits of working 'in-house' or as a consultant (Reiser 1972). However, given that occupational psychology has much to say about management techniques and skills, as well as training management skills (Alban Metcalfe and Wright 1986), the psychologist may have a role to play at this particular organizational level.

What training is needed by the psychologist aiming to work with the police? Reviewing the work discussed previously, the psychologist will need research skills, training and teaching skills, and clinical and occupational skills. At present there is no formal training programme for police psychology in this country; indeed police psychology does not have the same professional identity in this country as in the USA. It would be anticipated, however, that any expansion of police psychology would bring about some form of training for psychologists. It would also be anticipated that any psychologist entering police work, as in any other type of work, would not lose sight of ethical considerations. Horncastle for example offers the thought that 'With the current interest in communication skills and training, are psychologists in reality turning police officers into effective Machiavellians?' (1985: 255).

Finally, while psychology is becoming more involved in police work, some very basic issues remain. Ainsworth (1982) reported a survey of 177 British police officers' perceptions of psychology. It was found that over one-quarter of the officers could not adequately define psychology; while a similar proportion could not differentiate between psychology and psychiatry. Ninety per cent of the officers thought that psychology would be of value to police work, particularly in interviewing and hostage situations, but saw it as much less valuable for major incidents, sudden deaths, and crime detection. Almost 75 per cent thought that psychology should be part of police training, but less than 10 per cent said that the training should be presented by a psychologist. The officers were equally divided on the question of whether the police should employ psychologists. Given this somewhat mixed response, an appropriate step in the emergence of police psychology in this country would be first to attend to the misconceptions about psychology. With this achieved it might be easier to demonstrate, perhaps following M. Taylor's (1983) suggestions and building on the work exemplified by Bull *et al.* (1983) and Ainsworth and Pease (1987), how psychology can be applied in a constructive manner to police work.

Chapter six

Psychology in the courtroom

When a person is charged with a crime then a new set of actors enter the drama: the courtroom is the arena in which they perform, playing out decisions of guilt and innocence, liberty and custody, even life and death. While, as Sales and Hafemeister note, 'Since the 1970s we have witnessed a virtual explosion of interest in the law-psychology interface' (1985: 13), the involvement of psychologists in legal matters has a long history. Bartol and Bartol (1987) trace this history to Cattell's (1895) study of the psychology of testimony. This was the starting-point for a number of studies (e.g. Binet 1900; Bolton 1896) which eventually accumulated into a substantial body of evidence on witness memory, reviewed annually by Whipple (1909–15; 1917; 1918). Even Freud (1906) showed interest in this new application of psychology, with a paper titled 'psychoanalysis and the ascertaining of truth in courts of law'. The dominant figure of the period was the American-based German psychologist Hugo Münsterberg who, in 1908, published *On the Witness Stand* in which he proposed that psychology could be beneficially applied to courtroom issues and procedures. Münsterberg particularly drew attention to the psychologist's understanding of perception and memory, arguing that this gave the psychologist special insight into witness testimony. Münsterberg's claims drew fierce attack from the legal profession (Wigmore 1909), and accusations of 'yellow psychology' (Moore 1907). As chronicled by historians of the study of witness memory (Greer 1971; Sporer 1982), the late 1920s saw the interests of psychologists (but not lawyers; see M. Brown 1926) turn away from applied memory research. In the 1950s and 1960s only occasional relevant works appeared, with very little in the way of fresh empirical data (Haward 1963; Kubie 1959; J. Marshall 1966; Rouke 1957; Wall 1965). However, the late 1960s and early 1970s saw a full turn of the cycle, heralded by an upsurge of interest in memory for faces: while much of this work was theoretical in nature, it was but a short step to an applied orientation and a return of the study of eyewitness memory.

While Münsterberg emphasized the role of psychology in the study of witness testimony, he also saw the jury as a suitable topic for psychological investigation (Münsterberg 1914). Indeed, the study of the jury, in terms of selection, size, and decision-making, has never really gone out of fashion (Hans and Vidmar 1986; R.M. Hunter 1935). This line of research has since expanded to include other aspects of courtroom functioning such as judicial sentencing (Lovegrove 1984), magistrates' decision-making (Lawrence 1984), the defendant's testimony (Shaffer 1985), and courtroom interactions (Pomerantz and Atkinson 1984).

Not content with defining these two major research areas, Münsterberg — by all accounts a prolific and controversial writer (Hale 1980; Moskowitz 1977) — was influential in creating a role for the psychologist in the courtroom as an expert witness. While not actually testifying, as the 'expert witness' was not accepted in the American courts of the time, Münsterberg did act as a consultant in two murder cases. Since then the role of the psychologist as an expert witness has become established, although not without controversy, in many countries including England.

The focus of this chapter will therefore be on the three areas defined by Münsterberg — the witness, the jury, and the psychologist as expert witness — which have dominated psychology in the courtroom. It should be made clear that each of these areas has generated volumes of research and what follows should be seen as a selective overview: a number of extensive reviews are available (Kerr and Bray 1982; Loh 1981; Monahan and Loftus 1982; Sales and Hafemeister 1985).

The witness

Eyewitness memory

In reviewing studies of eyewitness memory a number of writers have drawn upon the three stages of *acquisition*, *retention*, and *retrieval* traditionally identified in human memory research (Goodman and Hahn 1987; Loftus 1981; Penrod et al. 1982). In the case of the eyewitness these stages correspond to the sequence: witnessing the incident, the waiting period prior to giving evidence, and finally giving evidence. Overlaying this sequence are a number of factors which may influence memory, some of which suggest themselves from the face memory literature (G.M. Davies *et al.* 1981; P.N. Shapiro and Penrod 1986), others from the nature of the eyewitness situation itself. A number of attempts have been made to categorize these factors: H.D. Ellis (1975) made the distinction between *stimulus* factors such as the length of viewing time, and *subject* factors such as the age and sex of the viewer. Similarly Loftus (1981) distinguished *event* and *witness* factors. Clifford (1979) offered *interrogational* factors as an additional category. A final reclassification of these various factors gives the comprehensive list of variables relevant to the study of eyewitness memory shown in Table 6.1.

Table 6.1 Variables in the study of eyewitness memory

Social	Situational	Individual	Interrogational
Attitudes	Complexity of event	Age	Artists' sketches
Conformity	Duration of event	Cognitive style	Computer systems
Prejudice	Illumination	Personality	ID parades
Status of	Time delay	Race	Mugshots
interrogator	Type of crime	Sex	Photofits
Stereotyping		Training	

The study of eyewitness memory has therefore been concerned with the effects of these variables at the stages of acquisition, retention, and retrieval. This endeavour has generated a vast body of research, summarized in several books on the subject (Clifford and Bull 1978; Lloyd-Bostock and Clifford 1983; Loftus 1979; J.W. Shepherd *et al.* 1982; Wells and Loftus 1984; Yarmey 1979). I have distilled this volume of work to give a flavour of this research and what it tells us of the reliability of eyewitness memory.

Acquisition The length of time given to observation appears to influence memory: Clifford and Richards (1977), as noted in Chapter 5, found better recall from policemen after 30 seconds rather than 15 seconds exposure to the target person. The illumination at the scene of the crime is also important. Kuehn (1974) found that witnesses made less complete statements when the incident took place at twilight as opposed to day or night. Yarmey (1986b) reported that the accuracy of both recall of the details of the incident and recognition of the people involved was better in daytime and at the start of twilight than at the end of twilight or at night.

The nature of the witnessed incident has been the concern of a number of studies. Clifford and Scott (1978) showed subjects one of two short filmed incidents; while both incidents involved the same people, in one the content was violent with scenes of physical assault. It was found that recall was significantly better for the non-violent incident. Clifford and Hollin (1981) carried out a study which looked at both the nature and complexity of the witnessed incident. Subjects were shown one of six different videotaped scenes: three showed a violent crime, in which a woman was attacked and her bag stolen, three a non-violent incident involving the same people: for each scene the male target was seen either alone, with two companions, or with four companions. It was found that the recall of the appearance of the target was significantly less accurate in the violent scenes. In the non-violent scenes recall was not affected by the number of people; however, in the violent scenes recall became progressively less accurate as the number of people increased. In a similar study Hollin (1981) replicated the effect for violence using a different experimental design, suggesting that the effect of violence is robust rather than simply the product of one particular experimental procedure. Loftus and Burns (1982) showed subjects a filmed bank robbery: in one version shots were fired but no injury occurred; in another a small boy was hit in the face and collapsed bleeding from the head. Those who saw the violent scenes gave less accurate recollections of the incident. Can it be concluded that serious crimes lead to poorer memory performance?

Leippe et al. (1978) staged a study in which subjects witnessed a live theft of either an expensive or inexpensive object. It was found that when subjects knew the object's value, and hence the seriousness of the offence, accurate identification of the thief was *more* likely. This appears to be contrary to the trend apparent in the other studies, in which the more serious crimes led to impaired memory. Deffenbacher (1983) attempted to reconcile these findings by drawing on the concept of arousal: as dictated by the Yerkes-Dodson Law, moderate levels of arousal lead to optimal performance, high and low levels of arousal impair performance. Thus crimes which induce moderate arousal, perhaps as in the Leippe et al. study, may lead to good memory performance; crimes which lead to high arousal, perhaps because of violence, lead to poorer performance. This theory has been expanded further with the suggestion — taken from the mainstream psychological literature (Easterbrook 1959) — that high arousal causes a narrowing of the range of factors to which the witness attends (Clifford and Hollin 1981). Indeed, attention to the incident may be influenced by powerful aspects of the crime: the notion of 'weapon focus' refers to a witness's concentration on a weapon to the exclusion of other details of a crime (Loftus *et al*. 1987). While there is tangential evidence in favour of an arousal hypothesis (Brigham *et al*. 1983; Hollin 1984), a complete investigation of eyewitness arousal and its relationship with memory performance remains to be carried out.

Retention The length of the period between acquisition and retrieval is the most obvious starting-point in considering the retention interval. The common-sense view may be that memory for an event becomes less accurate with the passage of time: indeed, this is often the case with memories for words, conversations, places visited, and so on. However, it seems that faces constitute a special class of stimulus, more resistant to decline in accuracy with time. As H.D. Ellis notes, 'Generally speaking, delay intervals as long as weeks or months do not automatically reduce recognition accuracy' (1984: 25). This is not to say that eyewitness identification is infallible despite long delays: J.W. Shepherd concluded from his review of the research evidence that the results

> seem to suggest that the lapse of time reduces the chances of errorless identification. If this is so, we should expect criminal cases in which there was a long delay between the offence and the identification parade to show more disagreement among witnesses and lower rates of identification than in those in which the delay was much shorter. (J.W. Shepherd 1983: 177)

While the length of delay is important, the events which occur in the retention interval may also be crucial. A number of events have been studied, such as the effects of changes in appearance of the target between viewing and identification (Patterson and Baddeley 1977), but two have proved particularly important: the effects of discussion among witnesses prior to giving testimony, and the effects of seeing 'mugshots' before making an identification.

Alper *et al*. (1976) reported a study in which witnesses to a staged incident first gave individual recall then, following a group discussion, contributed to an averaged group response. The group consensus descriptions were more complete than the averaged individual descriptions, but at the cost of an increase in errors of commission (reporting items not seen in the incident). Warnick and Sanders (1980) in a similar study found that witnesses who had discussed the incident gave more accurate recall than those who did not discuss what they had seen. Warnick and Sanders suggested that 'Group discussion prior to the delivery of testimony is probably an advantageous procedure' (1980: 235). Hollin and Clifford

(1983) expressed concern at this suggestion, arguing that group dynamics could equally well produce systematic errors in testimony. To test this concern Hollin and Clifford (1983) carried out a study in which witnesses to an incident first gave recall without discussion, then took part in a group discussion, then gave individual recall once again. Immediately prior to the group discussion two individuals were surreptitiously established as likely sources of correct answers: these two individuals were confederates of the experimenters with a number of prepared incorrect answers. Analysis of the real witnesses' recall revealed that after discussion significant numbers of witnesses changed their original responses to bring their answers into line with the (incorrect) responses of the confederates. The group discussion did produce a consensus — by changing correct responses to incorrect responses. A second study, reported in the same paper, showed that this change is selective in that it is most likely to occur for items which are difficult to recall. Hollin and Clifford concluded

> It would seem prudent to amend Warnick and Sanders' suggestion. We suggest it would be preferable to try to obtain uncontaminated testimony from each witness before he or she is allowed, or has had the opportunity to communicate with other witnesses. Where this is impossible, extreme caution should prevail; agreement, unanimous or otherwise, is not always an index of accuracy. (Hollin and Clifford 1983: 242)

The effects of giving verbal descriptions of faces and seeing photographs prior to making an identification have been examined in a number of studies. Loftus and Greene (1980) staged an incident in which witnesses viewed a central 'target': after the incident witnesses read an account of the events which contained misleading, erroneous details of the target's appearance. When later asked to recall the appearance of the target some witnesses incorporated the misleading information into their descriptions: straight hair became curly, a moustache was reported when none existed. If verbal descriptions may have a misleading effect, does the same apply when witnesses assist in making photofits, artist's impressions, and the like? It would seem not: several studies have found that this type of activity has little effect on later recognition performance (G.M. Davies *et al.* 1978). Indeed, the findings of Laughery and Fowler (1977) suggest that identification may well benefit from rehearsal soon after seeing the incident.

While this may be the case for attempts to reconstruct a face, either verbally or by artificial means, the same may not be true if 'mugshots' are viewed between acquisition and retrieval. G.M. Davies *et al.* (1979) found that even the act of looking at photographs of faces prior to a recognition task lowered memory performance. However, if subjects are told prior to the recognition task that the target had not been seen in the previously viewed mugshots, then this impairment was not found. The likely explanation therefore is that viewing the mugshots increases levels of caution and so leads to fewer identifications being made. If the same face is present in both the mugshots and the identification parade then matters change. E. Brown *et al.* (1977) found that witnesses most readily identified a person seen previously in both the incident and in mugshots: however, witnesses were as ready to identify a face seen in mugshots but not in the incident, as to identify a target who had not been seen in mugshots. It appears that a face may be correctly identified as having been previously seen, but the *context* is incorrect as the face has been seen in mugshots *not* at the incident. What might then happen if a witness selected a mugshot of an innocent person, and that innocent person was later seen in an identification parade? Gorenstein and Ellsworth (1980) experimentally tested such a situation and found that despite the presence of the real target, almost half the witnesses identified an innocent person they had previously picked out from a set of mugshots. It seems that once a choice is made, then it is maintained despite all else. In summarizing the evidence, J.W. Shepherd *et al.* note: 'The use of mugshots presents hazards . . . the showing of photographs to prospective witnesses should be limited to what is necessary to make a search effective' (1982: 69).

Retrieval At this stage the emphasis is on the witness's ability to gain access to and retrieve information from memory. In many cases this will be done by the process of questioning: a number of studies have investigated the effects of the type of question on eyewitness memory. It has been shown that even the most subtle changes in question wording can influence testimony (Harris 1973; Loftus 1977; Loftus *et al.* 1975; Loftus and Palmer 1974; Loftus and Zanni 1975). The study by Loftus and Palmer illustrates the general principle. Witnesses to a filmed automobile accident were asked to estimate the speed of the cars when 'they —— into each other'; for different groups of witnesses the blank contained one of the following verbs: 'contracted', 'hit', 'bumped', or 'smashed'. It was found that the witnesses' estimates of the speed increased with the severity of the verbs (in the order given above) from 31.8 mph to 40.8 mph. Further, in later questioning those subjects who had been asked about the 'smash' were more likely to say mistakenly that they had seen broken glass at the scene of the accident. Two studies have, however, failed to replicate some of these leading question effects (Read *et al.* 1978; Zanni and Offerman 1978).

The process of questioning may also be a source of misleading information which can produce later effects on the accuracy of testimony. A number of studies, again mainly by the American psychologist Elizabeth Loftus, have provided experimental evidence in this particular area (Loftus 1975; Loftus *et al.* 1978; D.G. Miller and Loftus 1976). In a typical study (Loftus 1975) subjects viewed a film in which, among other events, a car was seen on a country road; when questioned about the events, half the subjects were asked to judge the speed of the car 'as it passed the barn', the other subjects were asked the same question but without reference to the *fictitious* barn. One week later subjects were asked, along with other questions, if they had seen a barn: over 17 per cent of the 'primed' subjects wrongly said that they had compared to fewer than 3 per cent of the unprimed subjects. Further work has established that the misleading information is most likely to be accepted if the source is of high status (Bregman and McAllister 1982; Dodd and Bradshaw 1980); that peripheral detail rather than central events are more likely to be influenced (Read and Bruce 1984; Yuille 1980); and that if the witness is warned in advance about the possibility of misleading information the effects are much reduced (Christiaansen and Ochalek 1983; Greene *et al.* 1982).

In order to explain the effects of misleading questions Loftus drew on the idea that memory is malleable, as Loftus and Ketcham state: 'Human memory is a fragile and elusive creature. It can be supplemented, partially restructured, or even completely altered by post-event inputs' (1983: 168). Thus, for Loftus, misleading information contained in questions can cause memory changes to occur, so that the original material is lost from memory (Loftus 1981; Loftus and Loftus 1980). This theoretical position has sparked a fierce debate with a number of studies presenting evidence in support of the proposal that the effects found by Loftus are products of the questioning procedures themselves, rather than due to permanent changes in memory (Bekerian and Bowers 1983; McCloskey and Zaragoza 1985a; 1985b; Zaragoza *et al.* 1987). Counter-arguments and experimental data have been presented by proponents of the 'reconstructive school' (Loftus *et al.* 1985; Schooler *et al.* 1986). In summary, while the theoretical position is unclear, from a practical point of view it would seem prudent to acknowledge that misleading information may result in distortions and errors in eyewitness testimony.

The notion of *expectation*, that we tend to report seeing what we expect to see, has been applied to witness testimony. Penrod *et al.* (1982) suggested several types of expectation which might influence eyewitness accuracy including personal prejudices, expectations about emotional state, attributional biases, cultural or racial bias (but see Aronstam and Tyson 1980), and stereotypes (see Bull 1979).

The form in which testimony is given, as well as the status of the questioner (Hollin 1981; J. Marshall 1966), can be important. As long ago as 1900, Alfred Binet made the distinction between 'narrative' and 'interrogative' recall. In the former the witnesses tell what they saw in their own words; in the latter they give answers to specific questions. The overwhelming verdict of early research was that narrative reports are more accurate than interrogative reports, but at the cost of completeness (Stern 1939). This effect has been related to the 'difficulty' posed by a particular item for recall: 'easy' items, such as some aspects of appearance, are freely given in narrative report and correctly answered in interrogative questioning; 'difficult' items, such as actions, are omitted from narrative report and are usually answered incorrectly in direct questioning (Clifford and Scott 1978; J.P. Lipton 1977; J. Marshall *et al.* 1972).

Along with mode of recall, psychological research has also been concerned with the utility and effectiveness of various face recall methods such as the photofit and identikit systems for constructing likenesses of faces (G.M. Davies 1981; 1983), the line-up or identity parade (Malpass and Devine 1983; J.W. Shepherd *et al.* 1982; Wells *et al.* 1979a), and artist sketches (Laughery and Fowler 1980). More recent concern has been with the development of computer-based systems to aid face recognition (Laughery *et al.* 1981; Lenorovitz and Laughery 1984).

While some factors which may influence testimony are of importance at one of the stages of acquisition, retention, and retrieval, individual differences between witnesses may be important at any stage. As noted in Table 6.1, a range of individual differences have been linked with face memory, including intelligence, cognitive style, imagery ability, various aspects of personality, anxiety, sex, and race (Clifford and Bull 1978; J.W. Shepherd 1981). For these variables there is no evidence of their having any consistent effect on eyewitness memory. The exception to this is chronological age with the general finding that young children are more open to the effects of suggestion than older witnesses; and that the elderly are prone to more recognition errors. These are, of course, generalizations and other factors may be important in any given case (Ceci *et al*. 1987; Yarmey 1984). In a similar vein, it might be thought that being a victim, rather than a witness, would have an influence on testimony: two studies have, however, found similar levels of ability in witnesses and victims (Hosch and Cooper 1982; Hosch *et al*. 1984). In both studies the crime was theft; whether the same finding would appear with violent crime remains to be seen.

Finally, the relationship between accuracy of testimony and confidence has been reviewed by Wells and Murray: from the results of thirty-one separate studies they suggested that 'the eyewitness accuracy-confidence relationship is weak under good laboratory conditions and functionally useless in forensically representative settings' (1984: 165). However, it is important to note the suggestions of Stephenson (1984), that confidence is a complex construct and merits a more sophisticated analysis than it has been accorded in much of the eyewitness memory research.

The force of much of the research discussed above has been to point to the limitations and shortcomings of eyewitness memory: an outcome to be welcomed should it alert the legal profession to possible miscarriages of justice. More recently psychologists have turned to a more constructive task, seeking to develop ways of improving the quality of testimony. Training programmes in face recognition have been developed (Malpass 1981), along with interviewing techniques which use various memory-retrieval mnemonics to enhance recall (Geiselman *et al*. 1985). Hypnosis has also been used to gather evidence although not without controversy (Haward and Ashworth 1980; Orne *et al*. 1984; Scholder 1982): recent experimental evidence suggests however that hypnosis is not of great benefit in aiding witness memory (Sanders and Simmons 1983; Yuille and McEwan 1985). The use of the polygraph or lie detector has likewise generated considerable debate over the ethical and practical limitations to its use in assessing the validity of testimony (British Psychological Society 1986; Iacono and Patrick 1987).

In total the study of eyewitness testimony has grown both in scope and sophistication over the past decade. While the main thrust of this research has been to illuminate the factors which might influence the accuracy of testimony, a related line of research has considered the impact of eyewitness testimony on the jury. This field of research is one aspect of the study of the jury, and it is to the jury that attention is now turned.

The jury

The jury has proved a never-ending source of fascination, inspiring a steady stream of first-person accounts, films, and novels, with the film *Twelve Angry Men* perhaps the most famous of all. The jury has also been the subject of a great deal of research, including psychological research. This research has spanned decades, from the early investigations of Münsterberg, to more contemporary studies in both Britain (Baldwin and McConville 1979a; 1979b) and the USA (Hans and Vidmar 1986). The interests of psychologists have been principally in four areas: the impact of evidence, including expert evidence, on jury decisions; the effects of extra-evidential influences on jury decisions; the composition of the jury; and jury decision-making.

Evidence

Eyewitness testimony While psychological research has been concerned with various aspects of evidence in court, such as the use of live and videotaped evidence (Goodman and Jones 1988), the main topic of interest has been the impact of eyewitness testimony on jury decisions. Following research on the reliability of eyewitness memory, a number of studies were conducted to determine how much influence eyewitness testimony might have in court. Loftus (1974) reported a study in which subjects, acting as mock jurors, read one of three case summaries of an armed robbery and a murder. In one account there was no eyewitness, in a second the eyewitness evidence was not called into question, while in the third the eyewitness was revealed to have poor vision: in all three summaries there was circumstantial evidence of the defendant's guilt. In the 'no eyewitness' condition, 18 per cent of mock jurors said the defendant was guilty; in the 'unchallenged eyewitness' condition, 72 per cent said guilty; in the 'discredited eyewitness' condition, 68 per cent said guilty. Loftus drew two conclusions from these results: that eyewitness evidence is a powerful determinant of jury decisions, and that this power is virtually undiminished even when the witness is less than perfect. This finding has since been replicated, although the difference between the 'no witness' and 'discredited witness' conditions has not always been found (D.M. Saunders *et al.* 1983; Weinberg and Baron 1982). Whitley reported a meta-analysis of these studies (meta-analysis is a method by which the results of all studies on a particular topic can be pooled and analysed to find overall conclusions) and concluded that: 'A discredited witness does have an influence on mock jurors, albeit less of an influence than the unchallenged eyewitness' (1986: 213).

If decisions are swayed by positive eyewitness testimony, it might be expected that negative testimony will bias juries towards not guilty decisions (Wells and Lindsay 1980). A study by McAllister and Bregman (1986) suggests that this is not the case: they showed that non-identifications had significantly less impact on perceptions of guilt than either positive identification or fingerprint evidence. McAllister and Bregman suggested that positive information is accorded more significance than negative information in juror decision-making.

While the experimental evidence from investigations using mock juries shows that eyewitness evidence is important in jury decision-making, studies of actual jury performance suggest that eyewitness evidence is not seen by jurors as unduly problematic or influential (Baldwin and McConville 1979b; Kalven and Zeisel 1966; Visher 1987). This leads to two hypotheses: jurors are not sensitive to the strengths and weaknesses of eyewitness memory; or alternatively the experimental studies of the impact of eyewitness evidence on mock juries are at variance with the 'real world'. The latter point is addressed in detail later in this chapter; the former has been the subject of further research into 'lay knowledge' of eyewitness behaviour. Such studies typically ask subjects to select from a range of alternatives the answer which accords with research findings on some aspect of eyewitness memory. The results of American (Deffenbacher and Loftus 1982), Canadian (Yarmey and Tressillian Jones 1983), and English (Noon and Hollin 1987) investigations have shown that 'common sense' is not always in accord with the findings of empirical research. Similarly Hastie (cited in Wells 1984) found that while mock jurors were not naive about memory, they did express opinions and make some decisions which were at odds with research findings. A solution to this lack of knowledge is to bring a psychologist into court to inform the jury of relevant empirical findings. The psychologist as an expert witness is discussed fully in the next section of this chapter.

Expert testimony There are two rationales for expert testimony on eyewitness evidence: jurors are too ready to believe eyewitness evidence; jurors are unable always to discriminate between reliable and unreliable witnesses. An expert witness will, it is argued, be able to assist by presenting research findings to increase the jury's knowledge of eyewitness reliability. This might be done, say, if the witnesses had seen a violent crime, or if it was felt that leading questions had been used in taking statements. The effects of presenting such evidence have been evaluated in a number of studies, with the general finding that expert testimony has the effect of reducing juror belief in the reliability of eyewitness evidence (Fox and Walters 1986; Hosch 1980; Hosch et al. 1980; Loftus 1980; Wells et al. 1980). In a typical study, Loftus (1980) presented mock jurors with descriptions of two trials, a 'mild assault' and a murder, in which eyewitness testimony was an important part of the evidence. When jurors were informed of factors known to influence eyewitness reliability, the conviction rate fell from 68 per cent to 43 per cent in the murder, and from 47 per cent to 35 per cent in the assault.

Do these findings establish the case for expert testimony on eyewitness evidence? Egeth and McCloskey (1984) examined the two above rationales in great detail: with regard to overbelief they conclude that: 'It is by no means clear that there is a need for psychological testimony to make jurors more skeptical' (1984: 291). Indeed, they suggest that expert testimony may make jurors unduly sceptical without improving discrimination (McCloskey and Egeth 1983). Regarding discrimination, the second rationale, they express the view that 'At the present time there is no evidence that expert psychological evidence improves juror evaluation of eyewitness testimony' (1983: 294). While Wells (1984) offers some counters to this position, it is clear that there is considerable room for discussion of the exact impact of expert testimony. The fierce debate this has kindled is discussed later (see 'Perspective', pp. 176–80).

Extra-evidential influences

While evidence presented in the courtroom should form the basis of juror decision-making, it has been suggested that jurors can be affected by a range of extra-evidential influences. Three such influences are paramount: the effects of pre-trial publicity; the confidence expressed by a witness; and juror sentiments and prejudices towards others in the courtroom.

Pre-trial publicity In a number of trials the complaint has been made that adverse pre-trial publicity had influenced court proceedings. In an experimental study, Padawer-Singer and Barton (1974) gave a group of mock jurors newspaper cuttings about a defendant's criminal record and retracted confession. A second group of mock jurors read newspaper stories which omitted the biasing details. The two groups then listened to audio-tapes of the trial: of the jurors exposed to the pre-trial publicity, 78 per cent returned a guilty verdict; of the unexposed group, 55 per cent said guilty. Other studies have also found a similar effect of pre-trial material (Sue et al. 1975). Judicial instructions do not appear to eliminate the effects of the adverse material. While jury selection is one way to attempt to control for such publicity, this demands a reliable means of assessing the prejudice of each juror. As Penrod and Cutler note: 'The only certain safeguard against the effects of pretrial publicity is to impanel a jury which has not been exposed to pretrial publicity' (1987: 312). Easier said than done, one suspects.

Witness confidence Regardless of the accuracy of their evidence, are confident witnesses more likely to be believed? A number of experimental studies have suggested that mock jurors are more likely to return a guilty verdict on the basis of testimony from confident witnesses; and conversely to place less credibility on the testimony of the less confident witness (Brigham and Bothwell 1983; Wells and Lindsay 1983; Wells *et al.* 1979). Indeed, a recent study by Penrod and Cutler (1987) found that witness confidence was the single most important factor in mock juries' evaluation of witness evidence. This in itself is not a matter for concern if confidence is a reliable index of accuracy: the experimental evidence suggests, however, that at best confidence is but a weak predictor of witness accuracy (Wells and Murray 1984). The strength of the general belief in a positive relationship between confidence and accuracy is illustrated by the finding of Fox and Walters (1986) that even after expert testimony to the contrary, jurors continue to base judgements of witness accuracy on perceived confidence.

Interpersonal perception 'Critics have . . . claimed that the jury is swayed by subjective emotions, that its verdicts are often based upon unwarranted and irrational sympathies and prejudice' (Hans and Vidmar 1986: 131). What might stir such sympathies and prejudice? Elwork *et al.* (1981) reviewed the research evidence and suggested a number of potential influences: the attractiveness of the defendant can lead to a favourable outcome for the defendant (although attractive defendants who offered no justification for their offence were *more* severely sentenced than less attractive defendants); defendants of high socioeconomic status are judged to be less blameworthy for their offence; females are less likely than males to be found guilty for reasons of insanity. With regard to race, blacks are more likely to be found guilty than whites, although whites attract stiffer penalties. Other, more subtle influences can be found: Conley *et al.* (1978) reported that 'powerful speech' — speaking clearly and without prevarication — led to witnesses being judged as more convincing, competent, trustworthy, intelligent, and truthful. Other influences include the age of the witness, with children seen to be less credible than adults (Goodman *et al.* 1987), and the defendant's previous criminal record, perceived immorality, and demeanour in court (Hans and Vidmar 1986).

While the effects of prejudice and sympathy have been found to be effective in experimental studies, how much influence do these factors have in court? Kalven and Zeisel (1966) estimated that these biases account for only one-tenth of instances where a harsh verdict is returned. The biases appear most influential when guilt is seemingly well established and the evidence calls into question the defendant's trustworthiness. In keeping with this view, Tanford and Penrod (1982) found that mock jurors judged trial evidence to be more incriminating than character evidence. Visher gathered data from actual jurors to assess the relative impact of evidential and extra-evidential variables and suggested that 'Jurors' decisions are dominated by evidential issues . . . jurors were continually less responsive to characteristics of victims and defendants' (1987: 1).

Jurors

Selection There are, of course, formal selection procedures for jury service such as age, eligibility to vote, and so on. However, an individual may satisfy these criteria yet, arguably, still not be suited for the demands of jury service. As Hans and Vidmar pointedly ask: 'Can a person who believes that the police don't make mistakes and that the state doesn't charge an innocent person really hold the defendant innocent unless guilt is proved beyond a reasonable doubt?' (1986: 66). It would seem therefore advantageous to 'screen out' unsuitable jury candidates. In the USA the screening procedure, *voir dire*, has been extensively researched. Simply, this procedure consists of questioning prospective jurors to determine their knowledge from pre-trial publicity of the case for which the jury is being formed, to assess their attitudes towards the type of offence being tried, or to discover if they have a personal acquaintance with any of those involved in the case. Sales and Hafemeister (1985) add three further areas for consideration during selection: the personality, particularly authoritarianism (that is belief in the right of authority), of the prospective juror; assessment of non-verbal cues which may indicate undue anxiety; and demographic characteristics such as age, sex, and education. The process of selection can be a lengthy one, taking up weeks of court time. Kassin and Wrightsman (1983) constructed a Juror Bias Scale to measure individual differences in pre-trial bias among jurors. The scale, summarized in Table 6.2, assesses both the jurors' pre-trial expectancies that the defendant is guilty, and their values regarding conviction and punishment. In mock juror evaluation studies, the scale reliably detected individuals who were 'prosecution biased' in that they were more ready to return a guilty verdict and held less stringent standards on reasonable doubt. The scale could be used in selection to identify those who might be unsuitable for the jury but, as Kassin and Wrightsman note, 'One obvious and perhaps insurmountable problem would be eliciting the judge's approval for handing out a written questionnaire' (1983: 439).

Table 6.2 Items from the juror bias scale (after Kassin and Wrightsman 1983)

Probability of commission
1 If a suspect runs from the police then he probably committed the crime.
2 In most cases where the accused presents a strong defence, it is only because of a good lawyer.
3 Out of every 100 people brought to trial, at least 75 are guilty of the crime with which they are charged.
4 Defence lawyers don't really care about guilt or innocence; they are just in business to make money.
5 Generally the police make an arrest only when they are sure about who committed the crime.
6 Circumstantial evidence is too weak to use in court.
7 Many accident claims filed against insurance companies are phony.
8 The defendant is often a victim of his own bad reputation.
9 If the grand jury recommends that a person be brought to trial, then he probably committed the crime.

Reasonable doubt
1 A defendant should be found guilty if 11 out of 12 jurors vote guilty.
2 Too often jurors hesitate to convict someone who is guilty out of pure sympathy.
3 The death penalty is cruel and inhumane.
4 For serious crimes like murder, a defendant should be found guilty so long as there is a 90 per cent chance that he committed the crime.
5 Extenuating circumstances should not be considered — if a person commits a crime, then that person should be punished.
6 Too many innocent people are wrongfully imprisoned.
7 If a majority of the evidence — but not all of it — suggests that the defendant committed the crime, the jury should vote *not guilty*.
8 If the defendant committed a victimless crime like gambling or possession of marijuana he should never be convicted.

Kassin and Wrightsman hint at the considerable debate generated by jury selection. Should the selection be carried out by a judge or some other court official (Ginger 1975)? Should questioning be allowed to 'trap' unsuitable jurors (Fahringer 1980)? Is sophisticated psychological testing necessary or will simple demographic characteristics suffice (Baldwin and McConville 1980)? These questions have crystallized into the debate on 'scientific jury selection': proponents argue for a systematic, empirically based selection method; opponents maintain that the idea of selection is unfair, unsafe, unethical, and improper. As Hans and Vidmar conclude:

> There are no easy answers in this ethical quagmire, since the issues extend beyond the techniques themselves to the nature and functioning of the adversary system itself. But the ethical issues must constantly be confronted by those who conduct and by those who benefit from the new developments in jury selection. (Hans and Vidmar 1986: 94)

Numbers How many people are needed to make a jury? The centuries-long tradition, in both English and American courts, has been for 'twelve good men and true'. While twelve men and women still form a jury in this country, some American courts have experimented with five- and six-person juries. This has led to a number of studies on the relative merits of the smaller jury.

The basis of the change was that the use of twelve people was an anachronism, dating back to the time of King Henry II, and that a reduction in size would not impair jury functioning, would increase efficiency, and would reduce costs. A number of empirical studies concluded that a smaller jury is *less* likely to be representative of the community, to examine evidence in detail, and to engage in effective group discussion; they are *more* likely to hold secret ballots and to produce verdicts which favour the prosecution (Hans and Vidmar 1986; Kaye 1980; Saks 1977). Winick summarizes the functioning of the six-person jury: 'They are more likely to enter the jury room with their minds made up so that they are, in effect, polling their members rather than deliberating the case' (1979: 85). This may or may not be desirable, but it is a radical departure from the type of trial obtained with a twelve-person jury. It is for experts in jurisprudence to decide on the relative merits of different jury size. In the USA the small jury has been challenged as unconstitutional; what might happen in this country remains a matter only for speculation.

Competence Before retiring to reach their verdict, juries are presented with a range of facts, summaries, and points of law by the judge. This presentation is to ensure that the jury is certain of the facts in the case, has knowledge of the law, and knows how to apply the law to the facts. Critics of the jury system argue that this is too much to expect of the lay person; the alternative to a jury would be to entrust the decision solely to a judge, or to a panel of judges and lay people as in some European courts. Defenders of the jury system argue that the jurors' common sense will see them through, and that the collective judgement of twelve people is, by and large, superior to that of one person (Nizer 1978).

A number of studies have examined juror comprehension of judges' instructions: the principal finding is that style of language makes significant portions of the instructions incomprehensible to jurors (Charrow and Charrow 1979; Hastie *et al*. 1983; Penrod and Cutler 1987). Other research has found limited juror comprehension of complex evidence (J.L. Peterson *et al*. 1984). The implication of these findings is that if jurors do not fully understand the material germane to the case, then their decision cannot be fully informed and so is at greater risk of being incorrect. Elwork *et al*. (1981) found that 39 per cent of mock jurors who viewed a videotaped trial (in which the verdict was known) and received standard instructions made incorrect verdicts. If jurors were presented with instructions which were revised to increase their clarity, then the incorrect verdicts were reduced to 13 per cent of mock jurors. Thus a change in protocol, such as revised instructions, may improve accuracy. Other strategies for improvement have been suggested such as note-taking during instruction, or allowing jurors to ask questions to clarify issues. It is doubtful, however, that these strategies would silence critics of the jury: clearer instructions do not eliminate ignorance, bias, and prejudice.

Reaching a verdict

The process of deliberation The exact process of deliberation in a trial is, of course, impossible to research. The nearest that can be achieved is either to observe mock jury deliberations, or to interview jurors after a trial. The research which has been carried out has illuminated the group dynamics of structure, process, and decision-making by twelve people thrown together in a highly intense setting (Strasser *et al*. 1982).

The jury's first task is to appoint a foreman: as the title suggests, this person is most often a man, typically elected on the basis that they were the first person to be nominated. Having elected a leader, the jury must then decide where to begin: the evidence, the arguments heard in court, the legal points, and so on. A poll of views is often a starting-point: the poll may be carried out secretly, or by verbal announcement, or by a show of hands. Polling can influence outcome in that it increases the speed with which a verdict is reached, while secret ballots are more likely to culminate in a split decision. Following a poll, the typical sequence of events is to deliberate first the trial testimony, then the judge's instruction on the law, and finally the application of the law to the evidence. During the opening stages it is unlikely that the jury will agree on all the issues. As matters progress, with men speaking more than women, and the foreman most of all, conflicts become increasingly explicit. This can make some jurors anxious, angry, or uncomfortable: views become personalized, people refuse to change their opinion, insults may be exchanged, some jurors dissociate themselves by sitting apart, those in the minority feel persecuted. The defendant may be discussed in ways which are outside the jury's terms of reference: for example the defendant may be blamed for the disruption caused to everyone's life. The jurors may show that they are aware of the consequences of a guilty verdict and, while sentencing is not their concern, this may figure in their eventual decision (Goldman et al. 1975). In some cases the jury will be forced to grapple with the complexities of sanity and insanity, in others to come to terms with their emotional reactions to crimes against children and sexual offences (Hans and Vidmar 1986).

While jurors do change their minds during the course of the deliberations — research suggests that almost one-third of jurors change their views — the best predictor of the eventual verdict is the balance of opinion at the very start of the deliberations (Hastie et al. 1983). A jury sitting down with eleven votes for guilty, notwithstanding Henry Fonda, would be more than likely to return a guilty verdict: minorities can sway opinions, but this would appear to be an unusual event. With a verdict reached, the jury enters its final, reconciliatory phase: support for the group decision is asserted, rifts are healed, tension released often through humour, and arrangements made to meet after the trial.

While the study of jury deliberation is captivating as an exercise in group dynamics, there is considerable doubt about the importance of the deliberation in terms of its influence on the outcome of the trial. It seems that most jurors have made up their mind during the trial and the outcome is predetermined before a word is spoken in the jury chamber (Kalven and Zeisel 1966). Thus juries *may* be expensive, inefficient, and their deliberations of minimal importance; none of this matters terribly if they reach the correct verdict.

Outcome Again it is impossible to know exactly the frequency with which juries make wrong decisions: certainly innocent men and women have been imprisoned, even executed, because of a wrong jury decision; undoubtedly guilty people have been set free. The precise numbers will never be known. It is, however, possible to estimate the figures by comparing the judge's views with the jury verdict. An American study by Kalven and Zeisel (1966) compared the difference in convictions and acquittals between judges and juries. They found that in over 3,500 trials, the judge and jury agreed on the verdict in 78 per cent of cases. In the instances of disagreement, the jury acquitted in 19 per cent of cases when the judge would have convicted; and therefore in only 3 per cent of cases would the judge have acquitted when the jury returned a guilty verdict. An English study by Baldwin and McConville (1979a) arrived at similar findings to Kalven and Zeisel. Judges and juries agreed in the majority of cases and, where there was disagreement, the jury was more lenient. Kalven and Zeisel offered a number of observations to account for this leniency: if the defendant had no history of offending then this increased the benefit of doubt; if the jury felt sympathetic towards the defendant; and if the jury disagreed with the law. Baldwin and McConville add that doubtful decisions were reached when juries appeared not to appreciate the very high standard of proof needed to reach a decision, or when the jury did not understand the evidence or the judge's instructions.

In all, the jury appears reasonably reliable, although the difficulty with understanding evidence is noted by several authorities. The answer to this difficulty may be for the court to draw on the ability of an expert to assist in the proceedings. Recent years have seen a marked increase in the role of the psychologist as an expert witness and this is an aspect of psychology in the courtroom which is now addressed.

The psychologist

The role of the psychologist

As Haward (1987) notes, the matters on which the psychologist is called for an expert opinion fall into two classes, *medical* and *psychological*. The medical evidence includes three categories: *neurological*, as in assessment of the effects of brain injury; *psychiatric*, that is in relation to mental disorder; and *psychological medicine*, as in recovery from injury. The psychological evidence, Haward suggests, 'Is the very bedrock of the psychologist's scientific knowledge, concerning conation, cognition, affect, sensation and perception, individual differences and the distribution of human attributes' (1987: 12). While these areas define the scope of the psychologist's expertise, there are a variety of roles the psychologist might take in court proceedings. Haward (1981a) has defined four such roles; the experimental role, the clinical role, the actuarial role, and the advisory role.

The experimental role Haward (1981a) describes two aspects of the experimental role. In the first the psychologist informs the court of the findings of experimental research which are relevant to a given case: for example, pornography trials and cases involving eyewitness evidence have called on a psychologist to inform the court of relevant research findings. As Haward notes, 'Any competent academic psychologist is capable of filling this role' (1979: 46).

The second aspect to the experimental role, following the tradition started by Münsterberg, is for the psychologist to conduct laboratory or field studies to resolve some issue pertinent to the outcome of a trial. Haward (1979; 1981a; 1981b) presents a catalogue of cases in which experiments have been carried out to assist in proceedings. In the main, these experiments involve re-creating a given situation, then observing and recording performance in that setting to determine the degree of similarity between what is claimed in court and what the experimental results show. Among others, studies have been conducted to aid the court in questions of identification, the effects of drugs and alcohol, industrial hazards, faking of psychiatric symptoms, and accuracy of maritime vision. In a typical example, Haward (1979) reports testing whether a policeman could, as he claimed, have taken the registration numbers of four motor-cycles as they travelled at high speed through a village. Using 100 people with perfect eyesight as observers, with identical lighting conditions to those at the time of the incident, Haward found that the policeman's claims were not substantiated by the experimental results. However, as Haward notes, there is a caveat as the argument is by analogy:

> The fact that a hundred people found it impossible to see X in conditions Y does not prove that it was impossible for police constable Z. It may be highly improbable, but the impossibility of an event is beyond scientific proof. . . . When the forensic scientist is asked 'Could this policeman have possibly done it?', he, as a scientist, has to reply 'Yes, it is possible', however unlikely the event. (Haward 1979: 48)

The dichotomy between probabilistic statements and statements of 'fact' and 'truth' is one with which the court may be uneasy, and this in turn may influence the acceptability and standing of the psychologist's testimony.

The clinical role In this role, the psychologist's testimony may be given in conjunction with that of other experts. Thus in cases of brain injury, medical experts may testify on the nature and extent of the physical damage, while the psychologist informs the court of concomitant cognitive impairment or behaviour change (Ward 1982). Such cases are often related to compensation claims. On psychiatric matters, the psychologist may be concerned with an offender's state of mind, and so with issues of *mens rea*. Parenthetically the concept of *mens rea* can pose difficulties for the psychologist: while the law has a reasonably precise use of the term, the concept does not translate easily into psychological theory (Blackman 1981b; Crombag 1984). Clinical opinion has been given in a range of cases, including mental cruelty in divorce cases, estimates of intelligence, and the presence of phobias; as well as evidence in the juvenile court on care proceedings and non-school attendance (Lane 1987; H. Parker 1987). The clinical psychologist has a range of techniques to draw on, including the interview, case records, psychometric tests, and experimental evidence. Forensic hypnosis is also available, but this is rarely used in this country, and the rules on admissibility of this type of evidence are uncertain (Haward and Ashworth 1980).

The actuarial role In this capacity the psychologist is called upon to give the probability of an event, or to present an estimate of the average of something. The most frequent demand for this type of evidence is in the civil courts as, for example, in road traffic accident cases. The psychologist may be called, for example, to give evidence on the mean earnings of people of different levels of intelligence, relevant in cases where loss of earnings is to be calculated. In other instances the psychologist may be asked to comment on the frequency of certain types of social behaviour. While a statistician would be expected to give evidence of this type, the psychologist's knowledge of both human behaviour and qualitative methods relying on probability can on occasion prove an ideal combination.

The role of adviser In this role the psychologist does not testify on behalf of the defence or the prosecution, but is outside the adversarial process to inform the court on a technical matter. In the USA the psychologist as a 'Friend of the Court' is not uncommon; in England, while allowable, it is an option which is rarely exercised. The more common advisory role in this country is for the psychologist to sit with counsel, commenting on testimony and noting points which may need to be followed up in cross-examination of another expert witness. While the psychologist may in principle be asked to advise on a range of topics, eyewitness memory and clinical matters are the most frequent.

In conclusion it should be noted that the four roles described above are not exclusive of each other: for example, clinical-experimental evidence may be offered, or actuarial evidence may be informed by experimental findings. Indeed, Haward (1981a) notes a case in which the psychologist concerned took on all four roles.

Court work

The process of giving evidence, either in writing or verbally, demands an understanding of the functioning of the courtroom and its use of evidence (Haward 1981b), along with the necessary skills of presentation (T.H. Blau 1984). I.B. Weiner (1987) has discussed the writing of forensic reports. He begins with the wise advice that anyone involved in litigation may 'think whatever they like but write down only what they are prepared to testify in a court of law' (1987: 512). Given this consideration, Weiner suggests that the content of a report should be governed by the demands of the client, professional ethics, and courtroom protocol. A useful report will therefore communicate psychological information to the court in a clear, relevant, and informative manner to assist the court's deliberations.

Singer and Nievod (1987) discuss the presentation of verbal evidence and suggest two important steps. The first, which they term *orientation-delineation*, is the process of consultation between counsel and the psychologist. This consultation should define the role of the psychologist, the relevant psychological issues, and the nature of the evidence required from the psychologist. The second step involves *preparation* for direct testimony and cross-examination. As implied, this stage is concerned with planning to give evidence, discussing the material, noting points of strength and weakness, and arriving at strategies for ordering material so that it has maximum impact and memorability in court. Having given evidence the psychologist may well be cross-examined: Ziskin (1981) has presented a source-book for aiding cross-examination of psychologists. This contains a range of questioning strategies to discredit expert evidence: these include attacks on the personal skills of the expert; dismissal of psychology as a profession; attacks via issues on which the expert might be expected to have current knowledge; and drawing the expert into areas outside their special knowledge. Carson (1987) offers some helpful counter-strategies which might usefully be considered in preparing for cross-examination.

Current practice

Gudjonsson (1985) reported the results of a survey of British psychologists' involvement in presenting evidence in court. From an issue of over 2,500 questionnaires, 190 psychologists returned completed forms indicating that they had presented evidence to a court. The majority of respondents were clinical psychologists (71 per cent), with educational psychologists forming the next largest group (22 per cent); overall there were more males (67 per cent) than females. More than half the sample (57 per cent) had submitted court reports, while 95 per cent had appeared in person as an expert witness. Court appearances were equally divided between criminal cases and civil cases such as child and custody proceedings, and head injury and compensation.

The survey also asked what means the psychologists used to gather and prepare evidence. As shown in Table 6.3, interview and cognitive testing were most commonly used, with intelligence and neuropsychological tests employed most frequently. Over half (56 per cent) the psychologists who had appeared in court had been cross-examined, contributing to the general reported anxiety about making appearances in court. The overall evaluation was positive: almost all the psychologists (95 per cent) who had made a court appearance said that they saw the court as favourably disposed towards their evidence. In this light the rising demand for psychologists to appear as experts is liable to produce a favourable response from those approached.

Table 6.3 Type of evidence used in court: from most to least frequent (after Gudjonsson 1985)

1 Behavioural assessment/interviews
2 Cognitive test results
3 Considered opinions only
4 Personality questionnaires
5 Psychophysiological data
6 Projective test results

On a more disquieting note there is an unresolved controversy on the disclosure of psychometric test material in court. Gudjonsson (1985) reported that over one-quarter of psychologists had been asked to give details of test content in open court. This raises a number of problems: it may breach confidentiality; influence the validity and reliability of any further testing with a given client; it may adversely affect the psychometric properties of the test itself; and it produces a situation in which the general public has access to test material which is not available to psychologists without the appropriate postgraduate qualifications. If disclosure is requested by the court then it cannot be refused, which has proved a matter of both concern and acrimony for psychologists (Heim 1982; Tunstall et al. 1982a; 1982b). The distribution of psychological test material to open court raises another fundamental issue: this action implicitly states that the lay public acting as jurors are qualified to comment on the validity of any given psychometric test. In other words, the psychological evidence is simply 'common sense' and therefore can be dismissed out of hand by anyone, regardless of their lack of training in psychology. This introduces the topic of the standing of psychological evidence in court and, as might be expected, this has raised not inconsiderable debate. Thus while it appears that the psychologist is set to play a role of increasing importance in court proceedings, both by the production of research and in person as an expert witness, there remain some professional and ethical questions to be debated.

Perspective

The view which the court might hold that psychology is nothing more than common sense, that the qualified psychologist has no understanding or skills beyond a general level of knowledge, is of immediate concern. It follows that either psychologists are fooling themselves about their abilities, or alternatively that the court has an incomplete understanding of psychology. While I know of no studies which have specifically examined the court's level of understanding of psychology, studies with the police (Ainsworth 1982) and young people (Kirton et al. 1985) suggest that the general level of understanding about psychology is not accurate. I see no reason to suppose that the court is any different in this respect. Ward (1982) forcefully makes the point that the psychologist has discrete skills and knowledge, beyond that which might be expected of an 'ordinary person'; Ward cites two examples to make this point: the ability to conduct a neuropsychological assessment and an understanding of the working of memory. The list can be expanded to include, for example, psychological development in children, non-verbal communication, behaviour analysis, psychometric testing, psychopathology, and so on. This is not to say that such topics are the divine right of psychology, rather that a competent psychologist would be familiar with all of these in an informed manner, and would be a specialist in one or more at a highly informed level. Further, Colman (1981) lists over twenty examples of findings from psychological research which show that 'common sense' is not always correct in predicting human behaviour.

If it is accepted that there is a discrete body of knowledge which might be labelled 'psychological', should that knowledge be made available to the court? The sticking point here is the notion of *generalizability*, the degree to which the findings from psychological studies can be applied to the 'real world'. At issue is the 'realism' of experiments conducted to study real life performance. This issue of generalizability has been debated extensively for both jury studies (Bray and Kerr 1982) and eyewitness memory. Wth regard to the latter, Yuille and Cutshall (1986) point to experimental limitations such as the use of staged crimes, filmed sequences, subject awareness of the aims of the research, and the use of students as subjects. Aronson and Carlsmith (1968) suggested that the realism of an experiment can be seen in two ways: *experimental realism* refers to the degree of authenticity the experiment holds for the subjects; *mundane realism* is the extent to which laboratory conditions are likely to occur in real life. In applied research it is clearly necessary to have high levels of both experimental and mundane realism, and therefore each experiment must be judged on its own merits. A body of research, using different experimental designs, different subject groups, and different experimental materials, is required before strong statements about a particular topic can be made.

While much is made of generalization by critics of experimental studies (Konečni and Ebbesen 1986), it is not clear exactly why generalization might not be expected from the laboratory to the real world. Take, for example, the use of students as subjects: generally speaking, subjects are of above average intelligence, are familiar with laboratory and test conditions, and are used to having their performance assessed. To obtain poor memory performance with students, it might be argued, suggests equally poor, if not worse, performance in the remainder of the population. In truth the issue of generalizability is an empirical question: do people perform significantly differently in the laboratory from real life? The evidence is limited. Two studies which addressed this question for eyewitness memory found high levels of similarity between performance in laboratory and real conditions (Brigham *et al.* 1982; Sanders and Warnick 1981). Yuille and Cutshall (1986) adopted a different approach with a case study of eyewitness memory in which thirteen of twenty-one witnesses to a shooting incident were re-interviewed four to five months after the incident. The results were contrary to what might have been predicted on the basis of laboratory findings. While this is interesting, this type of field study falls prey to criticisms which are the very strength of laboratory research, that is the degree of *control* the investigator has over the study. Thus, in the Yuille and Cutshall study, it is not known how much witnesses have talked with each other, how accurate the missing 38 per cent of witnesses would be, and how much influence newspaper and television coverage has had. While it is easy to be enthusiastic about real-life studies, considerable caution is required. As Bray and Kerr note: 'Social scientists should not, in their zeal for realism, dismiss the utility of closely controlled experimental simulations, nor be unmindful of the practical and methodological drawbacks of more realistic methods' (1982: 318). The strongest approach is one which replaces squabbling about methodology with evidence from an amalgam of methodologies, including laboratory studies, case studies, field studies, and archival studies.

A further issue concerns the lack of predictive power of psychological research: it is a fact that psychological research cannot predict whether a given witness, offering a particular piece of evidence in a given case, is correct or incorrect in their testimony. There is no argument with this and there are few, if any, psychologists who would seek to disagree (see the quote above from Haward); a similar position was noted in Chapter 3 for the prediction of dangerousness, and indeed the debate cuts across many areas of psychology. We are therefore faced with a position in which some psychologists argue that the court can be informed by pro-babilistic statements based on empirical research (Loftus 1986), while others maintain that this is not good enough and offers nothing beyond common sense (Pachella 1986). Loftus cuts through the debate with the pragmatic suggestion that 'We take a Darwinian approach. Let the fittest expert evolve and survive' (1986: 259). While Loftus clearly feels able to support her position in open court, it is debatable whether a 'battle of experts' would be desirable (although it would undoubtedly be enter-taining) from either a professional or legal perspective.

At a more general level the debate extends from psychological evidence in court, to whether psychologists should even contemplate becoming involved in legal matters. Konečni and Ebbesen (1986) suggest that psychologists investigating eyewitness memory are wasting too much energy on the topic as the small number of wrongful convictions on the basis of witness testimony is an 'acceptable risk'. This undoubtedly depends on who is defining risk: a counter-argument would certainly be advanced by James Hanratty, Peter Hain, George Ince, Patrick Meehan, and all the others who have been imprisoned or even executed on the basis of mistaken eyewitness testimony (Hain 1976). It is not an exercise in risk but in ethics and morals: as Wells notes, 'we must consider the potential effects of *not* giving expert testimony' (1986: 83). Expert testimony, by definition, requires specialist knowledge of an area; knowledge which relies on an extensive research base.

From a practical viewpoint, Bray and Kerr see little to stand in the way of legal research: 'The study of the psychology of the courtroom is not qualitatively different from the study of other social phenomena' (1982: 318). King would not agree: 'The simple fact is that the knowledge and training of psychologists, even of social psychologists, make them no more competent to deal with legal issues and legal processes than the knowledge and training of astrophysicists makes them competent to take a spaceship to the moon' (1986: 85). It is evident that King does not hold psychologists in high regard: he suggests, for example, that some of those working in the field of legal psychology have failed to grasp fundamental issues such as the distinction between social and natural science. King is also critical of the research: 'I have often had the impression, when confronted with the mass of literature describing and sustaining experimental legal psychology, of facing single-handed not just Goliath but the whole of the Philistine army' (1986: 102).

From reading King's work there appear to be three principal objections to the development of legal psychology. The first, noted above, is that legal issues are somehow different from other issues which involve human behaviour and so fall into the province of psychological enquiry. It is less than clear why this should be the case; if King gives an explanation then I have missed it. What King does imply, and with which I agree, is that to attempt to study the 'legal system' is to chase shadows. However, I am less convinced than King that this is a 'dream fostered by many psychologists working on legal issues' (1986: 101). Applied psychologists are driven more by problems than dreams: if eyewitness evidence is problematical, then what can psychology say? If there is debate about sentencing, jury decision-making, or judicial instructions then how can psychology contribute? The competent applied psychologist will apply psychological theory and methods to augment the views of other parties, with the aim of advancing towards an analysis and understanding of a given situation thereby to generate solutions for the issue at hand.

King's second objection is towards experimentation as a means of gathering information. As has been pointed out throughout this text, it is widely recognized by all concerned that there are limitations to experimental methods: however, the argument against is far less clear cut than some critics maintain, and the limitations do not invalidate the use of experimental methods, they simply mean that additional methods have to be developed to use alongside experimentation. King's third objection lies in the general inadequacy of psychological theories, being particularly critical of 'mechanistic behaviourism': this rather has the quality of 'attacking straw men', mechanistic behaviourism, if it ever existed, disappeared a long time ago (cf. Lowe 1983; Skinner 1974). (It is rather ironic that King, in true Hullian fashion, suggests that the causes of people's behaviour can be explained by use of the formula FI(s)[S + R]!) Psychological theories are more advanced both philosophically and empirically than is generally acknowledged by critics such as King.

Faced with a situation which appears to have advanced little since the debate between Münsterberg and Moore at the turn of the century should psychologists maintain their involvement in legal issues? As Grisso (1987) points out, the involvement has probably reached the stage where it is irreversible and legal psychology is here to stay. Given that, two demands are evident: training for psychologists who enter legal work (Gudjonsson 1984b), and a drive towards educating those in the legal profession about psychology and what psychologists have to offer (Grisso 1987). Whether this will ever happen remains to be seen.

Chapter seven

Psychology and crime prevention

The offender provides the starting-point for a discussion of the role of psychology in attempts to prevent crime. As detailed in Chapter 2, there are a range of theories of crime which have, to a greater or lesser degree, a psychological component. These psychological theories, mainly of classical and positivist persuasion, are principally of a 'dispositional' nature: that is they seek to explain crime in terms of biological, cognitive, behavioural, or social differences between criminals and non-criminals. Taking this position it follows that in order to prevent crime, it is necessary to change the criminal's disposition towards offending. It is here that the therapist, particularly the clinical psychologist, comes into his or her own. Drawing on training, experience, and theories of psychopathology, vast numbers of clinical treatment programmes have been conducted with the aim of rehabilitating offenders back into 'normal' society. These treatments can be categorized in several ways: the focus may be on a treatment which follows a particular psychological theory such as behavioural approaches generally (E.K. Morris and Braukmann 1987) or social learning theory particularly (Nietzel 1979); the treatment may be aimed at a particular age group, such as juvenile delinquents (Burchard and Burchard 1987); or treatment may be for a particular type of offence, such as violent crime (Stuart 1981). A further consideration is the *setting* in which the intervention takes place, and it is this which I have used to structure the present discussion. With an emphasis on setting it is possible to place treatment in context, looking at not only the treatment programmes, but also the organizations in which treatment takes place. The weight of studies is too great to cover exhaustively here, so I have adopted the strategy of selecting examples to give an overall picture of the field of offender rehabilitation.

Offender rehabilitation

Secure institutions

If a convicted offender is sentenced to secure provision there are three options available: *prison, special hospital,* and *regional secure unit,* which are the product of 600 years of secure institutions in England (E. Parker 1985).

Prison It is claimed that imprisonment serves a number of functions: it acts as a general deterrent to society; it deters the person who experiences it; it protects the general population; and it assists the offender to return to a good and useful life. The penal structure which has evolved to meet these aims is complex, involving gradations of security and different regimes for both young and adult prisoners (Prins 1982). At the time of writing the prison population of England and Wales is as high as it has ever been, edging close to 50,000 people. The prison service employs a large number of people from a variety of professions to run this system, included in which is a relatively small number (about eighty) of psychologists.

Within any institution the distinction can be drawn between *institutional* and *inmate* needs: the former refers to the security and safe running of the institution, to staff training and development, management systems, and so forth; the latter to the medical, psychological, and social requirements of the individual held within the institution. It is evident that the two cannot be separated: a badly managed, poorly administered, under-staffed institution will not be able effectively to cater for the individual's needs. If institutions are to play a role in preventing crime through their effect on the offender then both sets of needs require attention. Thus Marcus (1982) defined four areas of work for prison psychologists: *organizational* work related to management of the institution; *staff training* for both psychologists and members of other professions; theoretical and applied *research*; and *clinical treatment* of offenders. A recent publication provides a great deal of detail about the work of prison psychologists in this country (McGurk *et al.* 1987).

In terms of organizational input, the advent of behaviour modification techniques — especially the token economy, a system in which 'good behaviour' is rewarded with points or tokens which can later be exchanged for rewards such as cigarettes, watching television and so on (Kazdin 1982) — provided the means to design programmes which could operate on a large scale. Prison token economies to increase compliance with institutional rules were used principally in the USA

(Nietzel 1979; Opton 1974). A number of highly sophisticated programmes were developed such as the Cell Block Token Economy (Milan
et al. 1974) and the START programme (Kennedy 1976). This use of
behaviour modification attracted a great deal of hostile criticism on both
legal and ethical grounds, culminating in lawsuits and hearings in the
USA's Congress. As Bartol (1980) notes, some of the criticism was
undoubtedly justified as techniques from clinical psychology were being
misused: however, some of the criticism was also due to a lack of
understanding of behaviour modification. In any event, funding for the
projects was discontinued and they quickly disappeared. There has been
nothing comparable in this country; psychologists have not been greatly
involved in the design of custodial regimes. Behaviour modification has
been used however for clinical purposes.

J.E. Cullen and Seddon (1981) designed a behavioural programme
based on a token economy for disturbed young offenders serving a borstal
sentence. (A recent change in legislation has renamed borstals 'Young
Offender Centres'.) The programme was successful in that the offenders
acquired new socially acceptable behaviours. However, Cullen and
Seddon encountered a familiar problem:

> The psychologists were criticised as being specialists whose working
> hours limited their effectiveness and perspective, while the hospital
> officers saw the trainees as they 'really are' . . . [a fundamental flaw
> was] we concentrated on the effect of the programme on the recipients
> rather than the staff involved in running the programme. (J.E. Cullen
> and Seddon 1981: 291)

This reinforces the point that institutional needs, in this case the need
to train and educate staff, cannot be separated from inmate needs. To
be successful intervention must work at both levels.

While a range of clinical methods have been used with incarcerated
offenders, especially delinquents (Blakely and Davidson 1984; Rutter
and Giller 1983), the use of social skills training (SST) has proved
particularly popular with both young offenders (M. Henderson and Hollin
1983; 1986; Huff 1987; Spence 1982) and adult offenders (Howells
1986; Priestley and McGuire 1985). With young offenders skills training
has been used mainly to increase levels of social competence (Hollin
et al. 1986), although skills training has also been used with sex offenders
(McGurk and Newell 1987), to increase job skills (Ashmore and Jarvie
1987), and to reduce institutional offending (J.E. Cullen 1987; Hollin
and Courtney 1983). While skills training programmes are generally

successful in changing the social behaviour at which they are aimed, there is very little evidence that this change prevents offending after discharge from custody. Given this, it is paradoxical that the May Report (Home Office, Scottish Office and Northern Ireland Office 1979), which effectively dismissed treatment from prison regimes, suggested that the use of SST should be 'enlarged substantially'. Hollin and Henderson (1984) argued that this suggestion should be resisted and drew attention to the experimental nature of the technique. There may be in many individual cases some justification for skills training, or any other form of treatment, on clinical grounds, but justification at a criminological level is altogether more problematical. SST may have a role to play in effective offender rehabilitation but the exact nature and extent of that role remains to be formulated. Similarly Howells (1986), noting the potential of SST for preventing both violent and sexual offences, listed a number of problems for SST with incarcerated offenders: the difficulties in maintaining and generalizing changes in skills; the poor motivation for change found in some prisoners; the inadequate theoretical integration of SST into analyses of offending; and institutional constraints, such as staff resistance, which pose problems for the implementation of treatment programmes (see also Priestley and McGuire 1985).

Moving on from SST, more broad-based treatments have been designed for violent (W. Davies 1982) and sexual offenders (Perkins 1982; 1987). The work of Derek Perkins with sex offenders, at a prison in Birmingham, England, provides a model for effective clinical treatment within a penal setting. The justification for the programme has been carefully described in clinical, ethical, preventive, and economic terms. Reliable assessment methods have been used to select offenders suitable for treatment; and a range of treatment techniques are used, drawn mainly from a cognitive-behavioural model of sex offending. Community links have been established to ensure that treatment does not stop when the offender leaves prison. Finally meticulous follow-up research has shown the effectiveness of the programme in reducing sexual offences. In stark economic terms, Perkins estimates that the cost of the programme 'amounted to £192 per reconviction prevented' (1987: 215). The cost in terms of preventing the distress of potential future victims is incalculable.

At another level, prison regimes have been designed to prevent recidivism. Two very different examples in this country are the implementation of the 'short sharp shock' regime for young offenders, and the regime at Grendon Prison which functions as a psychotherapeutic unit with the prison system in England and Wales. The 'short sharp shock' regime is based on the notion that a short, highly unpleasant custodial sentence will 'shock' young offenders and deter them from future crimes. The short sharp shock regimes, reintroduced by the present Conservative government, were evaluated by a team of Home Office psychologists (Thornton *et al.* 1984). They found that the regime had no effect on later offending as compared to any other type of regime; indeed, in theoretical terms, it is difficult to think why it should. The regime at Grendon Prison includes substantial input, in both management and treatment, from psychologists (Marcus 1982). An evaluation of Grendon Prison was reported by Gunn and Robertson in which they concluded that: 'Grendon is probably no better and no worse than any other prison in influencing the post-release offending behaviour' (1982: 302). American studies have fared little better. In a recent study Homant reported a ten-year follow-up of ninety-two prison inmates originally assigned to either group therapy or a no-treatment control condition: the study 'failed to find any significant differences between experimental and control subjects' (1986: 51). Gunn and Robertson argue strongly that it is not appropriate to expect any prison regime to 'cure' criminal conduct. They support the role of Grendon Prison in achieving clinical improvement in prisoners and for coping in a humane manner with some of the most difficult prisoners in the prison system.

Special hospitals In Chapter 4 the mentally disordered offender was discussed and three particular groups were noted; the mentally ill offender, the mentally handicapped offender, and the psychopathic offender. The dilemma posed by such offenders is that while their disorder requires treatment, the nature of their offences may justify close control and security. Psychiatric hospitals in the NHS are not equipped to manage such offenders; prisons are not appropriate because the disordered offender is not a 'criminal'. As documented by Greenland (1969), a solution to this dilemma was found in the setting up of the special hospitals: institutions which are not prisons but provide security within which treatment can take place. The first special hospital, Broadmoor in Berkshire, opened in 1863, followed by Rampton in Nottinghamshire in 1910. The institution at Moss Side, near Liverpool, dates back to 1914 in its history as an institution for mentally disordered people, although it became a special hospital as recently as 1960. Park Lane, adjacent to Moss Side, was opened in 1974 and is the newest special hospital. Scotland has its own special hospital at Carstairs.

In total the five special hospitals, which are not part of the NHS but which are administered by the DHSS, have provision for over 2,000 patients. All patients are detained under mental health legislation, not criminal law. Unlike psychiatric hospitals, security is crucial and special hospitals have walls, fences, locks, bolts, and bars to prevent escape. In common with psychiatric hospitals, a range of staff is employed in special hospitals, including medics (principally consultant psychiatrists), nursing staff, clinical psychologists, and social workers, as well as administrative, catering, and domestic staff. There are no prison officers, although nurses may join the Prison Officers Association. The numbers of clinical psychologists are relatively small: the average psychology department in a special hospital has about six qualified psychologists. In a review of the structure and management of special hospitals, J.R. Hamilton suggested that 'There is probably a need for a modest expansion of clinical psychology departments' (1985: 99).

The treatment offered in special hospitals is similar to that in any other psychiatric hospital; medication as appropriate, education, occupational therapy, psychotherapy, and behaviour therapy. D.A. Black (1984) suggested that psychologists have a particular role to play in 'psychosocial treatment'. Thus, as in prisons, SST has been a feature of clinical work in special hospitals, particularly with violent and sexual offenders (Crawford and Allen 1979; Howells 1976). As Howells (1987b) notes, other clinical techniques have been used with these offenders, including cognitive-behaviour therapy for violent offenders (Alves 1985), and comprehensive assessment and treatment programmes for sex offenders (Crawford 1979; Pratt 1986). Indeed, the psychological treatment of sex offenders has reached a considerable level of sophistication: the literature contains evaluations of interventions for different types of sex offence such as child molestation (Lanyon 1986) and exhibitionism (Blair and Lanyon 1981), as well as rape and sexual assault (Perkins 1982); there are a variety of different therapeutic approaches ranging from psychotherapy (Romero and Williams 1983) and behaviour therapy (Earls and Quinsey 1985), to approaches which combine biological and psychological methods (Grossman 1985); while the legal and ethical issues are debated at length (B.A. Weiner 1985). If the clinical treatment of 'normal' violent and sexual offenders is reasonably advanced, the same cannot be said for those offenders medically classified as psychopaths. As noted in Chapter 4, there are unresolved problems in the aetiology, classification, and theory of psychopathy; problems which have proved barriers to the formulation of effective intervention programmes (Blackburn 1984). As Bartol notes: 'Clinicians have yet to devise an effective treatment approach for the criminal psychopath' (1980: 382).

As well as treatment, psychologists have also been concerned with follow-up studies of the effectiveness of special hospitals. Black (1982) reported a five-year follow-up study of 125 male patients discharged from Broadmoor. This group contained similar numbers of mentally ill and psychopathic patients, but only five mentally handicapped patients. Of the 125 patients, 101 had had no readmission to any psychiatric hospital, 97 had no record of imprisonment, and 70 no further court appearances. Other outcome studies (not all conducted by psychologists) have also been cautiously optimistic: Bowden (1981) suggested that only 20 per cent of patients are readmitted to special hospital, and that while 50 per cent are subsequently convicted the offences are generally trivial (cf. Teplin 1984), with only about 10 per cent of those discharged involved in serious crimes. Similarly Tidmarsh (1982) calculated that the 'post-Broadmoor homicide rate' was about 1 per cent in a sample of 2,000 patients discharged over the previous twenty years. From his follow-up study D.A. Black (1982) was able to identify indicators of 'success' and 'failure', examples of which are shown in Table 7.1. Black has suggested that this knowledge could be built upon to develop units within special hospitals to cater therapeutically for selected patient groups such as 'for assertiveness and expressiveness in inhibited patients and for the control of impulsiveness in psychopathic patients' (1984: 379). The design of such units, building on empirical research and capitalizing on clinical skills and experience, is a task which might well have been devised for psychologists.

Table 7.1 Examples of indicators for success and failure following discharge from special hospital (after D.A. Black 1982)

Success
  Current offence homicide
  Diagnosed as 'affective disorder'
  Victim family or well known
  Older
  More social conformity and control

Failure
  Current offence property offender or non-homicidal assault
  Diagnosed as psychopathic disorder
  Victim stranger or casual acquaintance
  Younger
  More impulsive and extraverted

Regional secure units The type of patient detained in a special hospital has always presented difficulties for the NHS (Dell 1982). As psychiatric hospitals have proved unwilling to admit this type of patient, concern has been expressed that such individuals may be admitted to a special hospital simply because there is nowhere else for them. Further, there may be difficulties in finding provision for patients discharged from special hospital who no longer require high security but still need treatment. As various commentators have detailed (Bluglass 1985; W. Davies 1986; Higgins 1984), both the Glancy Committee (DHSS 1974) and the Butler Committee (Home Office and DHSS 1975) offered a similar solution to the problem of provision within the NHS for mentally disordered offenders. They proposed the setting up of a regional secure unit (RSU) within each NHS region. The RSU would provide security but ensure that patients remained close to their own home, while an out-patient service would mean that some degree of community care would also be available. The most serious patients would, of course, still be detained in a special hospital.

In the first instance regional interim secure units were established (Treasaden 1985), followed by the RSUs themselves. They have not proved the most popular of developments, and continue to experience difficulties in staff recruitment. Indeed, as Bluglass (1985) notes, some NHS regions have progressed only a little towards development of the units. The staffing in the RSUs is similar to special hospitals, including clinical psychologists engaged in institutional problems such as the management of violent patients (Gudjonsson and Drinkwater 1986) and assisting in the running of treatment regimes (Gudjonsson and Tibbles 1983). The RSUs are generating a great deal of research (Berry 1985) although at this early stage in their history no outcome studies are yet available.

Residential settings

There are many criticisms of closed institutions: that they reinforce criminal behaviour; that they label individuals; that they are, by their very nature, unsuitable for rehabilitation. An alternative may be found in a setting which is residential but in which the emphasis is transferred from security to treatment. The majority of such residential programmes have been for young offenders.

Therapeutic communities As Sinclair and Clarke (1982) note, a variety of therapeutic communities have been used in the treatment of offending.

A British study by Cornish and Clarke (1975) provides a typical example in comparing two regimes in an Approved School for 13–15-year-old boys. One was a traditional training and control regime, the other a therapeutic community based on Rapoport's (1960) four principles of communalism, democratization, permissiveness, and reality confrontation. The evaluation found that at a two-year follow-up the recidivism rate was 70 per cent for the boys from the therapeutic community and 69 per cent for the boys from the traditional regime.

In a similar American study by Jesness (1975) almost 1,000 convicted delinquents were randomly assigned to residential establishments based on the therapeutic techniques of either transactional analysis or behaviour modification. Therapeutically the regimes achieved most in the area they focused upon: on psychological measures the transactional analysis achieved most, behavioural measures favoured the behavioural regime. At two-year follow-up, 77 per cent of the sample had been arrested for further offences; there was no difference in recidivism between the two regimes. The picture is broadly similar across all studies of this type: therapeutic gains in the treatment setting which fail to be translated into a reduction in recidivism. A recent small-scale study by B. Brown (1985) describes the outcome from a residential regime based on principles from social learning theory. Brown reports that of eight young offenders referred to the unit from secure institutions, five have been successfully returned to the community with no indication of re-offending. The regime which Brown describes is similar to the American Achievement Place style of residential care.

Achievement Place The residential care at Achievement Place has two distinct points of emphasis: the consistent use of behavioural theory and associated clinical methods, giving the flexibility to conduct individual treatment programmes; and the maintaining of close community links. The work at Achievement Place has generated a wealth of research output (e.g. Phillips 1968; Phillips *et al.* 1974; Phillips *et al.* 1971; Phillips *et al.* 1973) for which a number of reviews are available (Burchard and Harig 1976; Hoefler and Bornstein 1975). The principal means of intervention is via 'teaching-parents': the young offender lives in residential accommodation, usually a house, with two adults who assume the joint roles of parent and teacher. Thus the teaching-parents not only provide a caring family environment, but also are responsible for administering individual treatment programmes. The system runs on a token economy, with various rewards available for achieving targets; the rewards vary from special recreation opportunities, time away from Achievement

Place to go shopping, see films and so on, and extra pocket money. As the offender makes progress, both in terms of satisfactory residential behaviour and achieving therapeutic targets (mainly through skills training), the rewards include time at home with natural parents. When this stage is reached, the (natural) parents are assisted to maintain the gains made at Achievement Place. In total Achievement Place builds on the token economy by incorporating individual skills training in a family-style environment; by targeting for individual responsibility as well as individual academic, social, and self-care skills; and by maintaining close community and natural family links. Rutter and Giller comment of Achievement Place that 'it is a highly imaginative, well thought out programme which includes a range of measures appropriately designed to maintain behavioural change after the youth leaves the institution' (1983: 278).

The apparent success of the Achievement Place style of residential care led to a number of similar programmes (R.N. Alexander *et al*. 1976; Davidson and Wolfred 1977; Liberman *et al*. 1975; Weber and Burke 1986; Wood and Flynn 1978). In this country there is the programme noted by B. Brown (1985), and also Glenthorne Youth Treatment Centre and at the Shape project (see pp. 190–2).

The success of Achievement Place as a residential establishment is not reflected in the outcome evidence. Kirigin *et al*. (1982) reported a one-year follow-up of 124 young offenders from twelve establishments using Achievement Place methods. The control group consisted of sixty-eight young offenders from establishments identified as typical, non-teaching-parent homes for delinquents. During their residential placement, the offenders in the teaching-parent homes had fewer contacts with the authorities. At follow-up this advantage had disappeared and there was no significant difference in recidivism between the two groups of offenders. In a similar study, Weinrott *et al*. (1982) examined twenty-six teaching-parent homes and twenty-five comparison homes and found little difference in outcome. In total the picture is not unlike that with treatment in institutions: the intervention is initially successful but fails, in the main, to generalize beyond the treatment setting to prevent offending. With this point in mind, two British programmes have modified the Achievement Place model to attempt to capitalize upon its strengths and amend the lack of generalization.

Glenthorne Youth Treatment Centre In any population there will be a minority who pose special problems: this may be because of the severity of their offence, or because of grave disturbance, or the residential management problems they present in, say, violence to staff and other residents. In this country such children and adolescents were often held in institutions, such as prisons or special hospitals, intended for adults. This was a source of continual disagreement and controversy such that, in 1969, the notion of a Youth Treatment Centre (YTC) was conceived: these were to be secure institutions for young people but firmly oriented towards treatment (Barlow 1979). Administered by the DHSS, the first YTC, St Charles in Brentwood, Essex, opened in 1971, followed by Glenthorne YTC, Birmingham, in 1978; the planned third YTC has not yet been built (and it is doubtful if it will be).

As described by Reid (1982), the decision was made at Glenthorne YTC to operate on an approach based on social learning theory, similar to Achievement Place and other American facilities such as Boys Town (Phillips 1978). In developing this regime three aspects of the Centre were considered: the staff, the management of the Centre, the treatment programme. The care staff are drawn from a range of professions, including nurses, psychologists, social workers, and teachers: all with the generic title 'groupworker' and all performing the same tasks. Specialist staff training in behavioural intervention takes place via a university-based course which leads to an academic qualification.

On arrival at Glenthorne YTC the young person, who may be on a Care Order or sentenced under criminal law, spends time on a secure assessment unit before progressing to another secure unit for treatment. The final move is to an open unit in which the target is a return to the community. The management needs are met through the use of behavioural methods, originally a token economy but now via a 'levels system' (Ostapiuk and Westwood 1986). In a similar fashion, the Centre has developed behaviourally based strategies for the management of institutional violence (Gentry and Ostapiuk 1988).

In terms of treatment, Reid (1982) suggests seven classes of behaviour which treatment programmes must consider; these are shown in Table 7.2. Given this multiplicity of potential targets for treatment, a priority system operates which specifies *major* and *minor* target programmes together with a *basic skills* programme. Individual programmes are designed following the initial assessment, to deal with major targets such as offending or violence: as Ostapiuk and Westwood note, treatment, which takes place either individually or in groups, 'include[s] offence counselling, anger control training, anxiety reduction, improving self-image, and so on' (1986: 51). Minor targets may be concerned with, say, aspects of social behaviour; while the basic skills programme deals with life skills and self-care. Each young person progresses at his or her own rate from security to an open setting; culminating in time spent away from the Centre on work experience schemes, family visits, and other activities in preparation for a permanent return to the community. As yet there are no outcome data from Glenthorne YTC; however, Ostapiuk and Westwood (1986) note that a DHSS-sponsored outcome study is in progress at present and should report in the near future. The results of this study will be of particular interest as they will reflect, to some degree, the generalization of the treatment aimed at the offence behaviour: a focus of treatment which appears to be lacking in other residential programmes.

Table 7.2 Behavioural targets in a youth treatment centre (after Reid 1982)

1 Major offence behaviours, e.g. murder, sexual assault
2 Minor offence behaviours, e.g. theft, burglary
3 'Clinical' problems, e.g. anxiety, enuresis
4 Behavioural deficits, e.g. lack of social skills, lack of education
5 Behavioural excesses, e.g. physical violence, verbal aggression
6 Institutional problem behaviours, e.g. attempted escapes, barricades
7 Problems of generalization, e.g. self-help skills, family conflicts

The Shape Project The Shape Project, based in Birmingham, England, is a non-secure residential facility for young offenders (Reid *et al.* 1980). Shape provides living accommodation, work training in preparation for employment (more recently preparing for unemployment), offence counselling, and individual life and social skills training. In the first instance the offender, generally referred by probation and social service departments, lives in a hostel with a structured daily routine; the next step is to semi-independent shared accommodation; moving finally to full independence in non-shared accommodation. Training and counselling take place at all stages. The project is selective in that it does not accept offenders with severe drug or alcohol problems, nor those with a history of severe violence. The most recently published re-offending statistics show a 78 per cent *success* rate, measured in terms of non-reconviction over a 6–18-month follow-up period (Ostapiuk 1982). Given this it is indeed ironic that, at the time of writing, Shape is in severe financial difficulties and unable to accept referrals.

Community programmes

If institutional and residential programmes are generally lacking the power to reduce recidivism, then perhaps the best option lies in treatment which takes place in the 'natural environment' — the community in which the offending occurs (Tharp and Wetzel 1969). Community intervention may take the form of individual or group treatment on an out-patient basis at a hospital or regional secure unit; or it can take place within an organized project.

Individual and group therapy A multitude of community-based treatments for offenders have been reported, from large-scale investigations to individual case studies (Glover 1985; Ostapiuk 1982). The American Cambridge-Somerville Youth Study (Powers and Witmar 1951) is perhaps the most widely quoted community programme. Young males living in a high delinquency area were recommended to the programme by welfare agencies, churches, and the police. When the recommendation was accepted, the young person was randomly assigned to either a treatment or no-treatment group. Starting in 1939, counsellors were assigned to the family to which each young male belonged, visiting on average twice a month. In addition, families were able to call for assistance when they thought it necessary. The intervention, for the treatment group, included academic teaching, medical and psychiatric care, counselling, and availability of various community programmes. The treatment lasted for between two and eight years. The control group simply provided information about themselves. The most recent follow-up traced over 500 men who had participated in the study (J. McCord 1978). While those in the treatment group expressed fond memories of the project and remembered their counsellors with affection, McCord's follow-up found no difference in the rate of offending, either as juveniles or adults, in treatment and control groups. Indeed, McCord notes that 'Unexpectedly, however, a higher proportion of criminals from the treatment group than of criminals from the control group committed more than one crime' (1978: 286). Yet further, McCord lists a string of seven *adverse* effects of treatment, including more signs of mental illness, more evidence of alcoholism, and even a tendency to die at a younger age. McCord suggests that the counsellors' different social values from the family with which they became involved may have led to internal conflicts in those treated and so produced the later disorder; alternatively the intervention may have fostered a dependency on outside assistance which caused problems when it was removed. McCord concludes with the stark statement: 'Intervention programmes risk damaging the individuals they are designed to assist' (1978: 289). Palamara *et al.* have expressed similar concern, reporting findings which revealed that: 'Police and mental health intervention had both independent and interactive effects in increasing juvenile deviance' (1986: 90). Commenting on the outcome evidence from counselling and psychotherapy with offenders, Rutter and Giller (1983) suggest that these methods are not 'particularly effective' in reducing recidivism.

Other treatment methods have been used with offenders. In an innovative project Fo and O'Donnell (1974; 1975) set up a 'buddy system' in which young offenders were paired with friendly adults in their own community. The aim was to increase the offender's socially acceptable behaviour by making both social and material rewards contingent upon good behaviour. The results were mixed: those young people with previous offences showed improvement, those without previous offences became worse. The full range of behavioural techniques have been used on a community basis with offenders, particularly young offenders; token economies, reinforcement programmes, and contracts have been successful at changing the target behaviour; instruction and modelling less so (Blakely and Davidson 1984). However, while successful in modifying targets such as academic skills and social behaviour, the impact of these interventions on recidivism is, at best, inconclusive.

As in prisons and residential establishments, SST has proved popular in community programmes with offenders (B.L. Hudson 1986). The outcome data do not lend themselves to the conclusion that SST is an effective intervention for offending. Spence and Marzillier (1981) reported that six months after training the SST group, compared with control groups, showed the lowest level of police convictions (although not statistically significant). On a self-report measure of offending, however, the SST group showed a *higher* level of offending than the controls. Spence and Marzillier would appear to have nurtured socially skilled delinquents.

Over the past few years the general enthusiasm for cognitive therapy has permeated treatment programmes for offenders (Ross and Fabiano 1985). It is, as yet, premature to judge the efficacy of this particular approach with offenders given the lack of long-term outcome studies. Kazdin (1987) has, however, reviewed a number of studies which have used 'Cognitive Problem-Solving Skills Training' with children who show antisocial behaviour. While noting the potential of the approach, Kazdin concludes that this 'has not been shown to be an effective treatment for antisocial behavior' (1987: 194). On a quite different line, Arbuthnot and Gordon (1986) reported that an intervention designed to raise moral reasoning development in young offenders had beneficial effects on police and court contacts. Again, long-term data are required.

Another group of studies has used *family therapy* as the treatment of choice in reducing delinquency. Kazdin (1987) identifies two broad types of family therapy: parent management training (PMT) and functional family therapy (FFT). In PMT the focus is on training the parental skills required to manage the child or adolescent's problem behaviour and to reinforce desirable behaviour. While hundreds of studies have testified to the utility of PMT (Kazdin 1985), the level of socioeconomic disadvantage and strength of the social support system are important predictors of outcome. As Kazdin suggests: 'Variables beyond the specific parent-child interaction need to be considered in treatment' (1987: 191). In FFT the focus shifts to the interactive processes within the family system: thus rather than parent skills, the aim is to increase the family's understanding of family issues, enabling them to generate effective and agreeable solutions to family problems (J.F. Alexander and Parsons 1982). The use of FFT with 'delinquent families' shows promise: Alexander and Parsons (1973) found lower recidivism at eighteen-months follow-up with an FFT group than a control group. Within FFT the technique of contingency contracting appears particularly useful (Welch 1985). Family therapy is increasingly being used with families in which child abuse has occurred (Bentovim *et al.* 1987; Elton *et al.* 1987).

Probation As documented by Prins (1982), the role of the probation officer is wide and varied, from court work to supervising offenders on probation, and in some instances carrying out treatment programmes. While a great deal of social work is involved, some treatment methods favoured by probation officers may be described as 'psychological'. Having said that, it is also true to say that, as with most alternatives to custody (Pointing 1986), a psychologist is rarely involved. In the USA the effectiveness of the probation officer has come under close scrutiny (Carney 1977), as has their use of behavioural and psychotherapeutic techniques (Nietzel 1979; Romero and Williams 1983). In Britain, as B.L. Hudson (1986) notes, behavioural casework is being reported with increasing frequency by probation officers, with SST proving particularly popular. McGuire and Priestley (1983) describe the use of a behavioural progamme, including both life and social skills training, by probation officers in a Day Training Centre for persistent petty recidivists. The re-offending rate was just over 50 per cent, which is an improvement on the predicted rate of 60 per cent from the figures from similar centres. In total the picture is not quite so optimistic: from their review of the outcome studies, Rutter and Giller comment that 'While no firm conclusions are warranted, the evidence provides no indication that probation makes any significant difference to recidivism' (1983: 298). Indeed, there is an increasingly outspoken view within probation that the individual treatment model is not an appropriate one for probation, given the dual roles of help and control inherent in probation work (Willis 1986).

, *Diversionary projects* During the 1960s concern was mounting about the numbers of young people held in custody. The concerns were twofold: the potentially damaging effects of custody on young people, and the financial costs of a growing prison population. Thus the Children and Young Persons Act, 1969, gave provision for the development of an alternative form of intervention with the dual aims of diverting offenders from the penal system and reducing offending. Similar steps were being taken in the USA (Lemart 1974). This was indeed a time of radical reform, nowhere more so than in Massachusetts where Jerome Miller, Director of the State's Youth Services, began a programme of closing all training schools and institutions for offenders under 17 years of age (A.D. Miller *et al.* 1977; Rutherford 1978). Despite spirited opposition the programme was successful and the process of decarceration continues today with little sign of being reversed (Rutherford 1986). As institutions closed so community programmes were developed: as B. Hudson (1987) notes, the boldness of Miller's approach lies in his perception that institutions had to close to allow successful community programmes to develop. A competition between institutions and community programmes, as is the case elsewhere, provides the community practitioners with the unenviable task of proving to judges and magistrates that institutions are redundant for young offenders. Clearly this extends beyond treatment issues into politics and social policy, areas into which psychologists have in large part been unwilling to be drawn.

Of the various diversionary measures, of which there are many, such as reparation (Blagg 1985) and community centres (Rutherford 1986), *intermediate treatment* (IT) has attracted a great deal of attention (Thorpe 1978). The term IT refers to an ideal rather than a set of techniques: IT projects aim to prevent both custody and offending, the manner in which they seek to achieve these goals differs from IT project to IT project. In a review, Preston notes that: 'IT schemes vary greatly, from playgroups for the under fives, through evening groups for young people who go to school, to day-care facilities for school truants and/or young offenders' (1982: 171). Preston continues, '[IT projects] tend to set very broad aims that are often both difficult to quantify and therefore to achieve' (1982: 172). This, in turn, means that the outcome data are, at best, uncertain. Preston describes an IT scheme in Birmingham, England, organized along behavioural principles; the one-year follow-up data appear promising. An American study by W.S. Davidson *et al.* (1987) reported the long-term effects of diversionary treatment for over 200 juvenile offenders. This study compared five intervention methods utilizing a range of outcome measures including both 'court recidivism' and self-reported recidivism. There were three important findings: regardless of theoretical basis, the interventions based on a specific treatment model produced lower court recidivism compared to a no-treatment control; any intervention conducted 'outside the influence of the court may beneficially influence (court) recidivism' (1987: 74); but that self-reported delinquency remained unchanged regardless of treatment or control condition.

In total the evidence regarding the effectiveness of psychological treatment is mixed: while there are undoubted successes (Garrett 1985; Gendreau and Ross 1979), the pooled data, as the major reviews conclude with monotonous regularity, show no consistent effectiveness of treatment. Whether this constitutes a 'failure of treatment' will be discussed presently: what has happened is that the perceived lack of therapeutic success has promoted a radically different approach to crime prevention.

Changing the environment

Attempts to prevent crime which are based on treatment of the offender are, as noted previously, based on a 'dispositional' view of crime in accord with positivist, classical and neo-classical, and interactionist theories of crime. Hough *et al.* suggest that

> This theoretical emphasis has had an unfortunate consequence. It has encouraged a view of crime whereby criminality in some way inheres in the personality of offenders, so that, come what may, they will seek out their opportunities for crime. In terms of prevention too much effort has been expended on unproductive attempts to change the 'criminal disposition' of offenders. (J.M. Hough *et al.* 1980: 3)

The dispositional argument extends to what can realistically be changed: there seems to be no acceptable means of modifying biological functioning; personality, as described by theorists such as Eysenck, appears largely resistant to change; and the resources for large-scale family and social changes are prohibitive (N. Morris and Hawkins 1970; J.Q. Wilson 1975). However, crime, or at least antisocial behaviour, is a social act in which the protagonist interacts with his or her environment. Following a rational-choice view, crime can be seen as an individual's response to a situation which offers the opportunity for successful offending (Cornish and Clarke 1986a). The 'situational' approach to crime prevention seeks to change the environment in two ways — reducing opportunity and increasing risk of detection — to prevent future offending. This approach to crime prevention has attracted a considerable amount of research over the past decade (R.V.G. Clarke 1982; 1983; 1985; R.V.G. Clarke and Mayhew 1980; Heal and Laycock 1986). In the following brief discussion examples of the approach are presented together with some objections to this style of prevention.

Reducing opportunity

Hardening the target One of the most obvious ways to reduce the opportunity for crime is physically to harden the target by use of stronger materials or locks and bars to obstruct the offender. The British Post Office has virtually eliminated theft of money from telephone kiosks by replacing aluminium coin boxes with steel boxes (Mayhew *et al.* 1976). A similar measure to prevent car theft was attempted in 1971 with the introduction of steering column locks on cars (Mayhew *et al.* 1980a). This British initiative followed West German legislation which had made such locks compulsory on *all* vehicles, old and new, in the early 1960s. The German figures showed a reduction of over 60 per cent in car thefts. In Britain the locks were compulsory only for *new* cars: as might have been predicted, thefts of new cars fell only for thefts of old cars to rise. Thus the effect of the target hardening was to *displace* theft from one type of car to another. It would be anticipated that as the proportion of vulnerable cars becomes less, so car theft will fall. Mayhew *et al.* suggest that vulnerable cars may begin to attract higher insurance premiums, leading owners to 'harden' them as well. The other side of the coin is that car thieves may become more sophisticated, or develop new strategies such as stealing parts from cars. However, as most cars are stolen for joy riding or convenience, the offender having missed the last bus home, this seems less likely to happen on a large scale. What is less certain is whether the crime will be displaced to another class of targets: do these offenders who stole from telephone kiosks now steal from another source?

There are instances in which target hardening has been quite fortuitous. The legislation requiring motor cycle riders to wear a crash helmet caused an immediate drop of about 24 per cent in the theft of two-wheeled vehicles. Unless the thief is equipped with a crash helmet, he or she increases the risk of detection by stealing a motor cycle and riding without a helmet. It is interesting to speculate how many frustrated motor cycle thieves stole cars without steering column locks.

Removing the target Rather than simply hardening the target, crime can be prevented by removing the target from the environment. Theft from coin boxes in telephone kiosks can be eliminated by a system which uses credit cards so that no money is available. Other coin boxes such as in gas meters and electricity meters can similarly be removed and replaced by, for example, quarterly bills. In a similar fashion, the payment of wages by cheque or bank credit removes the need to transport large amounts of cash, eliminating the opportunity for wage snatches and violent crime. Transport systems as arranged by some institutions such as universities and hospitals carry vulnerable people at night, so reducing the chances of assault and sexual attack. J.M. Hough *et al.* (1980) discuss several other examples to prevent theft in ports, theft of car radios, and robberies from public transport.

Allied to target removal is the strategy of removing the means to commit the crime. Wilkinson (1977) notes that the incidence of hijacking aeroplanes was cut dramatically by the introduction of screening of baggage and passengers to detect weapons or bombs. A similar argument applies to firearm control: if the availability of firearms is limited then the chances of abuse decline. In the same vein, legislation has made it illegal to sell certain commodities — alcohol, cigarettes, glue, and so forth — to children.

Increasing the risk of detection

Formal surveillance The police are the most obvious manifestation of formal surveillance; a police presence increases the risk of detection thereby reducing the opportunity of crime. The immediate problem is that it is doubtful whether sufficient police could ever be employed to maintain a presence at every potential criminal situation (R.V.G. Clarke and Hough 1980). One strategy has therefore been to focus police surveillance on particular situations in which crime is likely to occur. In this light, Ekblom (1980) discusses the operation of police truancy patrols. These patrols, working in conjunction with an education welfare officer (EWO), pick up children playing truant found on the streets. The justification for this is twofold: to prevent offending, given the link between truancy and delinquency (Belson 1975); and to return the child to school and allow the EWO to examine the reasons for the truancy. The effectiveness of the patrols has proved difficult to measure but, as Ekblom notes, the potential is certainly apparent for those children detected.

In the absence of formal police surveillance there are other possibilities for crime prevention. Sturman (1980) reports a study of vandalism on buses which has clear policy implications for reducing damage through formal surveillance. In comparing damage to different types of bus, Sturman found that vandalism was much greater on buses *without* a conductor; further, on all buses, with or without a conductor, damage was greatest at the rear on the upper deck. As Sturman suggests, bus companies must balance the costs of running defaced vehicles against the costs of repairs and of conductors to supervise passengers. Other studies have also pointed to the importance of an 'authority figure' in reducing crime. Walsh (1978) reported that the presence of a shop assistant reduces levels of shoplifting. Waller and Okihiro (1978) suggested that apartment blocks supervised by doormen are at less risk for burglary. R.V.G. Clarke (1982) notes that supervision of public telephones in public houses and launderettes is associated with low levels of vandalism; car parks with attendants have lower rates of damage to cars; while the presence of football club stewards reduces hooliganism on trains by supporters.

While the visible appearance of employees appears to be advantageous in reducing offending, the formality of the surveillance can be increased by the use of closed circuit television (CCTV); indeed, CCTV has become a feature in many shops, banks, and building societies. Burrows (1980) describes the use of CCTV to attempt to reduce robbery and theft on the London Underground. CCTV was installed at four Underground stations, positioned to give a view of the parts of the stations — platforms, ticket halls, escalators — which are high-risk areas for crime. In the stations with CCTV there were 252 reported offences in the twelve months prior to the installation of the CCTV: this fell to seventy-five offences in the twelve months after installation, which is 70 per cent fewer crimes. Over the same period, the comparable figure was a fall of just over 25 per cent in fifteen Underground stations geographically close to the four stations with CCTV. On 238 other stations over the whole of the Underground system the fall was 38 per cent. This pattern of figures clearly illustrates that while reported crime was falling throughout the system, the fall was greatest where the CCTV was in operation. However, the figures from the fifteen stations close to the CCTV-protected stations give some cause for concern. The significantly lower fall in offending in these stations suggests that displacement, particularly of theft, was occurring. As Burrows notes, if displacement was occurring then 'it may have nullified up to 85 per cent of the savings in theft offences apparently produced by CCTV installations' (1980: 81).

Informal surveillance The public are, as a general rule, slow to detect and report crime; although action is more likely if the aim is to protect personal property or the immediate neighbourhood. A number of innovations, such as 'Neighbourhood Watch' (Donnison *et al*. 1986; Kelling 1986), have tried to increase public involvement and willingness to report crimes. In this light, the architectural design of the environment may be an important determinant of public surveillance (Mayhew 1979; O. Newman 1972; 1980). A key concept from Newman's work has been the notion of 'defensible space': the area which individuals are able to survey and define as their territory and for which they take responsibility. Parts of large apartment blocks and high-rise flats have areas which are not anyone's defensible space: these 'semi-public' areas include internal and external access and circulation routes, lifts, and stairways. These impersonal areas are particularly prone to vandalism and liable to be 'no go' areas.

S. Wilson (1980) investigated vandalism and defensible space on a housing estate in an inner London borough. As might be predicted, vandalism occurred mainly on the ground floor, particularly in the areas where children played. Public areas such as entrances and underground garages were particularly heavily vandalized, with glazing the most common target. Wilson reported little overall variation in the levels of vandalism in housing blocks of different design. However, there were some variations of note: if entrances also acted as routes to other locations, thereby affording access to outsiders, vandalism was unduly high; alternatively, if the entrance design was such that it was exclusively for the use of residents then vandalism was lower. The child density in a given block was one of the best predictors of vandalism: when too great numbers of children were concentrated on a single estate, vandalism was at its peak. Wilson suggests that future design of housing estates might look to a number of points to increase surveillance and defensible space and so prevent vandalism:

> Dwellings should overlook outside areas so that children at play can be seen; impersonal space which is not part of residents' territory should be reduced; and entrances should be made discrete for residents' use only. Reducing child densities through dispersal of families with children is problematic but may have a significant part to play in prevention. Where possible, families with children should be housed in buildings small enough not to need lifts or much semi-public access space. . . . More robust materials should be used in construction and repair . . . and where possible the use of glazing reduced. (S. Wilson 1980: 61–2)

In a similar study of vandalism to telephone kiosks, Mayhew *et al.* (1980b) tested the hypothesis that kiosks would be less of a target for vandalism if they were overlooked by people's homes. Analysis of the frequency of vandalism showed, as predicted, that there was less vandalism when the kiosk could be seen from a home. The effect was not however of high magnitude and, as R.V.G. Clarke notes, this 'perhaps emphasises that defensible space is only part of the solution to crime in public housing settings' (1982: 224). It is probably more than coincidence that, as in Wilson's (1980) study, the major determinant of vandalism was the number of children living in the vicinity. With children in mind, Hope (1986) discusses the prevention of school burglary through design of the school buildings.

Objections

A number of objections to situational measures of crime prevention have been voiced. The first is that they ignore the 'person' side of the person and environment interaction. Farrington, with particular emphasis on delinquency prevention through schools, is firmly of the opinion that 'it is just as plausible to locate the causes of delinquency in the individual as in the environment' (1985: 40), a point which is recognized by proponents of environmental measures, who point to social factors alongside architectural design (O. Newman 1980). It must be emphasized that the theoretical stance in situational prevention, which has a great deal in common with social learning theory (R.V.G. Clarke 1982), postulates an *interaction* between the person and the environment. To prevent or reduce crime both sides of the interaction must be considered. In a critique of situational crime control, Trasler works towards just such a position:

> Policies of crime reduction really demand two strategies: deterring occasional or low-rate offenders from committing crimes . . . and identifying and incapacitating high-rate, persistent offenders. Situational crime control offers effective measures for the first, but is likely to have little impact on the second group. (Trasler 1986: 24)

A second objection lies in the domain of civil liberties; recordings on videotape, photographs on credit cards, and so on. (Although, as Laycock (1986) describes, the marking of personal property can reduce the incidence of domestic burglary.) This is clearly an area in which moral and political decisions have to be made, as R.V.G. Clarke notes: 'A certain level of crime may be the inevitable consequence of practices and institutions we cherish or find convenient and the costs of reducing crime below this level may be unacceptable' (1982: 227). A similar argument applies to objections concerning the aesthetics of an environment at worst bristling with guard dogs, barbed wire, and security cameras. Situational measures can have an effect but their implementation requires caution, planning, debate and consultation.

The final objection centres around the notion of 'displacement', that the criminal, frustrated by situational measures, will change either the time, place, method, or form of the crime (Reppetto 1976). Displacement is difficult to measure accurately, but there is little doubt that the studies of car steering locks (Mayhew *et al.* 1980a) and CCTV (Burrows 1980) did show evidence of this phenomenon. The nature and extent of the displacement will certainly be determined by a number of factors. The motivation of the offender may be important: the 'opportunistic offender' may be deterred by situational measures, whereas the 'professional criminal' is forced to devise other strategies and more sophisticated techniques. The level of implementation is important, so that only partial prevention (as with steering locks) influences displacement. In addition, removing a target may lead to opportunities for other offences: the shift to credit cards may reduce robbery or pilfering but opens the door to computer crime, accounting frauds, and so on. In the final analysis it is a question of balance: if the gains in crime prevention, in both financial and human terms, outweigh the effects of displacement, in a manner acceptable to the majority, then situational measures may be worthwhile. The great problem is the difficulty in measuring the exact effects of situational interventions, so that in the final analysis their implementation becomes something of a social gamble.

Perspective

Is criminal behaviour a suitable target for clinical intervention? The question is an important one at theoretical, practical, and policy levels. The outcome evidence provides a suitable starting-point in looking for answers. A number of reviews of the effects of treatment have suggested that clinical intervention does not always lead to reduced recidivism (Bailey 1966; Brody 1976; Rutter and Giller 1983); as was the general force of the brief review at the beginning of this chapter. The ambiguity in the clinical outcome studies has been used in some quarters, both in this country and the USA, to fuel the doctrine of 'nothing works'; that is any attempt at rehabilitation is doomed to failure.

In a highly influential paper, Martinson (1974) argued that only a small proportion of outcome studies indicated any efficacy of clinical intervention, and of those that did sampling and methodological errors could explain the 'successes'. This research is often quoted by those in favour of therapeutic nihilism and so a recent re-examination by Thornton (1987) of Martinson's data is of particular interest. Referring to the same source as Martinson, a review of 231 studies by D. Lipton *et al.* (1975), Thornton extracted studies on three criteria: (1) the use of recidivism as an outcome variable; (2) a research design involving either random allocation to conditions or matching across conditions; (3) a level of methodological sophistication acceptable by criteria defined by Lipton *et al.* Thornton found that of the 231 studies, only 38 satisfied all three criteria. The majority of the 38 (34) involved a comparison between psychological therapies, such as counselling and psychotherapy, and an untreated control group. As Thornton notes, the small number of acceptable studies immediately limits the data base from which any conclusions can be drawn; while the subject matter of the studies says nothing about other forms of treatment based, for example, on vocational training or behaviour modification. In examining the outcome of these 34 studies, Thornton found that sixteen studies showed a significant advantage following treatment; seventeen studies showed no significant difference between treated offenders and controls; one study showed a significant disadvantage following treatment. Concluding his discussion of this re-analysis, Thornton states:

> Either the catalogue of studies on which Martinson based his assertions may properly be read as indicating that psychological therapy can have positive effects on recidivism, or it can be read as indicating that no conclusion can safely be drawn. The one interpretation that

is not acceptable is that it has been shown that 'Nothing Works' (Thornton 1987: 188)

The spirit of Thornton's work is to be found in other reviews of the clinical outcome data with offenders (e.g. Garrett 1985; Gendreau and Ross 1979), leading to the position that clinical intervention works with some offenders, some of the time. The major difficulty, from a clinical perspective, is the inability to devise interventions with a consistently high success rate. While this is undoubtedly the force of the empirical studies, the view that nothing works continues to prevail in many quarters. There are, I think, two prime reasons for this continuing state of affairs: conceptual and research difficulties in the experimental-clinical literature; and a political and ideological struggle for a dominant model of crime and the associated social policies.

Looking first at the design of clinical treatment programmes, one is often struck by the lack of *criminological* justification for the intervention. For example, in reviewing the behavioural literature the question keeps arising as to why the target behaviour — academic ability, institutional performance, social competence — was selected. For example, if social skills training is being evaluated in terms of its effects on recidivism, then this necessarily implies a causal relationship between social skills and offending. Evidence for such a relationship is sorely lacking in the empirical literature. As discussed previously, there are studies which suggest that, on average, young offenders are less socially skilled than non-offenders: however, the co-existence of two factors, skills difficulties and offending, does not necessarily demonstrate a causal link; both may be the product of a third factor such as intelligence, a broken home, social class, and so forth. This point applies, of course, to all types of clinical intervention which assume a relationship between some individual variable — skills level, ego dysfunction, personality, emotional lability, cognition, etc. — and the criminal behaviour. The issue is complicated still further by the possible effects of individual differences: for example, *some* offenders may commit crimes because of skills deficits, and they will be the successes of skills training programmes; but in other cases, perhaps the majority, a skills deficit (when it exists) has no causal relationship with offending. In total, these points call into question the model of crime being utilized by many clinical programmes.

It is undoubtedly the case that by focusing the intervention on the offender, treatment is locating the cause of offending within the individual (occasionally also including the offender's peers or family). This is a clear classical or positivistic stance, implying that the clinical intervention can 'put right' the individual aberration which has caused the offending. However, as discussed previously, criminological theories suggest the involvement of a whole range of other factors, economic, sociological, legal, political, and so on. Given that there may well be reasons other than preventing crime for conducting clinical interventions with offenders, some laudable, others less so (Emery and Marholin 1977), and notwithstanding several strong statements on the topic (Hollin and Howells 1986; West 1980; 1986), a strong *criminological* case for clinical intervention remains to be elucidated. The promising findings coming from the clinical work with sex offenders may point to the way in which this might be achieved: a sound empirical base from which to generate clinical hypotheses concerning the offence behaviour; the inclusion of a wide range of criminologically relevant variables in theories of sexual offending; well-developed assessment methods; and the setting of realistic targets in the design of clinical programmes.

In terms of research the greatest difficulty lies in an accurate measure of recidivism. Studies have used a variety of indices of offending, including arrest rate, reconviction rate, rate of reinstitutionalization, offence type, and self-report measures. There are advantages and disadvantages to all these measures (Hollin and Henderson 1984), although their varied use does pose considerable difficulty when comparing across studies. The major issue lies in the distinction between 'official' and 'unofficial' (i.e. self-report) measures of offending: studies repeatedly discover considerable differences in outcome depending on which type of measure is used (e.g. W.S. Davidson *et al.* 1987; Spence and Marzillier 1981). There is no ready answer to which measure to use, but it is perhaps worth noting that there is considerable dissatisfaction with the use of official figures as an outcome measure. Indeed, Braukmann and Fixsen (1975) suggest that official figures provide a better measure of the court's behaviour than of the offender's.

While part of the debate hinges around the empirical data, at another level the struggle is for a dominant model of crime. A treatment philosophy is often associated with liberal political values, stemming from the belief that individuals can be helped to overcome their difficulties and become a useful member of society. This liberal ideal has taken a terrible pounding over the past decade: the ambiguity of the treatment outcome studies has not assisted greatly, but other forces have been at work. The political tone, in both this country and the USA, has become more conservative: Bayer (1981) writes of the shattering of the optimism of post-war liberalism and the emergence of the new pessimism of the conservative perspective. Proponents of neoclassical views of crime offer a quite different perspective on crime prevention, a view which removes the need to consider the finer points of individuality by reducing human motivation and behaviour to economic terms. Van Den Haag argues against the notion of rehabilitation in just this way:

> I do not see any relevant difference between dentistry and prostitution or car theft, except that the latter activities do not require a license. . . . The frequency of rape, or of mugging, is essentially determined by the expected comparative net advantage, just as is the rate of dentistry and burglary. The comparative net advantage consists in the satisfaction (produced by the money or by the violative act itself) expected from the crime, less the expected cost of achieving it, compared to the net satisfaction expected from other activities in which the offender has the opportunity to engage. Cost in the main equals the expected penalty divided by the risk of suffering it. (Van Den Haag 1982: 1,026–7)

Such a position clearly pays little heed to any sophisticated psychological or sociological analysis of crime; offending is seen principally in terms of costs and benefits. It is not difficult to see where this leads; Van Den Haag again:

> Our only hope for reducing the burgeoning crime rate lies in decreasing the expected net advantage of committing crimes (compared to lawful activities) by increasing the cost through increasing the expected severity of punishment and the probability of suffering them. (Van Den Haag 1982: 1,035)

These views, encapsulated in the justice model (B. Hudson 1987), have obvious implications for social policy. The response to crime is not couched in terms of rehabilitation but rather in terms of 'tougher' punishments (F.T. Cullen *et al.* 1985). Thus we witness the return of custodial regimes such as the 'short sharp shock' for young offenders, repeated calls for the return of corporal and capital punishment, and the abandonment of treatment and training in prisons for the ideal of 'humane containment'.

I find this a bleak scenario, bleak in a humanitarian sense as well as in preventive terms: it is perhaps the greatest irony of all that with harsh, punitive measures 'nothing works' (e.g. Thornton *et al.* 1984), while the possibilities of treatment have been prematurely discarded. Although fighting a rearguard action, the treatment ideal is not defeated and with the right tactics could yet emerge with honour. These tactics might profitably include the following: strong counter-arguments to an 'economic' model of human behaviour (e.g. Trasler 1986); a greater emphasis on criminological targets (e.g. Barth 1986); the use of multi-component, individually tailored programmes (e.g. Perkins 1982); a sense of realism and acknowledgement of forces other than just the psychological in crime; greater lobbying at political and legal levels; an awareness of the potential harm of labelling (e.g. J. McCord 1978) and therefore a willingness to discriminate in offering treatment; organization of effective institutional systems (e.g. T. Williams *et al.* 1984); a reappraisal of research methodologies; and a greater emphasis on criminology in the training of psychologists who work with offenders. In the debate about responses to crime, Lord Windlesham offers a view which all concerned might consider: 'Common humanity is the moral sieve through which criminal policies aimed at protecting the public must pass if they are to be regarded as deserving the title "justice" ' (1987: 341).

Epilogue

Stepping back from the expanse of material covered in this text, two points deserve immediate attention: What has psychology contributed to the understanding of crime? How useful is this contribution?

It would be a harsh critic indeed who would dismiss all of the psychological literature on crime as meaningless or irrelevant. My overwhelming impression from the literature has been that psychological research into crime has achieved most in precisely the areas in which mainstream psychology is the strongest: that is in the study of the individual (and to a lesser extent the social group) in terms of motivation, behaviour, perception, psychopathology, personality, group dynamics, and so on. Psychology is at its best in studying the individual offender, in the development of empirically based offender taxonomies, in studies of witness memory, jury deliberation, and interpersonal skills training for police officers. However, along with these strengths, there are a number of pitfalls of which two merit particular discussion.

For better or worse, and with some notable dissenters, mainstream psychology is closely wedded to a 'scientific' ethos, with its research centred around an experimental, laboratory-based methodology. While there are criticisms and limitations to such a methodology, it also has undoubted strengths. One such strength is that it allows any given topic to be examined in depth in a highly controlled manner. While this can lead to a greater understanding of a given topic, it also sets the problem of whether the laboratory setting has produced artificial results. At worst this may mean that experimental results are meaningless, or alternatively that the results are in some way distorted. The former is an empirical matter, as highlighted by the debate on the applicability of laboratory research to witness memory, and each case will demand examination in its own right. As regards the latter question of distortion, it is almost certainly the case that this occurs in some, if not all, laboratory studies. The focus on a single factor or variable in an experimental study, controlling for other influences, may well act to magnify or to diminish the effect of the variable of interest. Thus jury studies in the laboratory may demonstrate the influence of different types of evidence but, in the courtroom, this effect does not appear to be of the same magnitude. The single variable in the laboratory loses some of its power when other variables are also present and exerting their influence. I suspect that the effects of leading questions with eyewitnesses are another example of a phenomenon which is powerful in the laboratory when all else is equal, but in practice its effects are attenuated by other variables. To design experiments which are meaningful, in that they include all the relevant variables and so point to interactive effects, while remaining manageable, is a perennial difficulty in any experimental science.

Experimental methodology also brings difficulties when psychology comes into contact with other disciplines which prefer different methods of enquiry. Thus there has proved to be ground for only a limited exchange with sociology and almost no common language with law. Further, in terms of both a relationship between the various areas of research and in generating theories, psychology has tended to maintain a piecemeal, isolationist stance. There is little or no attempt to draw together the various aspects of psychological enquiry, such as say on the police, the courts and the offender, in a unified way so as to make sense of the overall picture. Psychological theories of criminal behaviour can similarly be criticized for concentrating too much on the individual, to the neglect of the context of the crime. In short, psychology has in the main been *about* crime: what is lacking is a psychology of and for crime, in other words, a *criminological psychology*.

A true criminological psychology would attempt to integrate its methodologies and findings with criminological theories. I. Taylor *et al.* (1973) have presented a model of how this might be achieved. Their emphasis is on a social account of crime: 'The formal requirement . . . is for a *social psychology of crime*' (1973: 271); in understanding the act of crime, 'The formal requirement . . . is for an account of real *social dynamics* surrounding the actual acts' (1973: 272); and with regard to social reaction to crime, 'The requirement . . . is for a *social psychology of social reaction*: an account of the contingencies and the conditions which are crucial to the decision to act against the deviant' (1973: 272–3). As Taylor *et al.* stress, these social accounts need themselves to be placed within a political and economic context.

The emphasis on social psychology is an important one, so that the movement is away from positivistic explanations which focus almost exclusively on the offender, to interactive explanations which see individual differences within a social (and political and economic) environment. This type of study is to be found (e.g. Elmer *et al.* 1987) and hopefully is an approach which will continue to be employed by researchers. It is not feasible at present to detail a genuine criminological psychology — although R.V.G. Clarke (1977) gives a tantalizing glimpse of what might be achieved. Following Clarke's lead, such an account of crime would need to include the myriad of relationships between individual factors, both psychological and biological, socialization and development, social behaviour and social cognition, social reactions to crime, education, labelling, lay explanations for crime, media reactions to crime, and social control of crime; all set within or alongside political and economic considerations. Such an ambitious account would need to rely on information from a range of methodologies and a willingness to break down professional barriers in both training and co-operation between researchers. Even then, of course, there will remain philosophical problems, such as the nature and role of free will (Glaser 1977; Schafer 1977). This is a daunting project but, I suggest, a necessary one if a real criminological psychology is to evolve.

In conclusion I hope the process of gathering together the material here will, in itself, be valuable for all those interested in both psychology and crime. Should the book prove useful in informing the practice of those who work with offenders I will be especially pleased. If my final musing goes even a little way towards promoting a new style of psychology, in the form of criminological psychology, then that will indeed be a bonus.

References

Abel, G.G., Barlow, D.H., Blanchard, E.B., and Guild, D. (1977) 'The components of rapists' sexual arousal', *Archives of General Psychiatry 34*: 895–903.

Abel, G.G., Becker, J.V., and Cunningham-Rather, J. (1984) 'Complications, consent, and cognitions in sex between children and adults', *International Journal of Psychiatry and Law 7*: 89–103.

Abel, G.G., Becker, J.V., Murphey, W.D., and Flanagan, B. (1981a) 'Identifying dangerous child molesters', in R.B. Stuart (ed.) *Violent Behavior: Social Learning Approaches to Prediction, Management and Treatment*, New York: Brunner/Mazel.

Abel, G.G., Blanchard, E.B., and Barlow, D.H. (1981b) 'Measurement of sexual arousal in several paraphilias: the effects of stimulus modality, instructional set and stimulus content', *Behaviour Research and Therapy 19*: 25–33.

Abrahamson, D. (1944) *Crime and the Human Mind*, New York: Columbia University Press.

Adlam, R.C.A. (1981) 'The police personality', in D.W. Pope and N.L. Weiner (eds) *Modern Policing*, London: Croom Helm.

Ahlstrom, W.M. and Havinghurst, R.J. (1971) *400 Losers*, San Francisco, Calif: Jossey-Bass.

Aichhorn, A. (1955) *Wayward Youth* (trans.), New York: Meridian Books (original work published in 1925).

Ainsworth, P.B. (1981) 'Incident perception by British police officers', *Law and Human Behavior 5*: 231–6.

—— (1982) *British Police Officers' Perceptions of Psychology*, paper presented at the International Conference on Psychology and Law, Swansea, Wales.

Ainsworth, P.B. and Pease, K. (1987) *Police Work*, Leicester/London: British Psychological Society/Methuen.

Akers, R.L. (1977) *Deviant Behavior: A Social Learning Approach* (2nd edn), Belmont, Calif: Wadsworth.

Akers, R.L., Krohn, M.D., Lanza-Kaduce, L., and Radosevich, M. (1979) 'Social learning and deviant behavior: a specific test of a general theory', *American Sociological Review 44*: 636–55.

Alban Metcalfe, B.M. and Wright, P. (1986) 'Social skills training for managers', in C.R. Hollin and P. Trower (eds) *Handbook of Social Skills Training, vol. 1: Applications across the Life Span*, Oxford: Pergamon.

Alder, C. (1984) 'The convicted rapist: a sexual or violent offender?', *Criminal Justice and Behavior 11*: 157–77.

Alexander, F. and Healy, W. (1935) *Roots of Crime*, New York: Knopf.

Alexander, F. and Staub, H. (1931) *The Criminal, the Judge and the Public*, New York: Macmillan.

Alexander, J.F. and Parsons, B.V. (1973) 'Short-term behavioral intervention with delinquent families: impact on family processes and recidivism', *Journal of Abnormal Psychology 81*: 219–25.

—— (1982) *Functional Family Therapy*, Monterey, Calif: Brooks/Cole.

Alexander, R.N., Corbett, T.F., and Smigel, J. (1976) 'The effects of individual and group consequences on school attendance and curfew violations with pre-delinquent adolescents', *Journal of Applied Behavior Analysis 9*: 221–6.

Allsopp, J.F. and Feldman, M.P. (1975) 'Extraversion, neuroticism and psychoticism and anti-social behaviour in school girls', *Social Behaviour and Personality 2*: 184–8.

—— (1976) 'Personality and anti-social behaviour in school-boys', *British Journal of Criminology 16*: 337–51.

Alper, A., Buckhout, R., Chern, S., Harwood, R., and Slomovits, M. (1976) 'Eyewitness identification: accuracy of individual vs. composite recollection of a crime', *Bulletin of the Psychonomic Society 8*: 147–9.

Alter-Reid, K., Gibbs, M.S., Lachenmeyer, J.R., Sigal, J., and Massoth, N.A. (1986) 'Sexual abuse of children: a review of the empirical findings', *Clinical Psychology Review 6*: 249–66.

Alterman, A.I., Druley, K.A., Connolly, R.B., and Bush, D. (1978) 'A comparison of moral reasoning in drug addicts and non-addicts', *Journal of Clinical Psychology 34*: 790–4.

Alves, E.A. (1985) 'The control of anger in the ''mentally abnormal'' offender', in E. Karas (ed.) *Current Issues in Clinical Psychology*, vol. 2, New York: Plenum.

American Psychiatric Association (1980) *Diagnostic and Statistical Manual of Mental Disorders* (3rd edn), Washington, DC: American Psychiatric Association.

Amir, M. (1971) *Patterns in Forcible Rape*, Chicago, Ill: Chicago University Press.

Anderson, C.A. (1987) 'Temperature and aggression: effects on quarterly, yearly, and city rates of violent and nonviolent crime', *Journal of Personality and Social Psychology 52*: 1,161–73.

Andrew, J.M. (1977) 'Delinquency: intellectual imbalance?', *Criminal Justice and Behavior 4*: 99–104.

Arbuthnot, J. and Gordon, D.A. (1986) 'Behavioral and cognitive effects of a moral reasoning development intervention for high-risk behavior-disordered adolescents', *Journal of Consulting and Clinical Psychology 54*: 208–16.

Argyle, M. (1967) *The Psychology of Interpersonal Behaviour*, Harmondsworth: Pelican.

Argyle, M. and Kendon, A. (1967) 'The experimental analysis of social performance', in L. Berkowitz (ed.) *Advances in Experimental Social Psychology*, vol. 3, New York: Academic Press.

Aromaa, K. (1974) *The Replication of a Survey of Victimization to Violence*, Helsinki: Institute of Criminology.

Aronfreed, J. (1968) *Conduct and Conscience*, New York: Academic Press.

Aronson, E. and Carlsmith, J.M. (1968) 'Experimentation in social psychology', in G.D. Lindzey and E. Aronson (eds) *Handbook of Social Psychology*, Reading, Mass: Addison-Wesley.

Aronstam, D. and Tyson, G.A. (1980) 'Racial bias in eyewitness perception', *Journal of Social Psychology 110*: 177–82.

Asch, S.E. (1952) *Social Psychology*, Englewood Cliffs, NJ: Prentice-Hall.

Ashmore, Z. and Jarvie, J. (1987) 'Job skills for young offenders', in B.J. McGurk, D.M. Thornton, and M. Williams (eds) *Applying Psychology to Imprisonment: Theory & Practice*, London: HMSO.

Ashworth, A. and Gostin, L. (1985) 'Mentally disordered offenders and the sentencing process', in L. Gostin (ed.) *Secure Provision: A Review of Special Services for the Mentally Ill and Mentally Handicapped in England and Wales*, London: Tavistock.

Atkinson, R.L., Atkinson, R.C., and Hilgard, E.R. (1983) *Introduction to Psychology* (8th edn), New York: Harcourt Brace Jovanovich.

Austin, T.L., Hale, D.C., and Ramsey, L.J. (1987) 'The effect of layoff on police authoritarianism', *Criminal Justice and Behavior 14*: 194–210.

Ausubel, D. (1958) *Theories and Problems of Child Development*, New York: Grune & Stratton.

Avery-Clarke, C.A. and Laws, D.R. (1984) 'Differential erection response patterns of sexual child abusers to stimuli describing activities with children', *Behavior Therapy 15*: 71–83.

Bailey, W. (1966) 'Correctional outcome: an evaluation of 100 reports', *Journal of Criminal Law, Criminology and Police Science 57*: 153–60.

Baldwin, J. and McConville, M. (1979a) *Jury Trials*, Oxford: Oxford University Press.

—— (1979b) 'Trial by jury: some empirical evidence on contested criminal cases in England', *Law and Society Review 13*: 861–90.

—— (1980) 'Does the composition of an English jury affect its verdict?', *Judicature 64*: 133–9.

Bales, K.B. (1982) 'Contrast and complementarity in three theories of criminal behavior', *Deviant Behavior: An Interdisciplinary Journal 3*: 155–73.

Bandura, A. (1973a) *Aggression: A Social Learning Analysis*, Englewood Cliffs, NJ: Prentice-Hall.

—— (1973b) 'Social learning theory of aggression', in J.F. Kautson (ed.) *The Control of Aggression: Implications from Basic Research*, Chicago, Ill: Aldine.

—— (1976) 'Social learning analysis of aggression', in E. Ribes-Inesta and A. Bandura (eds) *Analysis of Delinquency and Aggression*, Hillsdale, NJ: Lawrence Erlbaum.

—— (1977) *Social Learning Theory*, New York: Prentice-Hall.

Bandura, A., Ross, D., and Ross, S.A. (1963) 'Imitation of film-mediated aggressive models', *Journal of Abnormal and Social Psychology 66*: 3-11.

Banton, M. (1986) *Investigating Robbery*, Aldershot, Hants: Gower.

Barbaree, H.E., Marshall, W.L., and Lanthier, R.K. (1979) 'Deviant sexual arousal in rapists', *Behaviour Research and Therapy 17*: 215-22.

Barbaree, H.E., Marshall, W.L., Yates, E., and Lightfoot, L.O. (1983) 'Alcohol intoxication and deviant sexual arousal in male social drinkers', *Behaviour Research and Therapy 21*: 365-73.

Barlow, G. (1979) 'Youth Treatment Centre', in C. Payne and K.J. White (eds) *Caring for Deprived Children*, London: Croom Helm.

Barnes, C., Hollin, C.R., and Martin, G. (1984) 'Changes in young offender scores over time on measures of literacy and intelligence', *Directorate of Psychological Services Report*, series II, no. 130, Home Office, London.

Baron, R.A. (1977) *Human Aggression*, New York: Plenum.

Barth, R.P. (1986) 'Assessment and treatment of stealing', in B.B. Lahey and A.E. Kazdin (eds) *Advances in Clinical Child Psychology*, vol. 10, New York: Plenum.

Bartol, C.R. (1980) *Criminal Behavior: A Psychosocial Approach*, Englewood Cliffs, NJ: Prentice-Hall.

Bartol, C.R. and Bartol, A.M. (1987) 'History of forensic psychology', in I.B. Weiner and A.K. Hess (eds) *Handbook of Forensic Psychology*, New York: Wiley.

Baxter, D.J., Barbaree, H.E., and Marshall, W.L. (1986) 'Sexual responses to consenting and forced sex in a large sample of rapists and nonrapists', *Behaviour Research and Therapy 24*: 513-20.

Bayer, R. (1981) 'Crime, punishment and the decline of liberal optimism', *Crime and Delinquency 27*: 169-90.

Bean, P.T. (1980) *Compulsory Admissions to Mental Hospitals*, Chichester: Wiley.

Beck, S.J. and Ollendick, T.H. (1976) 'Personal space, sex of experimenter, and locus of control in normal and delinquent adolescents', *Psychological Reports 38*: 383-7.

Becker, H. (1963) *Outsiders: Studies in the Sociology of Deviance*, New York: Free Press.

Bekerian, D.A. and Bowers, J.M. (1983) 'Eyewitness testimony: were we misled?', *Journal of Experimental Psychology: Learning, Memory and Cognition 9*: 139-45.

Belson, W. (1975) *Juvenile Theft: The Causal Factors*, New York: Harper & Row.

Bennett, L., Sorensen, D., and Forshay, H. (1971) 'The application of self-steem measures in a correctional setting: I. Reliability of the scale and relationship to other measures', *Journal of Research in Crime and Delinquency 8*: 1-10.

Bennett, T. (1986) 'A decision-making approach to opioid addiction', in D.B. Cornish and R.V.G. Clarke (eds) *The Reasoning Criminal: Rational Choice Perspectives on Offending*, New York: Springer-Verlag.

Bentovim, A., Elton, A., and Tranter, M. (1987) 'Prognosis for rehabilitation after abuse', *Adoption and Fostering 11*(1): 26-31.

Benyon, J. and Bourn, C. (eds) (1986) *The Police: Powers, Procedures and*

Proprieties, Oxford, Pergamon.

Beran, N.J. and Toomey, B.G. (1979) *Mentally Ill Offenders and the Criminal Justice System: Issues in Forensic Services*, New York: Praeger.

Berkowitz, L. (1965) 'The concept of aggressive drive: some additional considerations', in L. Berkowitz (ed.) *Advances in Experimental Social Psychology*, vol. 2, New York: Academic Press.

—— (1974) 'Some determinants of impulsive aggression: role of mediated associations with reinforcement for aggression', *Psychological Review 81*: 165–76.

Berry, M.J. (1985) 'Secure units: a bibliography', *Special Hospitals Research Report, No. 18*, London: Special Hospitals Research Unit.

Berryman, J.C., Hargreaves, D.J., Hollin, C.R., and Howells, K. (1987) *Psychology and You: An Informal Introduction*, Leicester/London: British Psychological Society/Methuen.

Biederman, A.D., Johnson, L., McIntyre, J., and Weir, A. (1967) *Report on a Pilot Study in the District of Columbia on Victimization and Attitudes to Law Enforcement*, Washington, DC: US Government Printing Office.

Billig, M. and Milner, D. (1976) 'A spade is a spade in the eyes of the law', *Psychology Today 2*: 13–15; 62.

Binet, A. (1900) *La Suggestibilité*, Paris: Schleicher.

Black, D.A. (1982) 'A 5-year follow-up study of male patients discharged from Broadmoor Hospital', in J. Gunn and D.P. Farrington (eds) *Abnormal Offenders, Delinquency, and the Criminal Justice System*, Chichester: Wiley.

—— (1984) 'Treatment in maximum security settings', in M. Craft and A. Craft (eds) *Mentally Abnormal Offenders*, London: Baillière Tindall.

Blackburn, R. (1968) 'Personality in relation to extreme aggression in psychiatric offenders', *British Journal of Psychiatry 114*: 821–8.

—— (1971) 'Personality types among abnormal homicides', *British Journal of Criminology 11*: 14–31.

—— (1975a) 'An empirical classification of psychopathic personality', *British Journal of Psychiatry 127*: 456–60.

—— (1975b) 'Aggression and the EEG: a qualitative analysis', *Journal of Abnormal Psychology 84*: 358–65.

—— (1979) 'Cortical and autonomic arousal in primary and secondary psychopaths', *Psychophysiology 16*: 143–50.

—— (1982) 'On the relevance of the concept of the psychopath', in D.A. Black (ed.) *Symposium: Broadmoor Psychology Department's 21st birthday, Issues in Criminological and Legal Psychology, No. 2*, Leicester: British Psychological Society.

—— (1983) 'Psychopathy, delinquency and crime', in A. Gale and J.A. Edwards (eds) *Physiological Correlates of Human Behaviour, vol. 3: Individual Differences and Psychopathology*, London: Academic Press.

—— (1984) 'Are personality disorders treatable?', in J. Shapland and T. Williams (eds) *Mental Disorder and the Law: Effects of the New Legislation, Issues in Criminological and Legal Psychology, No. 4*, Leicester: British Psychological Society.

—— (1986) 'Patterns of personality deviation among violent offenders', *British*

Journal of Criminology 26: 254–69.

Blackburn, R. and Lee-Evans, J.M. (1985) 'Reactions of primary and secondary psychopaths to anger-evoking situations', *British Journal of Clinical Psychology* 24: 93–100.

Blackburn, R. and Maybury, C. (1985) 'Identifying the psychopath: the relation of Cleckley's criteria to the interpersonal domain', *Personality and Individual Differences* 6: 375–86.

Blackman, D.E. (1981a) 'The experimental analysis of behaviour and its relevance to applied psychology', in G. Davey (ed.) *Applications of Conditioning Theory*, London: Methuen.

—— (1981b) 'On mental elements and their place in psychology and law', in J. Shapland (ed.) *Lawyers and Psychologists — The Way Forward, Issues in Criminological and Legal Psychology, No. 1*, Leicester: British Psychological Society.

Blackmore, J. (1974) 'The relationship between self-reported delinquency and official convictions amongst adolescent boys', *British Journal of Criminology* 14: 172–6.

Blader, J.C. and Marshall, W.L. (1984) 'The relationship between cognitive and erectile measures of sexual arousal in non-rapist males as a function of depicted aggression', *Behavioral Research and Therapy* 22: 623–30.

Blagg, H. (1985) 'Reparation and justice for juveniles', *British Journal of Criminology* 25: 267–79.

Blair, C.D. and Lanyon, R.I. (1981) 'Exhibitionism: etiology and treatment', *Psychological Bulletin* 89: 439–63.

Blakely, C.H. and Davidson, W.S. (1984) 'Behavioral approaches to delinquency: a review', in P. Karoly and S.J. Steffen (eds) *Adolescent Behavior Disorders: Foundations and Contemporary Concerns*, Lexington, Mass: Lexington Books.

Blasi, A. (1980) 'Bridging moral cognition and moral action: a critical review of the literature', *Psychological Bulletin* 88: 1–45.

Blatt, S.J. and Lerner, H. (1983) 'Psychodynamic perspectives on personality theory', in M. Hersen, A.E. Kazdin, and A.S. Bellack (eds) *The Clinical Psychology Handbook*, Oxford: Pergamon.

Blau, J. and Blau, P. (1982) 'The cost of inequality: metropolitan structure and violent crime', *American Sociological Review* 47: 113–29.

Blau, T.H. (1984) *The Psychologist as Expert Witness*, New York: Wiley.

Block, R. (1977) *Violent Crime*, Lexington, Mass: Lexington Books.

—— (1979) 'Community, environment and violent crime', *Criminology* 17: 46–57.

Bluglass, R. (1985) 'The development of regional secure units', in L. Gostin (ed.) *Secure Provision: A Review of Special Services for the Mentally Ill and Mentally Handicapped in England and Wales*, London: Tavistock.

Blumberg, N.H. (1981) 'Arson update: A review of the literature on firesetting', *Bulletin of the American Academy of Psychiatry and the Law* 9: 255–65.

Blumer, H. (1969) *Symbolic Interactionism*, Englewood Cliffs, NJ: Prentice-Hall.

Bohman, M. (1978) 'Some genetic aspects of alcoholism and criminality', *Archives of General Psychiatry* 35: 269–76.

Bohman, M., Cloninger, C.R., Sigvardsson, S., and van Knorring, A-L. (1983)

'Gene-environment interaction in the psychopathology of adoptees: some recent studies of the origin of alcoholism and criminality', in D. Magnusson and V. Allen (eds) *Human Development: An Interactional Perspective*, London: Academic Press.

Bolton, F.E. (1896) 'The accuracy of recollection and observation', *Psychological Review 3*: 286-95.

Borgstrom, C.A. (1939) 'Eine Serie von kriminellen Zwillingen', *Archiv für Rassenbiologie*.

Borkowski, M., Murch, M., and Walker, V. (1983) *Marital Violence: The Community Response*, London: Tavistock.

Bornstein, P.H., Hamilton, S.B., and McFall, M.E. (1981) 'Modification of adult aggression: a critical review of theory, research, and practice', in M. Hersen, R.M. Eisler, and P.M. Miller (eds) *Progress in Behavior Modification*, vol. 12, London: Academic Press.

Bottomley, K. and Pease, K. (1986) *Crime and Punishment: Interpreting the Data*, Milton Keynes: Open University Press.

Bowden, P. (1981) 'What happens to patients released from special hospitals?', *British Journal of Psychiatry 138*: 350-4.

Bowlby, J. (1944) 'Forty-four juvenile thieves', *International Journal of Psychoanalysis 25*: 1-57.

—— (1946) *Forty-Four Juvenile Thieves: Their Characters and Home-Life*, London: Baillière, Tindall, & Cox.

—— (1951) *Maternal Care and Mental Health*, Geneva: World Health Organisation.

—— (1979) *The Making and Breaking of Affectional Bonds*, London: Tavistock.

Bowlby, J. and Salter-Ainsworth, M.D. (1965) *Child Care and the Growth of Love*, Harmondsworth: Penguin.

Bowlby, J., Ainsworth, M.D., Boston, M., and Rosenbluth, D. (1956) 'The effects of mother-child separation: a follow-up study', *British Journal of Medical Psychology 29*: 211-47.

Box, S. (1971) *Deviance, Reality and Society*, London: Holt, Rinehart, & Winston.

—— (1983) *Power, Crime and Mystification*, London: Tavistock.

Braukmann, C.J. and Fixsen, D.L. (1975) 'Behavior modification with delinquents', in M. Hersen, R.M. Eisler, and P.M. Miller (eds) *Progress in Behavior Modification*, vol. 1, New York: Academic Press.

Bray, R.M. and Kerr, N.L. (1982) 'Methodological considerations in the study of the psychology of the courtroom', in N.L. Kerr and R.M. Bray (eds) *The Psychology of the Courtroom*, New York: Academic Press.

Bregman, N.J. and McAllister, H.A. (1982) 'Eyewitness testimony: the role of commitment in increasing reliability', *Social Psychology Quarterly 45*: 181-4.

Brigham, J.C. and Bothwell, R.K. (1983) 'The ability of prospective jurors to estimate the accuracy of eyewitness identifications', *Law and Human Behavior 7*: 19-30.

Brigham, J.C., Maass, A., Snyder, L.D., and Spaulding, K. (1982) 'Accuracy of eyewitness identification in a field setting', *Journal of Personality and Social Psychology 42*: 673-81.

Brigham, J.C., Maass, A., Martinez, D., and Whittenberger, G. (1983) 'The effect of arousal on facial recognition', *Basic and Applied Social Psychology* 4: 279–93.

British Psychological Society (1986) 'Report of the working group on the use of the polygraph in criminal investigation and personnel screening', *Bulletin of the British Psychological Society 39*: 81–94.

Brody, S. (1976) *The Effectiveness of Sentencing: A Review of the Literature*, London: HMSO.

Brown, B. (1985) 'An application of social learning methods in a residential programme for young offenders', *Journal of Adolescence 8*: 321–31.

Brown, E., Deffenbacher, K.A., and Sturgill, W. (1977) 'Memory for faces and the circumstances of the encounter', *Journal of Applied Psychology 62*: 311–18.

Brown, L. and Willis, A. (1985) 'Authoritarianism in British police recruits: importation, socialization or myth?', *Journal of Occupational Psychology 58*: 97–108.

Brown, M. (1926) *Legal Psychology*, Indianapolis, Ind: Bobbs-Merrill.

Brown, W.C. (1961) *Freud and the Post-Freudians*, Harmondsworth: Penguin.

Brownmiller, S. (1975) *Against our Will: Men, Women and Rape*, New York: Simon & Schuster.

Buchanan, D.R. (1985) 'Enhancing eyewitness identification: applied psychology for law enforcement officers', *Journal of Police Science and Administration 13*: 303–9.

Bukstel, L.H. and Kilman, P.R. (1980) 'Psychological effects of imprisonment on confined individuals', *Psychological Bulletin 88*: 469–93.

Bull, R.H.C. (1979) 'The influence of stereotypes on person perception', in D.P. Farrington, K. Hawkins, and S.M.A. Lloyd-Bostock (eds) *Psychology, Law and Legal Processes*, London: Macmillan.

—— (1982) 'Physical appearance and criminality', *Current Psychological Reviews* 2: 269–81.

—— (1984) 'Psychology's contribution to policing', in D.J. Müller, D.E. Blackman, and A.J. Chapman (eds) *Psychology and Law*, Chichester: Wiley.

—— (1985) 'Police awareness training', *Policing 1*: 109–23.

—— (1986a) 'Police psychology: the world conference', *Policing 2*: 56–67.

—— (1986b) 'An evaluation of police recruit training in human awareness', in J.C. Yuille (ed.) *Police Selection and Training: The Role of Psychology*, Dordrecht: Martinus Nijhoff.

Bull, R.H.C. and Horncastle, P. (1986) *Metropolitan Police Recruit Training: An Independent Evaluation*, London: Police Foundation.

—— (1987) 'Evaluating training: the London Metropolitan police's recruit training in human awareness/policing skills', in P. Southgate (ed.) *New Directions in Police Training*, London: HMSO.

Bull, R.H.C. and Reid, R.L. (1975) 'Police officers' recall of information', *Journal of Occupational Psychology 48*: 73–8.

Bull, R.H.C., Bustin, B., Evans, P., and Gahagan, D. (1983) *Psychology for Police Officers*, Chichester: Wiley.

Bull, R.H.C., Horncastle, P., Jones, C., and Mason, D. (1987) *Metropolitan Police Recruit Training in 'Policing Skills' (Phase 2): An Independent Evaluation. Executive Summary*, London: Police Foundation.

Burbeck, E. and Furnham, A. (1984) 'Personality and police selection: trait differences in successful and non-successful applicants to the Metropolitan Police', *Personality and Individual Differences 5*: 257–63.

Burchard, J.D. and Burchard, S.N. (eds) (1987) *Prevention of Delinquent Behavior*, Beverly Hills, Calif: Sage.

Burchard, J. and Harig, P.T. (1976) 'Behavior modification and juvenile delinquency', in H. Leitenberg (ed.) *Handbook of Behavior Modification and Behavior Therapy*, Englewood Cliffs, NJ: Prentice-Hall.

Burrows, J. (1980) 'Closed circuit television and crime on the London Underground', in R.V.G. Clarke and P. Mayhew (eds) *Designing out Crime*, London: HMSO.

Burt, C. (1925) *The Young Delinquent*, London: University of London Press.

Burt, M. (1980) 'Cultural myths and support for rape', *Journal of Personality and Social Psychology 39*: 217–30.

Burton, L. (1968) *Vulnerable Children*, London: Routledge & Kegan Paul.

Buss, A.H. (1961) *The Psychology of Aggression*, New York: Wiley.

Butler, A.J.P. (1986) 'The limits of police community relations training', in J.C. Yuille (ed.) *Police Selection and Training: The Role of Psychology*, Dordrecht: Martinus Nijhoff.

Butler, A.J.P. and Cochrane, R. (1977) 'An examination of some elements of the personality of police officers and their implications', *Journal of Police Science and Administration 5*: 441–50.

Byrne, J.M. and Sampson, R.J. (eds) (1986) *The Social Ecology of Crime*, London: Springer-Verlag.

Cadoret, R.J. (1986) 'Epidemiology of antisocial personality', in W.H. Reid, D. Door, J.I. Walker, and J.W. Bonner (eds) *Unmasking the Psychopath: Antisocial Personality and Related Syndromes*, London: W.W. Norton.

Cadoret, R.J. and Cain, C. (1980) 'Sex differences in predictors of antisocial behavior in adoptees', *Archives of General Psychiatry 37*: 1,171–5.

—— (1981) 'Environmental and genetic factors in predicting antisocial behaviors in adoptees', *Psychiatric Journal of the University of Ottawa 6*: 220–5.

Cadoret, R.J., Cain, C.A., and Crowe, R.R. (1983) 'Evidence for gene-environment interaction in the development of adolescent antisocial behaviour', *Behavior Genetics 13*: 301–10.

Campagna, A.F. and Harter, S. (1975) 'Moral judgement in sociopathic and normal children', *Journal of Personality and Social Psychology 31*: 199–205.

Campbell, A. and Gibbs, J.J. (eds) (1986) *Violent Transactions: The Limits of Personality*, Oxford: Blackwell.

Cantwell, D.P. (1975) 'A medical model for research and clinical use with hyperactive children', in D.P. Cantwell (ed.) *The Hyperactive Child*, New York: Spectrum.

Carney, L.P. (1977) *Probation and Parole: Legal and Social Dimensions*, New York: McGraw-Hill.

Carroll, J. and Weaver, F. (1986) 'Shoplifters' perceptions of crime opportunities: a process-tracing study', in D.B. Cornish and R.V.G. Clarke (eds) *The Reasoning Criminal: Rational Choice Perspectives on Offending*, New York: Springer-Verlag.

Carroll, L. and Jackson, P.I. (1983) 'Inequality, opportunity and crime rates in central cities', *Criminology 21*: 178–93.

Carson, D. (1987) 'In the witness box', in G. Gudjonsson and J. Drinkwater (eds) *Psychological Evidence in Court, Issues in Criminological and Legal Psychology, No. 11*, Leicester: British Psychological Society.

Cattell, J.M. (1895) 'Measurements of the accuracy of recollection', *Science 2*: 761–6.

Ceci, S., Toglia, M., and Ross, D. (eds) (1987) *Children's Eyewitness Memory*, New York: Springer-Verlag.

Chambliss, W. and Seidman, R. (1971) *Law, Order and Power*, Reading, Mass: Addison-Wesley.

Chandler, M.J. (1973) 'Egocentrism and anti-social behavior: the assessment and training of social perspective-taking skills', *Developmental Psychology 9*: 326–32.

Chapman, A.J. and Jones, D.M. (eds) (1980) *Models of Man*, Leicester: British Psychological Society.

Chappell, D. and Singer, S. (1977) 'Rape in New York city: a study of material in the police files and its meaning', in D. Chappell, R. Geis, and S. Feis (eds) *Forcible Rape: The Crime, the Victim, and the Offender*, New York: Columbia University Press.

Chappell, D., Geis, G., Schafer, S., and Siegal, L. (1977) 'A comparative study of forcible rape offences known to the police in Boston and Los Angeles', in D. Chappell, R. Geis, and G. Geis (eds) *Forcible Rape: The Crime, the Victim, and the Offender*, New York: Columbia University Press.

Charrow, R.P. and Charrow, V.R. (1979) 'Making legal language understandable: a psycholinguistic study of jury instructions', *Columbia Law Review 79*: 1,306–74.

Check, J.V.P. and Malamuth, N.M. (1985) 'Sex role stereotyping and reactions to depiction of stranger versus acquaintance rape', *Journal of Personality and Social Psychology 45*: 344–56.

Cheek, J. and Hogan, R. (1982) 'Self-concept, self-presentation and moral judgement', in J. Suls and A. Greenwald (eds) *Psychological Perspectives on the Self*, vol. 2, Hillsdale, NJ: Lawrence Erlbaum.

Chesno, F.A. and Kilmann, P.R. (1975) 'Effects of stimulation intensity on sociopathic avoidance learning', *Journal of Abnormal Psychology 84*: 144–50.

Chilton, R. and Galvin, J. (1985) 'Race, crime and criminal justice', *Crime and Delinquency 31*: 3–14.

Christiaansen, R.E. and Ochalek, K. (1983) 'Editing misleading information from memory: evidence for the coexistence of original and postevent information', *Memory and Cognition 11*: 467–75.

Christiansen, K.O. (1977) 'A preliminary study of criminality among twins', in S. Mednick and K.O. Christiansen (eds) *Biosocial Bases of Criminal Behavior*, New York: Gardner Press.

Ciminero, A.R., Calhoun, K.S., and Adams, H.E. (eds) (1986) *Handbook of Behavioral Assessment* (2nd edn), Chichester: Wiley.

Clare, A. (1976) *Psychiatry in Dissent: Controversial Issues in Thought and Practice*, London: Tavistock.

Clarke, A. and Clarke, A. (eds) (1976) *Early Experience: Myth and Evidence*, London: Open Books.

Clarke, R.V.G. (1977) 'Psychology and crime', *Bulletin of the British Psychological Association 30*: 280–3.

—— (1982) 'Crime prevention through environmental management and design', in J. Gunn and D.P. Farrington (eds) *Abnormal Offenders, Delinquency, and the Criminal Justice System*, Chichester: Wiley.

—— (1983) 'Situational crime prevention: its theoretical basis and practical scope', in N. Morris and M. Tonry (eds) *Crime and Justice: An Annual Review of Research*, vol. 4, Chicago, Ill: University of Chicago Press.

—— (1985) 'Jack Tizard memorial lecture: delinquency, environment and intervention', *Journal of Child Psychology and Psychiatry 26*: 505–23.

Clarke, R.V.G. and Hough, J.M. (eds) (1980) *The Effectiveness of Policing*, Aldershot, Hants: Gower.

Clarke, R.V.G. and Mayhew, P. (1980) (eds) *Designing Out Crime*, London: HMSO.

Cleckley, H. (1964) *The Mask of Sanity* (4th edn), St Louis, Mo: C.V. Mosby.

—— (1976) *The Mask of Sanity* (5th edn), St Louis, Mo: C.V. Mosby.

Clifford, B.R. (1976) 'Police as eyewitnesses', *New Society 36*: 176–7.

—— (1979) 'The relevance of psychological investigation to legal issues in testimony and identification', *Criminal Law Review* 153–63.

Clifford, B.R. and Bull, R. (1978) *The Psychology of Person Identification*, London: Routledge & Kegan Paul.

Clifford, B.R. and Hollin, C.R. (1981) 'Effects of the type of incident and the number of perpetrators on eyewitness memory', *Journal of Applied Psychology 66*: 364–70.

Clifford, B.R. and Richards, V.J. (1977) 'Comparison of recall of policemen and civilians under conditions of long and short durations of exposure', *Perceptual and Motor Skills 45*: 503–12.

Clifford, B.R. and Scott, J. (1978) 'Individual and situational factors in eyewitness testimony', *Journal of Applied Psychology 63*: 352–9.

Cochrane, R. and Butler, A.J.P. (1980) 'The values of police officers, recruits, and civilians in England', *Journal of Police Science and Administration 8*: 205–11.

Cohen, L.E. and Felson, M. (1979) 'Social change and crime rate trends: a routine activity approach', *American Sociological Review 44*: 588–608.

Cohen, L.H. and Freeman, H. (1945) 'How dangerous to the community are State Hospital patients?', *Connecticut State Medical Journal 9*: 697–700.

Cohen, M.L., Garofalo, R.F., Boucher, R., and Seghorn, T. (1971) 'The psychology of rapists', *Seminars in Psychiatry 3*: 307–27.

Coid, J. (1984) 'How many psychiatric patients in prison?', *British Journal of Psychiatry 145*: 78–86.

Colman, A.M. (1981) *What is Psychology?*, London: Kogan Page.

—— (1983) 'Attitudes of British police officers: a rejoinder', *Sociology 17*: 388–91.

Colman, A.M. and Gorman, L.P. (1982) 'Conservatism, dogmatism, and authoritarianism in British police officers', *Sociology 16*: 1–11.

Congalton, A.A. and Najman, J.M. (1974) *Unreported Crime*, Sydney: New South Wales Bureau of Crime Statistics and Research.

Conklin, J. (1972) *Robbery and the Criminal Justice System*, New York: Lippincott.

Conley, J., O'Barr, W., and Lind, A. (1978) 'The power of language: presentation style in courtroom', *Duke Law Journal* 1,375–99.

Conte, J.R. (1985) 'Clinical dimensions of adult sexual interest in children', *Behavioral Sciences and the Law 3*: 341–54.

Cook, P.M. (1977) 'Empirical survey of police attitudes', *Police Review 85*: 1,042; 1,078; 1,114; 1,140.

Cooper, C.L., Davidson, M.J., and Robinson, P. (1982) 'Stress in the police service', *Journal of Occupational Medicine 24*: 30–6.

Cooper, D. (1967) *Psychiatry and Anti-Psychiatry*, London: Tavistock.

Cornish, D.B. and Clarke, R.V.G. (1975) *Residential Treatment and its Effects on Delinquency*, Home Office Research Study, no. 32, London: HMSO.

—— (eds) (1986a) *The Reasoning Criminal: Rational Choice Perspectives on Crime*, New York: Springer-Verlag.

—— (1986b) 'Introduction', in D.B. Cornish and R.V.G. Clarke (eds) *The Reasoning Criminal: Rational Choice Perspectives on Offending*, New York: Springer-Verlag.

Cortes, J.B. and Gatti, F.M. (1972) *Delinquency and Crime: A Biopsychosocial Approach*, New York: Seminar Press.

Cox, T. (1978) *Stress*, London: Macmillan.

Craft, M. (1984) 'Low intelligence, mental handicap and criminality', in M. Craft and A. Craft (eds) *Mentally Abnormal Offenders*, London: Baillière Tindall.

Craft, M. and Craft, A. (1978) *Sex and the Mentally Handicapped*, London: Routledge & Kegan Paul.

—— (eds) (1984) *Mentally Abnormal Offenders*, London: Baillière Tindall.

Crawford, D.A. (1977) 'The HDHQ results of long-term prisoners: relationships with criminal and institutional behaviour', *British Journal of Social and Clinical Psychology 16*: 391–4.

—— (1979) 'Modification of deviant sexual behaviour: the need for a comprehensive approach', *British Journal of Medical Psychology 52*: 151–6.

—— (1980) 'Applications of penile response monitoring to the assessment of sexual offenders', in D.J. West (ed.) *Sex Offenders in the Criminal Justice System*, Cambridge: University of Cambridge, Institute of Criminology.

Crawford, D.A. and Allen, J.V. (1979) 'A social skills training programme with sex offenders', in M. Cook and G. Wilson (eds) *Love and Attraction*, Oxford: Pergamon.

Crombag, H.F.M. (1984) 'Some psychological observations on mens rea', in D.J. Müller, D.E. Blackman, and A.J. Chapman (eds) *Psychology and Law*, Chichester: Wiley.

Crowe, R.R. (1974) 'An adoption study of antisocial personality', *Archives of General Psychiatry 31*: 785–91.

Cullen, F.T., Clark, G.A., and Wozniak, J.F. (1985) 'Explaining the get tough movement: can the public be blamed?', *Federal Probation 49*: 16–24.

Cullen, J.E. (1987) 'Group-based treatment for serious institutional offending', in B.J. McGurk, D.M. Thornton, and M. Williams (eds) *Applying Psychology to Imprisonment: Theory & Practice*, London: HMSO.

Cullen, J.E. and Seddon, J.W. (1981) 'The application of a behavioural regime to disturbed young offenders', *Personality and Individual Differences 2*: 285–92.

Cumberbatch, W.G. (1984) 'Community policing in Britain', in D.J. Müller, D.E. Blackman, and A.J. Chapman (eds) *Psychology and Law*, Chichester: Wiley.

Cusson, M. and Pinsonneault, P. (1986) 'The decision to give up crime', in D.B. Cornish and R.V.G. Clarke (eds) *The Reasoning Criminal: Rational Choice Perspectives in Offending*, New York: Springer-Verlag.

Cutting, J. (1985) *The Psychology of Schizophrenia*, London: Churchill.

Dahrendorf, R. (1959) *Class and Class Conflict in Industrial Society*, Stanford, Conn: Stanford University Press.

Dalgaard, O.S. and Kringlen, E. (1976) 'A Norwegian twin study of criminality', *British Journal of Criminology 16*: 213–33.

David, O., Hoffman, S., Sverd, J., Clark, J., and Voeller, K. (1976) 'Lead and hyperactivity. Behavior response to Chelation: a pilot study', *American Journal of Psychiatry 133*: 1,155–8.

Davidson, M.S. and Veno, A. (1980) 'Stress and the policeman', in C.L. Cooper and J. Marshall (eds) *White Collar and Professional Stress*, Chichester: Wiley.

Davidson, W.S. and Wolfred, T.R. (1977) 'Evaluation of a community-based behavior modification program for prevention of delinquency: the failure of success', *Community Mental Health Journal 13*: 296–306.

Davidson, W.S., Redner, R., Blakely, C.H., Mitchell, C.M., and Emshoff, J.G. (1987) 'Diversion of juvenile offenders: an experimental comparison', *Journal of Consulting and Clinical Psychology 55*: 68–75.

Davies, G.M. (1981) 'Face recall systems', in G.M. Davies, H.D. Ellis, and J.W. Shepherd (eds) *Perceiving and Remembering Faces*, London: Academic Press.

—— (1983) 'Forensic face recall: the role of visual and verbal information', in S.M.A. Lloyd-Bostock and B.R. Clifford (eds) *Evaluating Witness Evidence: Recent Psychological Research and New Perspectives*, Chichester: Wiley.

Davies, G.M., Ellis, H.D., and Shepherd, J.W. (1978) 'Face recognition accuracy as a function of mode of representation', *Journal of Applied Psychology 63*: 180–7.

Davies, G.M., Shepherd, J.W., and Ellis, H.D. (1979) 'Effects of interpolated mugshot exposure on accuracy of eyewitness identification', *Journal of Applied Psychology 64*: 232–7.

Davies, G.M., Ellis, H.D., and Shepherd, J.W. (eds) (1981) *Perceiving and Remembering Faces*, New York: Academic Press.

Davies, W. (1982) 'Violence in prisons', in P. Feldman (ed.) *Developments in the Study of Criminal Behaviour, vol. 2: Violence*, Chichester: Wiley.

—— (1986) 'The development and operation of regional secure units', in C.R. Hollin and K. Howells (eds) *Clinical Approaches to Criminal Behaviour, Issues in Criminological and Legal Psychology, No. 9*, Leicester: British Psychological Society.

Davies, W. and Feldman, P. (1981) 'The diagnosis of psychopathy by forensic specialists', *British Journal of Psychiatry 138*: 329–31.

Davis, G.E. and Leitenberg, H. (1987) 'Adolescent sex offenders' *Psychological Bulletin 101*: 417–27.

Davison, G.C. and Neale, J.M. (1986) *Abnormal Psychology: An Experimental Clinical Approach* (4th edn), Chichester: Wiley.

Deardroff, P.A., Kendall, P.C., Finch, A.J., and Sitarz, A.M. (1977) 'Empathy, locus of control, and anxiety in college students', *Psychological Reports 40*: 1,236-8.

deChesnay, M. (1985) 'Father-daughter incest: an overview', *Behavioral Sciences and the Law 3*: 391-402.

Deffenbacher, K.A. (1983) 'The influence of arousal on reliability of testimony', in S.M.A. Lloyd-Bostock and B.R. Clifford (eds) *Evaluating Witness Evidence: Recent Psychological Research and New Perspectives*, Chichester: Wiley.

Deffenbacher, K.A. and Loftus, E.F. (1982) 'Do jurors share a common understanding concerning eyewitness behavior?', *Law and Human Behavior 6*: 15-30.

De Francis, V. (1969) *Protecting the Child Victims of Sex Crimes Committed by Adults*, Denver, Colo: American Humane Society.

Dell, S. (1982) 'Transfer of special hospital patients into National Health Service hospitals', in J. Gunn and D.P. Farrington (eds) *Abnormal Offenders, Delinquency, and the Criminal Justice System*, Chichester: Wiley.

Deming, M.B. and Eppy, A. (1981) 'The sociology of rape', *Sociology and Social Research 65*: 357-80.

Dengerink, H.A., Schnedler, R.W., and Covey, M.V. (1978) 'The role of avoidance in aggressive responses to attack and no attack', *Journal of Personality and Social Psychology 36*: 1,044-53.

Denkowski, G.C. and Denkowski, K.M. (1985) 'The mentally retarded offender in the state prison system: identification, prevalence, adjustment, and rehabilitation', *Criminal Justice and Behavior 12*: 55-70.

DHSS (1974) *Report of the Working Party on Security in NHS Psychiatric Hospitals (Glancy Report)*, London: DHSS.

DHSS and Home Office (1986) *Offenders Suffering from Psychopathic Disorder*, London: DHSS and Home Office.

Dinitz, S., Dynes, R. and Clarke, A. (1975) *Deviance*, Oxford: Oxford University Press.

Dobash, R.E. and Dobash, R.P. (1984) 'The nature and antecedents of violent events', *British Journal of Criminology 24*: 269-88.

Dodd, D.H. and Bradshaw, J.M. (1980) 'Leading questions and memory: pragmatic constraints', *Journal of Verbal Learning and Verbal Behavior 21*: 207-19.

Dohrenwend, B.S. and Dohrenwend, B.P. (ed.) (1974) *Conference on Stressful Life Events: Their Nature and Effect*, Chichester: Wiley.

Dollard, J., Doob, L.W., Miller, N.E., Mowrer, O.H., and Sears, R.R. (1939) *Frustration and Aggression*, New Haven, Conn: Yale University Press.

Donnison, H., Scola, J., and Thomas, P. (1986) *Neighbourhood Watch: Policing the People*, London: Libertarian Research and Education Trust.

Dorr, D. and Woodhall, P.K. (1986) 'Ego dysfunction in psychopathic psychiatric impatients', in W.H. Reid, D. Dorr, J.I. Walker, and J.W. Bonner (eds) *Unmasking the Psychopath: Antisocial Personality and Related Syndromes*, London: W.W. Norton.

Drasgow, F., Palau, J., Taibi, R., and Drasgow, J. (1974) 'Levels of function-ing and locus of control', *Journal of Clinical Psychology 30*: 365-9.

Drinkwater, J. (1982) 'Violence in psychiatric hospitals', in P. Feldman (ed.) *Developments in the Study of Criminal Behaviour, vol. 2: Violence*, Chichester: Wiley.

Dugdale, R. (1910) *The Jukes*, New York: Putnam.

Earls, C.M. and Marshall, W.L. (1983) 'The current state of technology in the laboratory assessment of sexual arousal patterns', in J.G. Greer and I.R. Stuart (eds) *Sexual Aggression: Current Perspectives on Treatment*, New York: Van Nostrand Reinhold.

Earls, C.M. and Quinsey, V.L. (1985) 'What is to be done? Future research on the assessment and behavioural treatment of sex offenders', *Behavioral Sciences and the Law 3*: 377-90.

Easterbrook, J.A. (1959) 'The effect of emotion on cue utilization and the organization of behavior', *Psychological Review 66*: 183-201.

Eastwood, L. (1985) 'Personality, intelligence and personal space among violent and non-violent delinquents', *Personality and Individual Differences 6*: 717-23.

Egeth, H.E. and McCloskey, M. (1984) 'Expert testimony about eyewitness behavior: Is it safe and effective?', in G.L. Wells and E.F. Loftus (eds) *Eyewitness Testimony: Psychological Perspectives*, Cambridge: Cambridge University Press.

Ekblom, P. (1980) 'Police truancy patrols', in R.V.G. Clarke and P. Mayhew (eds) *Designing Out Crime*, London: HMSO.

Ellis, H.D. (1975) 'Recognising faces', *British Journal of Psychology 66*: 409-26.

—— (1984) 'Practical aspects of face memory', in G.L. Wells and E.F. Loftus (eds) *Eyewitness Testimony: Psychological Perspectives*, Cambridge: Cambridge University Press.

Ellis, P.L. (1982) 'Empathy: a factor in antisocial behavior', *Journal of Abnormal Child Psychology 2*: 123-33.

Elmer, N., Reicher, S., and Ross, A. (1987) 'The social context of delinquent conduct', *Journal of Child Psychology and Psychiatry 28*: 99-109.

Elton, A., Bentovim, A., and Tranter, M. (1987) 'Child sexual abuse: treat-ment stages', *Adoption and Fostering 11*(2): 30-2.

Elwork, A., Sales, B.D., and Alfini, J.J. (1982) *Making Jury Instructions Understandable*, Charlottesville, Va: Michie.

Elwork, A., Sales, B.D., and Suggs, D. (1981) 'The trial: a research review', in B.D. Sales (ed.) *The Trial Process*, New York: Plenum.

Emery, R.E. and Marholin, D. (1977) 'An applied behavior analysis of delinquency: the irrelevancy of relevant behavior', *American Psychologist 6*: 860-73.

Ennis, P.H. (1967) *Criminal Victimization in the United States: A Report of a National Survey*, Washington, DC: US Government Printing Office.

Estabrook, A. (1916) *The Jukes in 1915*, Washington, DC: Carnegie Institute of Washington.

Eysenck, H.J. (1959) *Manual of the Maudsley Personality Inventory*, London: University of London Press.

—— (1964) *Crime and Personality*, London: Routledge & Kegan Paul.

—— (1970) *Crime and Personality* (2nd edn), London: Granada.

—— (1973) *The Inequality of Man*, London: Temple Smith.

—— (1977) *Crime and Personality* (3rd edn), London: Routledge & Kegan Paul.

—— (1984) 'Crime and personality', in D.J. Müller, D.E. Blackman, and A.J. Chapman (eds) *Psychology and Law*, Chichester: Wiley.

—— (1987) 'Personality theory and the problems of criminality', in B.J. McGurk, D.M. Thornton, and M. Williams (eds) *Applying Psychology to Imprisonment: Theory & Practice*, London: HMSO.

Eysenck, H.J. and Eysenck, S.B.G. (1968) 'A factorial study of psychoticism as a dimension of personality', *Multivariate Behavioural Research* (special issue): 15–31.

—— (1976) *Psychoticism as a Dimension of Personality*, London: Hodder & Stoughton.

Eysenck, M.W. (1984) *Handbook of Cognitive Psychology*, London: Lawrence Erlbaum.

Eysenck, S.B.G. and Eysenck, H.J. (1971) 'Crime and personality: item analysis of questionnaire responses', *British Journal of Criminology 11*: 49–62.

—— (1972) 'The questionnaire measurement of psychoticism', *Psychological Medicine 2*: 50–5.

Eysenck, S.B.G., Eysenck, H.J., and Barrett, P. (1985) 'A revised version of the psychoticism scale', *Personality and Individual Differences 6*: 21–9.

Eysenck, S.B.G. and McGurk, B.J. (1980) 'Impulsiveness and venturesomeness in a detention centre population', *Psychological Reports 47*: 1,299–1,306.

Eysenck, S.B.G., Rust, J., and Eysenck, H.J. (1977) 'Personality and the classification of adult offenders', *British Journal of Criminology 17*: 169–79.

Fahringer, H.P. (1980) ' "In the valley of the blind" — jury selection in a criminal case', *Trial Diplomacy Journal 3*: 34–9; 48–54.

Farrington, D.P. (1983) 'Offending from 10 to 25 years of age', in K.T. Van Dusen and S.A. Mednick (eds) *Prospective Studies of Crime and Delinquency*, The Hague: Kluwer-Nijhoff.

—— (1985) 'Delinquency prevention in the 1980s', *Journal of Adolescence 8*: 3–16.

Farrington, D.P. and Bennett, T. (1981) 'Police cautioning of juveniles in London', *British Journal of Criminology 21*: 123–35.

Farrington, D.P. and Dowds, E.A. (1985) 'Disentangling criminal behaviour and police reaction', in D.P. Farrington and J. Gunn (eds) *Reactions to Crime: The Police, Courts and Prisons*, Chichester: Wiley.

Farrington, D.P., Ohlin, L.E., and Wilson, J.Q. (1986) *Understanding and Controlling Crime: Toward a New Research Strategy*, New York: Springer-Verlag.

Feeney, F. (1986) 'Robbers as decision-makers', in D.B. Cornish and R.V.G. Clarke (eds) *The Reasoning Criminal: Rational Choice Perspectives on Offending*, New York: Springer-Verlag.

Feldman, M.P. (1977) *Criminal Behaviour: A Psychological Analysis*, Chichester: Wiley.

Field, H.S. (1978) 'Attitudes towards rape: a comparative analysis of police, rapists, crisis counselors and citizens', *Journal of Personality and Social Psychology 36*: 156–79.

Finkelhor, D. (1979) *Sexually Victimized Children*, New York: Free Press.
—— (1984) *Child Sexual Abuse: New Theory and Research*, New York: Free Press.
—— (1986) *A Sourcebook on Child Sexual Abuse*, Beverly Hills, Calif: Sage.
Fo, W.S.O. and O'Donnell, C.R. (1974) 'The buddy system: relationship and contingency conditions in a community intervention program for youth and non-professionals as behavior change agents', *Journal of Consulting and Clinical Psychology 42*: 163–8.
—— (1975) 'The buddy system: effect of community intervention on delinquent offences', *Behavior Therapy 6*: 522–4.
Fodor, E.M. (1972) 'Delinquency and susceptibility to social influence among adolescents as a function of level of moral development', *Journal of Social Psychology 86*: 257–60.
Fox, S.G. and Walters, H.A. (1986) 'The impact of general versus specific expert testimony and eyewitness confidence upon mock juror judgements', *Law and Human Behavior 10*: 215–28.
Fraas, L.A. and Price, R.L. (1972) 'The Jesness Inventory as a predictor of AWOL recidivism', *Psychological Reports 31*: 741–2.
Freedman, B.J., Rosenthal, L., Donahoe, C.P., Schlundt, D.G., and McFall, R.M. (1978) 'A social-behavioral analysis of skills deficits in delinquent and non-delinquent adolescent boys', *Journal of Consulting and Clinical Psychology 46*: 1,448–62.
Freud, S. (1906) 'Psychoanalysis and the ascertaining of truth in courts of law', *Collected Papers*, vol. 2, New York: Basic Books.
Freund, K. (1967) 'Diagnosing homo- or heterosexuality and erotic age preference by means of a psychophysiological test', *Behaviour Research and Therapy 5*: 209–28.
Freund, K. and Langevin, R. (1976) 'Bisexuality in homosexual pedophilia', *Archives of Sexual Behavior 5*: 415–23.
Friedlander, K. (1947) *The Psychoanalytic Approach to Juvenile Delinquency*, London: Routledge & Kegan Paul.
Fromm, E. (1977) *The Anatomy of Human Destructiveness*, Harmondsworth: Penguin.
Frude, N. (ed.) (1980) *Psychological Approaches to Child Abuse*, London: Batsford Academic & Educational.
—— (1988) 'The physical abuse of children', in K. Howells and C.R. Hollin (eds) *Clinical Approaches to Aggression and Violence, Issues in Criminological and Legal Psychology, No. 12*, Leicester: British Psychological Society.
Furnham, A. (1984) 'Personality, social skills, anomie and delinquency: a self-report study of a group of normal non-delinquent adolescents', *Journal of Child Psychology and Psychiatry 25*: 409–20.
Furnham, A. and Henderson, M. (1982) 'The good, the bad and the mad: response bias in self-report measures', *Personality and Individual Differences 3*: 311–20.
—— (1983) 'Lay theories of delinquency', *European Journal of Social Psychology 13*: 107–20.
Gaffney, L.R. and McFall, R.M. (1981) 'A comparison of social skills in delinquent and non-delinquent adolescent girls using a behavioral role-playing

inventory', *Journal of Consulting and Clinical Psychology 49*: 959–67.

Garrett, C.J. (1985) 'Effects of residential treatment on adjudicated delinquents: a meta-analysis', *Journal of Research on Crime and Delinquency 22*: 287–308.

Gebhard, P.H., Gagnon, J.H., Pomeroy, W.B., and Christenson, C.V. (1965) *Sex Offenders: An Analysis of Types*, New York: Harper & Row.

Geiselman, R.E., Fisher, R.P., MacKinnon, D.P., and Holland, H.L. (1985) 'Eyewitness memory enhancement in the police interview: cognitive retrieval mnemonics versus hypnosis', *Journal of Applied Psychology 7*: 401–12.

Gelles, R.J. (1982)' Domestic criminal violence', in M.E. Wolfgang and N.A. Weiner (eds) *Criminal Violence*, Beverly Hills, Calif: Sage.

Gendreau, P. and Ross, B. (1979) 'Effective correctional treatment: bibliotherapy for cynics', *Crime and Delinquency 25*: 463–89.

Gendreau, P., Gibson, M., Surridge, C., and Hug, J. (1973) 'The application of self-esteem measures in corrections: a further report on the SEI', *Journal of Community Psychology 1*: 423–5.

Gentry, M. and Ostapiuk, E.B. (1988) 'Management of violence in a Youth Treatment Centre', in K. Howells and C.R. Hollin (eds) *Clinical Approaches to Aggression and Violence, Issues in Criminological and Legal Psychology, No. 12*, Leicester: British Psychological Society.

Genz, L.J. and Lester, D. (1976) 'Authoritarianism in policemen as a function of experience', *Journal of Police Science and Administration 7*: 53–64.

Gibbens, T.C.N., Way, C., and Soothill, K.L. (1977) 'Behavioural types of rape', *British Journal of Psychiatry 130*: 32–42.

Gibson, E. and Kline, S. (1961) *Murder*, London: HMSO.

Gilbert, P. (1984) *Depression: From Psychology to Brain State*, London: Lawrence Erlbaum.

Gilligan, C. (1982) *In a Different Voice*, Cambridge, Mass: Harvard University Press.

Gilmartin-Zena, P. (1985) 'Rape impact: immediately and two months later', *Deviant Behavior 6*: 347–61.

Ginger, A.F. (ed.) (1975) *Jury Selection in Criminal Trials*, Tiburon, Calif: Law Press.

Ginsberg, M. (1965) *On Justice in Society*, Harmondsworth: Pelican.

Glaser, D. (1977) 'The compatibility of free will and determinism in criminology: comments on an alleged problem', *Journal of Criminal Law and Criminology 67*: 486–90.

Glasser, W. (1965) *Reality Therapy: A New Approach to Psychiatry*, New York: Harper & Row.

Glover, J.H. (1985) 'A case of kleptomania treated by covert sensitization', *British Journal of Clinical Psychology 24*: 213–14.

Glueck, B. (1918) 'A study of 608 admissions to Sing Sing Prison', *Mental Hygiene 2*: 85–151.

Glueck, S. and Glueck, E. (1950) *Unraveling Juvenile Delinquency*, New York: Harper & Row.

—— (1956) *Physique and Delinquency*, New York: Harper & Row.

Goldman, J., Maitland, K.A., and Norton, P.L. (1975) 'Pschological aspects of jury performance', *Journal of Psychiatry and Law 3*: 367–79.

Goldstein, A.G., Chance, J.E., and Gilbert, B. (1984) 'Facial stereotypes of good guys and bad guys: a replication and extension', *Bulletin of the Psychonomic Society 22*: 549–52.

Goldstein, A.P., Monti, P.J., Sardino, T.J., and Green, D.J. (1979) *Police Crisis Intervention*, New York: Pergamon.

Goldstein, J.H. (1986) *Aggression and Crimes of Violence* (2nd edn), Oxford: Oxford University Press.

Goodman, G.S. and Hahn, A. (1987) 'Evaluating eyewitness testimony', in I.B. Weiner and A.K. Hess (eds) *Handbook of Forensic Psychology*, New York: Wiley.

Goodman, G.S. and Jones, D.P.H. (1988) 'The emotional effects of criminal court testimony on child sexual assault victims: a preliminary report', in G. Davies and J. Drinkwater (eds) *The Child Witness: Do the Courts Abuse Children?*, *Issues in Criminological and Legal Psychology, No. 13*, Leicester: British Psychological Society.

Goodman, G.S., Golding, J.M., Helgeson, V.S., Haith, M.M., and Michelli, J. (1987) 'When a child takes the stand: jurors' perceptions of children's eyewitness testimony', *Law and Human Behavior 11*: 27–40.

Gorenstein, G.W. and Ellsworth, P.C. (1980) 'Effect of choosing an incorrect photograph on a later identification by an eyewitness', *Journal of Applied Psychology 65*: 616–22.

Gostin, L. (1975) *A Human Condition*, vol. 1, London: MIND.

—— (1977) *A Human Condition*, vol. 2, London: MIND.

Gove, W. (ed.) (1975) *The Labeling of Deviance: Evaluating a Perspective*, New York: Wiley.

Graham, J.R. (1977) *The MMPI: A Practical Guide*, Oxford: Oxford University Press.

Green, C.M. (1981) 'Matricide by sons', *Medicine, Science and the Law 21*: 207–14.

Greene, E., Flynn, M.S., and Loftus, E.F. (1982) 'Inducing resistance to misleading information', *'Journal of Verbal Learning and Verbal Behavior 21:* 207–19.

Greenland, C. (1969) 'The three special hospitals in England and Wales and patients with dangerous, violent or criminal propensities', *Medicine, Science and the Law 9*: 253–64.

Greer, D.S. (1971) 'The reliability of testimony in criminal trials', *British Journal of Criminology 11*: 131–54.

Griffith, J.E., Pennington-Averett, A., and Bryan, I. (1981) 'Women prisoners' multidimensional locus of control', *Criminal Justice and Behavior 8*: 375–89.

Grisso, T. (1987) 'The economic and scientific future of forensic psychological assessment', *American Psychologist 42*: 831–9.

Groh, T.R. and Goldenberg, E.E. (1976) 'Locus of control with subgroups in a correctional population', *Criminal Justice and Behavior 3*: 169–79.

Grossman, L.S. (1985) 'Research directions in the evaluation and treatment of sex offenders: an analysis', *Behavioral Sciences and the Law 3*: 421–40.

Groth, A.N. (1979) *Men who Rape: The Psychology of the Offender*, New York: Plenum.

Groth, A.N. and Hobson, W.F. (1983) 'The dynamics of sexual assault', in L.B. Schlesinger and E. Revitch (eds) *Sexual Dynamics of Anti-Social Behaviour*, Springfield, Ill: C.C. Thomas.

Groth, A.N., Hobson, W.F., and Gary, T.S. (1982a) 'The child molester: clinical observations', in J. Conte and D. Shore (eds) *Social Work and Child Sexual Abuse*, New York: Haworth.

Groth, A.N., Longo, R.E., and McFadin, J.B. (1982b) 'Undetected recidivism among rapists and child molesters', *Crime and Delinquency 3*: 450–8.

Gruber, K. and Jones, R. (1983) 'Identifying determinants of risk of sexual victimization of youth', *Child Abuse and Neglect 7*: 17–24.

Grygier, T., Chesley, J., and Tuters, E.W. (1970) 'Parental deprivation: a study of delinquent children', *British Journal of Criminology 9*: 209–53.

Gudjonsson, G.H. (1983a) 'Life events stressors and physical reactions in senior British police officers', *Police Journal 56*: 66–7.

—— (1983b) 'Factors reducing occupational stress in police officers: junior officers' view', *Police Journal 56*: 251–5.

—— (1984a) 'Fear of "failure" and "tissue damage" in police recruits, constables, sergeants and senior officers', *Personality and Individual Differences 5*: 233–6.

—— (1984b) 'The current status of the psychologist as an expert witness in criminal trials', *Bulletin of the British Psychological Society 37*: 80–2.

—— (1985) 'Psychological evidence in court: results from the BPS survey', *Bulletin of the British Psychological Society 38*: 327–30.

Gudjonsson, G.H. and Adlam, K.R.C. (1982) 'Factors reducing occupational stress in police officers: senior officers' view', *Police Journal 55*: 365–9.

—— (1983a) 'Personality patterns of British police officers', *Personality and Individual Differences 4*: 507–12.

—— (1983b) 'A stressful lot', *Police Review 91*; 1,931.

—— (1985) 'Occupational stressors among British police officers', *Police Journal 58*: 73–80.

Gudjonsson, G.H. and Drinkwater, J. (1986) 'Intervention techniques for violent behaviour', in C.R. Hollin and K. Howells (eds) *Clinical Approaches to Criminal Behaviour, Issues in Criminological and Legal Psychology, No. 9*, Leicester: British Psychological Society.

Gudjonsson, G.H. and Tibbles, P. (1983) 'Behaviour modification in an interim secure unit', *Nursing Times 79*: 25–7.

Gunderson, J. (1974) 'Management of manic states: the problem of firesetting', *Psychiatry 37*: 137–46.

Gunn, J. (1977) 'Criminal behaviour and mental disorder', *British Journal of Psychiatry 130*: 317–29.

Gunn, J. and Robertson, G. (1982) 'An evaluation of Grendon Prison', in J. Gunn and D.P. Farrington (eds) *Abnormal Offenders, Delinquency, and the Criminal Justice System*, Chichester: Wiley.

Gunn, J., Robertson, G., Dell, S., and Way, C. (1978) *Psychiatric Aspects of Imprisonment*, London: Academic Press.

Guttmacher, M.S. (1951) *Sex Offenses: The Problem, Causes, and Prevention*, New York: W.W. Norton.

Guze, S.B. (1976) *Criminality and Psychiatric Disorders*, Oxford: Oxford

University Press.

Häfner, H. and Böker, W. (1982) *Crimes of Violence by Mentally Abnormal Offenders: A Psychiatric and Epidemiological Study in the Federal German Republic* (trans. H. Marshall), Cambridge: Cambridge University Press (original work published 1973).

Hain, P. (1976) *Mistaken Identity: The Wrong Face of the Law*, London: Quartet Books.

Hale, M. (1980) *Human Science and Social Order: Hugo Münsterberg and the Origins of Applied Psychology*, Philadelphia, PA: Temple University Press.

Halleck, S. (1971) *Psychiatry and the Dilemmas of Crime*, Berkeley, Calif: University of California Press.

Hall Williams, J.E. (1981) *Criminology and Criminal Justice*, London: Butterworths.

Hamilton, J. (1981) 'Diminished responsibility', *British Journal of Psychiatry* *138*: 434–6.

Hamilton, J.R. (1985) 'The special hospitals', in L. Gostin (ed.) *Secure Provision: A Review of Special Services for the Mentally Ill and Mentally Handicapped in England and Wales*, London: Tavistock.

Hans, V.P. and Vidmar, N. (1986) *Judging the Jury*, New York: Plenum.

Hare, R.D. (1978) 'Electrodermal and cardiovascular correlates of psychopathology', in R.D. Hare and D. Schalling (eds) *Psychopathic Behaviour: Approaches to Research*, Chichester: Wiley.

—— (1980) 'A research scale for the assessment of psychopathy in criminal populations', *Personality and Individual Differences 1*: 111–19.

—— (1985) 'Comparison of procedures for the assessment of psychopathy', *Journal of Consulting and Clinical Psychology 53*: 7–16.

—— (1986) 'Twenty years of experience with the Cleckley psychopath', in W.H. Reid, D. Dorr, J.I. Walker, and J.W. Bonner (eds) *Unmasking the Psychopath: Antisocial Personality and Related Syndromes*, New York: W.W. Norton.

Harris, R. (1973) 'Answering questions containing marked and unmarked adjectives and verbs', *Journal of Experimental Psychology 97*: 399–401.

Hastie, R., Penrod, S.D., and Pennington, N. (1983) *Inside the Jury*, Cambridge, Mass: Harvard University Press.

Hathaway, S.R. and McKinley, J.C. (1940) 'A multiphasic personality schedule (Minnesota): I. Construction of the schedule', *Journal of Psychology 10*: 249–54.

Haward, L.R.C. (1963) 'Some psychological aspects of oral evidence', *British Journal of Criminology 3*: 342–58.

—— (1979) 'The psychologist as expert witness', in D.P. Farrington, K. Hawkins, and S.M.A. Lloyd-Bostock (eds) *Psychology, Law and Legal Processes*, London: Macmillan.

—— (1981a) 'The psychologist as expert witness: I', in J. Shapland (ed.) *Lawyers and Psychologists — The Way Forward, Issues in Criminological and Legal Psychology, No. 1*, Leicester: British Psychological Society.

—— (1981b) *Forensic Psychology*, London: Batsford.

—— (1987) 'The uses and misuses of psychological evidence', in G. Gudjonsson and J. Drinkwater (eds) *Psychological Evidence in Court, Issues in*

Criminological and Legal Psychology, No. 11, Leicester: British Psychological Society.

Haward, L. and Ashworth, A. (1980) 'Some problems of evidence obtained by hypnosis', *Criminal Law Review* 469–85.

Hawley, C. and Buckley, R.E. (1974) 'Food dyes and hyperkinetic children', *Academy Therapy 10*: 27–32.

Hayashi, S. (1967) 'A study of juvenile delinquency in twins', in H. Mitsuda (ed.) *Clinical Genetics in Psychiatry*, Tokyo: Igaku Shoin.

Hayes, S.C., Rincover, A., and Volosin, D. (1980) 'Variables influencing the acquisition and maintenance of aggressive behaviour: modeling versus sensory reinforcement', *Journal of Abnormal Psychology 89*: 254–62.

Heal, K. and Laycock, G. (eds) (1986) *Situational Crime Prevention: From Theory into Practice*, London: HMSO.

Healy, W. and Bronner, A.F. (1936) *New Light on Delinquency and its Treatment*, New Haven, Conn: Yale University Press.

Heidensohn, F. (1985) *Women and Crime*, London: Macmillan.

Heim, A. (1982) 'Professional issues arising from psychological evidence in court: a reply', *Bulletin of the British Psychological Society 35*: 332–3.

Henderson, M. (1982) 'An empirical classification of convicted violent offenders', *British Journal of Criminology 22*: 1–20.

—— (1983a) 'Self-reported assertion and aggression among violent offenders with high or low levels of overcontrolled hostility', *Personality and Individual Differences 4*: 113–15.

—— (1983b) 'An empirical classification of non-violent offenders using the MMPI', *Personality and Individual Differences 4*: 671–7.

—— (1986) 'An empirical typology of violent incidents reported by prison inmates with convictions for violence', *Aggressive Behavior 12*: 21–32.

Henderson, M. and Hewstone, M. (1984) 'Prison inmates' explanations for interpersonal violence: accounts and attributions', *Journal of Consulting and Clinical Psychology 52*: 789–94.

Henderson, M. and Hollin, C.R. (1983) 'A critical review of social skills training with young offenders', *Criminal Justice and Behavior 10*: 316–41.

—— (1986) 'Social skills training and delinquency', in C.R. Hollin and P. Trower (eds) *Handbook of Social Skills Training, vol. 1: Applications across the Life Span*, Oxford: Pergamon.

Henderson, N.D. (1979) 'Criterion-related validity of personality and aptitude scales', in C.D. Speilberger (ed.) *Police Selection and Evaluation*, New York: Praeger.

Henn, F.A., Herjanic, M., and Vanderpearl, R.H. (1976) 'Forensic psychiatry: profiles of two types of sex offender', *American Journal of Psychiatry 133*: 694–6.

Herbert, M. (1987) *Behavioural Treatment of Children with Problems: A Practice Manual* (2nd edn), London: Academic Press.

Herman, J. (1981) *Father-Daughter Incest*, Cambridge, Mass: Harvard University Press.

Higgins, J. (1984) 'The regional secure unit', in M. Craft and A. Craft (eds) *Mentally Abnormal Offenders*, London: Baillière Tindall.

Higgins, J.P. and Thies, A.P. (1981) 'Social effectiveness and problem-solving thinking of reformatory inmates', *Journal of Offender Counselling Services and Rehabilitation* 5: 93–8.

Hill, D. and Pond, D.A. (1952) 'Reflections on a hundred capital cases submitted to electroencephalography', *Journal of Mental Science* 98: 23–43.

Hill, R.W., Langevin, R., Paitich, D., Handy, L., Russon, A., and Wilkinson, L. (1982) 'Is arson an aggressive act or a property offence? A controlled study of psychiatric referrals', *Canadian Journal of Psychiatry* 27: 648–58.

Hindelang, M.J. and Weis, J.G. (1972) 'Personality and self-reported delinquency: an application of cluster analysis', *Criminology* 10: 268–94.

Hindelang, M.J., Hirschi, T., and Weis, J. (1981) *Measuring Delinquency*, Beverly Hills, Calif: Sage.

Hinton, J. (ed.) (1983) *Dangerousness: Problems of Assessment and Prediction*, London: Allen & Unwin.

Hippchen, L. (ed.) (1978) *Ecologic-Biochemical Approaches to Treatment of Delinquents and Criminals*, New York: Van Nostrand Reinhold.

Hirschi, T. (1969) *Causes of Delinquency*, Berkeley and Los Angeles, Calif: University of California Press.

Hirschi, T. and Hindelang, M.J. (1977) 'Intelligence and delinquency: a revisionist review', *American Sociological Review* 42: 571–87.

Hochstedler, E. (1981) 'Testing types: a review and test of police types', *Journal of Criminal Justice* 9: 451–66.

Hoefler, S.A. and Bornstein, P.A. (1975) 'Achievement Place: an evaluative review', *Criminal Justice and Behavior* 2: 146–68.

Holdaway, S. (ed.) (1979) *The British Police*, London: Edward Arnold.

Holland, T.R. and Holt, N. (1975) 'Personality patterns among short-term prisoners undergoing pre-sentence evaluations', *Psychological Reports* 37: 827–36.

Hollin, C.R. (1981) 'Nature of the witnessed incident and status of interviewer as variables influencing eyewitness recall', *British Journal of Social Psychology* 20: 295–6.

—— (1982) *Legal Psychology: The Strength of Experiments in Legal Psychology*, paper presented at the International Conference on Psychology and Law, Swansea, Wales.

—— (1984) 'Arousal and eyewitness memory', *Perceptual and Motor Skills* 58: 266.

Hollin, C.R. and Clifford, B.R. (1983) 'Eyewitness testimony: the effects of discussion on recall accuracy and agreement', *Journal of Applied Social Psychology* 13: 234–44.

Hollin, C.R. and Courtney, S.A. (1983) 'A skills training approach to the reduction of institutional offending', *Personality and Individual Differences* 4: 257–64.

Hollin, C.R. and Henderson, M. (1984) 'Social skills training with young offenders: false expectations and the "failure of treatment" ', *Behavioural Psychotherapy* 12: 331–41.

Hollin, C.R. and Howells, K. (eds) (1986) *Clinical Approaches to Criminal Behaviour, Issues in Criminological and Legal Psychology, No. 9*, Leicester: British Psychological Society.

—— (1987) 'Lay explanations of delinquency: global or offence-specific?', *British Journal of Social Psychology* 26: 203–10.

Hollin, C.R. and Trower, P. (1986) 'Social skills training: critique and future development', in C.R. Hollin and P. Trower (eds) *Handbook of Social Skills Training, vol. 2: Clinical Applications and New Directions*, Oxford: Pergamon.

Hollin, C.R. and Wheeler, H.M. (1982) 'The violent young offender: a small group study of a Borstal population', *Journal of Adolescence* 5: 247–57.

Hollin, C.R., Huff, G.J., Clarkson, F., and Edmondson, A.C. (1986) 'Social skills training with young offenders in a borstal: an evaluative study', *Journal of Community Psychology* 14: 289–99.

Holmstrom, L.L. and Burgess, A.W. (1978) *The Victim of Rape: Institutional Reactions*, New York: Wiley.

Homant, R.J. (1986) 'Ten years after: a follow-up of therapy effectiveness', *Journal of Offender Counseling, Services and Rehabilitation* 10: 51–7.

Home Office (1981) *Selection Procedures*, Circular 59 (ref. Pol/75–103/4/54), London: Home Office.

—— (1984) *Code of Practice on Selection Procedures*, Circular 17 (ref. Pol/83–130/4/6), London: Home Office.

—— (1985) *Criminal Statistics England and Wales: Supplementary Tables, vol. 4, Convictions, Cautions, Specific Aspects of Sentencing, DPP Prosecutions, Appeals, Prerogative of Mercy*, London: HMSO.

Home Office and DHSS (1975) *Report of the Committee on Mentally Abnormal Offenders (Butler Committee)*, Cmdn 6244, London: HMSO.

Home Office, Scottish Office and Northern Ireland Office (1979) *Committee of Inquiry into the United Kingdom Prison Services (May Report)*, Cmnd 7673, London: HMSO.

Hood, R. and Sparks, R. (1970) *Key Issues in Criminology*, London: Weidenfeld & Nicolson.

Hooton, E. (1939) *The American Criminal*, Cambridge, Mass: Harvard University Press.

Hope, T. (1986) 'School design and burglary', in K. Heal and G. Laycock (eds) *Situational Crime Prevention: From Theory into Practice*, London: HMSO.

Horncastle, P. (1985) 'Psychology and police training', *Policing* 1:254–66.

Hosch, H.M. (1980) 'A comparison of three studies of the influence of expert testimony on jurors', *Law and Human Behavior* 4: 297–302.

Hosch, H.M. and Cooper, S.D. (1982) 'Victimization as a determinant of eyewitness accuracy', *Journal of Applied Psychology* 67: 649–52.

Hosch, H.M., Beck, E.L., and McIntyre, P. (1980) 'Influence of expert testimony regarding eyewitness accuracy on jury decisions', *Law and Human Behavior* 4: 287–96.

Hosch, H.M., Leippe, M.R., Marchioni, P.M., and Cooper, D.S (1984) 'Victimization, self-monitoring, and eyewitness identification', *Journal of Applied Psychology* 69: 280–8.

Hough, J.M., Clarke, R.V.G., and Mayhew, P. (1980) 'Introduction', in R.V.G. Clarke and P. Mayhew (eds) *Designing out Crime*, London: HMSO.

Hough, M. and Mayhew, P. (1983) *The British Crime Survey: First Report*,

London: HMSO.

—— (1985) *Taking Account of Crime: Key Findings from the Second British Crime Survey*, London: HMSO.

Howarth, E. (1986) 'What does Eysenck's psychoticism scale really measure?', *British Journal of Psychology* 77: 223-7.

Howells, K. (1976) 'Interpersonal aggression', *International Journal of Criminology and Penology* 4: 319-30.

—— (1981) 'Adult sexual interest in children: considerations relevant to theories of etiology', in M. Cook and K. Howells (eds) *Adult Sexual Interest in Children*, London: Academic Press.

—— (1982) 'Mental disorder and violent behaviour', in P. Feldman (ed.) *Developments in the Study of Criminal Behaviour, vol. 2: Violence*, Chichester: Wiley.

—— (ed.) (1984a) *The Psychology of Sexual Diversity*, Oxford: Blackwell.

—— (1984b) 'Coercive sexual behaviour', in K. Howells (ed.) *The Psychology of Sexual Diversity*, Oxford: Blackwell.

—— (1986) 'Social skills training and criminal and antisocial behaviour in adults', in C.R. Hollin and P. Trower (eds) *Handbook of Social Skills Training, Vol. 1: Applications across the Life Span*, Oxford: Pergamon.

—— (1987a) 'Forensic problems: investigation', in S.J.E. Lindsay and G.E. Powell (eds) *Handbook of Clinical Psychology*, Aldershot, Hants: Gower.

—— (1987b) 'Forensic problems: treatment', in S.J.E. Lindsay and G.E. Powell (eds) *Handbook of Clinical Psychology*, Aldershot, Hants: Gower.

Hsu, L.K.G., Wisner, K., Richey, E.T., and Goldstein, C. (1985) 'Is juvenile delinquency related to abnormal EEG? A study of EEG abnormalities in juvenile delinquents and adolescent psychiatric inpatients', *Journal of the American Academy of Child Psychiatry* 24: 310-15.

Hudson, B. (1987) *Justice through Punishment: A Critique of the 'Justice' Model of Corrections*, London: Macmillan.

Hudson, B.L. (1986) 'Community applications of social skills training', in C.R. Hollin and P. Trower (eds) *Handbook of Social Skills Training, vol. 1: Applications across the Life Span*, Oxford: Pergamon.

Huff, G. (1987) 'Social skills training', in B.J. McGurk, D.M. Thornton, and M. Williams (eds) *Applying Psychology to Imprisonment: Theory & Practice*, London: HMSO.

Hunt, Y.C. (1971) *Minority Recruiting in the New York City Police Department: Part I, The Attraction of Candidates*, New York: New York City-Rand Institute.

Hunter, N. and Kelley, C.K. (1986) 'Examination of the validity of the Adolescent Problems Inventory among incarcerated juvenile delinquents', *Journal of Consulting and Clinical Psychology* 54: 301-2.

Hunter, R.M. (1935) 'Law in the jury room', *Ohio State Law Journal* 1: 1-19.

Hurwitz, S. and Christiansen, K.O. (1983) *Criminology*, London: Allen & Unwin.

Hutchings, B. and Mednick, S.A. (1975) 'Registered criminality in the adoptive and biological parents of registered male criminal adoptees', in R.R. Fieve, D. Rosenthal, and H. Brill (eds) *Genetic Research in Psychiatry*, Baltimore, Md: Johns Hopkins University Press.

—— (1977) 'Criminality in adoptees and their adoptive and biological parents: a pilot study', in S.A. Mednick and K.A. Christiansen (eds) *Biological Bases of Criminal Behavior*, New York: Gardner Press.

Iacono, W.G. and Patrick, C.J. (1987) 'What psychologists should know about lie detection', in I.B. Weiner and A.K. Hess (eds) *Handbook of Forensic Psychology*, New York: Wiley.

Ions, E. (1977) *Against Behaviouralism: A Critique of Behavioural Science*, Oxford: Blackwell.

Irving, B. and Hilgendorf, E. (1980) *Police Interrogation: The Psychological Approach*, Research Study No. 1, Royal Commission on Criminal Procedure, London: HMSO.

James, S.P., Campbell, I.M., and Lovegrove, S.A. (1984) 'Personality differentiation in a police-selection interview', *Journal of Applied Psychology 69*: 129–34.

Jarvik, L.F., Klodin, V., and Matsuyama, S.S. (1973) 'Human aggression and the extra Y chromosome', *American Psychologist 28*: 674–82.

Jeffery, C.R. (1965) 'Criminal behavior and learning theory', *Journal of Criminal Law, Criminology and Police Science 56*: 294–300.

Jennings, W.S., Kilkenny, R., and Kohlberg, L. (1983) 'Moral development theory and practice for youthful and adult offenders', in W.S. Laufer and J.M. Day (eds) *Personality Theory, Moral Development, and Criminal Behavior*, Toronto: Lexington Books.

Jesness, C.F. (1975) 'Comparative effectiveness of behavior modification and transactional analysis programs for delinquents', *Journal of Consulting and Clinical Psychology 43*: 758–79.

Jesness, C.F., DeRisi, W., McCormick, P., and Wedge, R. (1972) *The Youth Center Research Project*, Sacramento, Calif: California Youth Authority.

Johnson, A. and Szurek, S. (1952) 'The genesis of antisocial acting out in children and adults', *Psychoanalytic Quarterly 21*: 223–43.

Jones, T., MacLean, B., and Young, J. (1986) *The Islington Crime Survey: Crime, Victimization and Policing in Inner-City London*, Aldershot, Hants: Gower.

Jurkovic, G.J. (1980) 'The juvenile delinquent as a moral philosopher: a structural-developmental approach', *Psychological Bulletin 88*: 709–27.

Jutai, J.W. and Hare, R.D. (1983) 'Psychopathy and selective attention during performance of a complex perceptual-motor task', *Psychophysiology 20*: 146–51.

Kalven, H. and Zeisel, H. (1966) *The American Jury*, Boston, Mass: Little, Brown.

Kaplan, P.J. and Arbuthnot, J. (1985) 'Affective empathy and cognitive role-taking in delinquent and nondelinquent youth', *Adolescence 20*: 323–33.

Kassin, S.M. and Wrightsman, L.S. (1983) 'The construction and validation of a juror bias scale', *Journal of Research in Personality 17*: 423–42.

Kaye, D. (1980) 'And then there were twelve: statistical reasoning, the Supreme Court, and the size of the jury', *California Law Review 68*: 1,004–43.

Kazdin, A.E. (1982) 'The token economy: a decade later', *Journal of Applied*

Behavior Analysis 15: 431–45.

—— (1985) *Treatment of Antisocial Behavior in Children and Adolescents*, Holmwood, Ill: Dorsey Press.

—— (1987) 'Treatment of antisocial behavior in children: current status and future directions', *Psychological Bulletin 102*: 187–203.

Kegan, R.G. (1986) 'The child behind the mask: sociopathy as developmental delay', in W.H. Reid, D. Dorr, J.I. Walker, and J.W. Bonner (eds) *Unmasking the Psychopath: Antisocial Personality and Related Syndromes*, London: W.W. Norton.

Keilitz, I. and Dunivant, N. (1986) 'The relationship between learning disability and juvenile delinquency: current state of knowledge', *Remedial and Special Education 7*: 18–26.

Kelling, G. (1986) 'Neighbourhood crime control and the police: a view of the American experience', in K. Heal and G. Laycock (eds) *Situational Crime Prevention: From Theory into Practice*, London: HMSO.

Kempe, C.H. and Helfer, R.E. (eds) (1980) *The Battered Child* (3rd edn), Chicago, Ill: University of Chicago Press.

Kennedy, R.E. (1976) 'Behavior modification in prisons', in W.E. Craighead, A.E. Kazdin, and J.M. Mahoney (eds) *Behavior Modification: Principles, Issues, and Applications*, Boston, Mass: Houghton-Mifflin.

Kerr, N.L. and Bray, R.M. (eds) (1982) *The Psychology of the Courtroom*, New York: Academic Press.

Kiesler, S., Siegal, J., and McGuire, T.W. (1984) 'Social psychological aspects of computer-mediated communications', *American Psychologist 59*: 1,123–34.

Kiessel, S. (1966) 'Juvenile delinquency and psychological differentiation: difference between social and solitary delinquency', *Journal of Clinical Psychology 22*: 442.

Killeen, P.R. (1984) 'Emergent behaviorism', *Behaviorism 12*: 25–39.

King, M. (1986) *Psychology in and out of Court: A Critical Examination of Legal Psychology*, Oxford: Pergamon.

Kinsey, R. (1984) *Merseyside Crime Survey: First Report, November 1984*, Liverpool: Merseyside County Council.

Kirigin, K.A., Braukmann, C.J., Atwater, J.D., and Wolf, M.M. (1982) 'An evaluation of teaching family (Achievement Place) group homes for juvenile offenders', *Journal of Applied Behavior Analysis 15*: 1–16.

Kirkham, G. (1981) 'A professor's street lessons', in R. Culbertson and M. Tezak (eds) *Order under Law*, Prospect Heights, Ill: Waveland Press.

Kirmeyer, S.L. and Diamond, A. (1985) 'Coping by police officers: a study of role stress and type A and type B behavior patterns', *Journal of Occupational Behaviour 6*: 183–95.

Kirton, M., Hollin, C.R. and Radford, J. (1985) 'School pupils' image of psychology: general knowledge and opinions', in A. Gale, J. Radford, and M. Taylor (eds) *Bulletin of the Association for the Teaching of Psychology*, Leicester: British Psychological Society.

Klaus, P. and DeBerry, M. (1985) *The Crime of Rape*, Washington, DC: Bureau of Justice Statistics.

Klemmack, S.H. and Klemmack, D.L. (1976) 'The social definition of rape', in M.J. Walker and S.L. Brodsky (eds) *Sexual Assault: The Victim and the Rapist*, Lexington, Mass: Lexington Books.

Kletschka, H.D. (1966) 'Violent behavior associated with brain tumours', *Minnesota Medicine 49*: 1,853–5.

Kline, P. (1984) *Psychology and Freudian Theory*, London: Methuen.

Klockars, C. (1980) 'The contemporary crises of Marxist criminology', in J. Inciardi (ed.) *Radical Criminology: The Coming Crisis*, Beverly Hills, Calif: Sage.

Kohlberg, L. (1964) 'Development of moral character and moral ideology', in M. Hoffman and L. Hoffman (eds) *Review of Child Development Research*, vol. 1, New York: Russell Sage Foundation.

—— (1978) 'Revisions in the theory and practice of mental development', in W. Damon (ed.) *New Directions in Child Development: Moral Development*, San Francisco, Calif: Jossey-Bass.

Konečni, V.J. and Ebbesen, E.B. (1986) 'Courtroom testimony by psychologists on eyewitness identification issues', *Law and Human Behavior 10*: 117–26.'

Kovel, J. (1976) *A Complete Guide to Therapy: From Psychoanalysis to Behaviour Modification*, Harmondsworth: Pelican.

Kranz, H. (1936) *Lebensschicksale kriminellen zwillinge*, Berlin: Julius Springer.

Kroes, W., Margolis, B., and Hurrell, J. (1974) 'Job stress in policemen', *Journal of Police Science and Administration 2*: 145–55.

Kubie, L, (1959) 'Implications for legal procedure of the fallibility of human memory', *University of Pasadena Law Review 108*: 59–75.

Kuehn, L. (1974) 'Looking down a gun barrel: person perception and violent crime', *Perceptual and Motor Skills 39*: 1,159–64.

Kumchy, C. and Sayer, L.A. (1980) 'Locus of control and delinquent adolescent populations', *Psychological Reports 46*: 1,307–10.

Kutash, S.B. (1978) 'Psychoanalytic theories of aggression', in I.L. Kutash, S.B. Kutash, and L.B. Schlesinger (eds) *Violence: Perspectives on Murder and Aggression*, San Francisco, Calif: Jossey-Bass.

Laing, R.D. (1967) *The Politics of Experience*, Harmondsworth: Penguin.

Lane, D.A. (1987) 'Psychological evidence in the juvenile court', in G. Gudjonsson and J. Drinkwater (eds) *Psychological Evidence in Court, Issues in Criminological and Legal Psychology, No. 11*, Leicester: British Psychological Society.

Lange, J. (1929) *Verbrechen als Sochicksal*, Leipzig: Verlag.

Langevin, R. (1983) *Sexual Strands: Understanding and Treating Sexual Anomalies in Men*, Hillsdale, NJ: Lawrence Erlbaum.

Langevin, R. and Lang, R.A. (1985) 'Psychological treatment of pedophiles', *Behavioral Sciences and the Law 3*: 403–19.

Langevin, R., Handy, L., Russon, A.E., and Day, D. (1985) 'Are incestuous fathers pedophilic, aggressive, or alcoholic?', in R. Langevin (ed.) *Erotic Preference, Gender, Identity, and Aggression in Men*, Hillsdale, NJ: Lawrence Erlbaum.

Lanyon, R.I. (1986) 'Theory and treatment in child molestation', *Journal of Consulting and Clinical Psychology 54*: 176–82.

Laughery, K.R. and Fowler, R.H. (1977) *Factors Affecting Facial Recognition*, Mug File Project (Report Number UHMUG-3), University of Houston, Houston, Texas.

—— (1980) 'Sketch artist and Identi-kit procedures for recalling faces', *Journal of Applied Psychology* 65: 307–16.

Laughery, K.R., Rhodes, B., and Batten, G. (1981) 'Computer-guided recognition and retrieval of facial images', in G.M. Davies, H.D. Ellis, and J.W. Shepherd (eds) *Perceiving and Remembering Faces*, London: Academic Press.

Lawrence, J.A. (1984) 'Magisterial decision-making: cognitive perspectives and processes used in courtroom information processing', in D.J. Müller, D.E. Blackman, and A.J. Chapman (eds) *Psychology and Law*, Chichester: Wiley.

Laws, D.R. (1984) 'The assessment of dangerous sexual behaviour in males', *Medicine and Law 3*: 127–40.

Lawson, W.K. (1984) 'Depression and crime: a discursive approach', in M. Craft and A. Craft (eds) *Mentally Abnormal Offenders*, London: Baillière Tindall.

Laycock, G. (1986) 'Property marking as a deterrent to domestic burglary', in K. Heal and G. Laycock (eds) *Situational Crime Prevention: From Theory into Practice*, London: HMSO.

Lea, J. (1986) 'Police racism: some theories and their policy implications', in R. Matthews and J. Young (eds) *Confronting Crime*, London: Sage.

Le Doux, J.C. and Hazlewood, R.R. (1985) 'Police attitudes and beliefs toward rape', *Journal of Police Science and Administration 13*: 211–20.

Lefcourt, H.M. and Ladwig, G.W. (1965) 'The American Negro: a problem in expectancies', *Journal of Personality and Social Psychology 1*: 377–80.

Lefkowitz, J. (1975) 'Psychological attributes of policemen: a review of research and opinion', *Journal of Social Issues 31*: 3–26.

Legras, A.M. (1932) *Psychese en criminaliteit bij twellingen*, Utrecht: Keminken Zoon N.V.

Leippe, M.R., Wells, G.L., and Ostrom, T.M. (1978) 'Crime seriousness as a determinant of accuracy in eyewitness identification', *Journal of Applied Psychology 63*: 345–51.

Lemart, E. (1951) *Social Pathology*, New York: McGraw-Hill.

—— (1974) 'Beyond Mead: the societal reaction to deviance', *Social Problems 21*: 457–61.

Lenorovitz, D.R. and Laughery, K.R. (1984) 'A witness-computer interactive system for searching mug files', in G.L. Wells and E.F. Loftus (eds) *Eyewitness Testimony: Psychological Perspectives*, Cambridge: Cambridge University Press.

Levi, M. (1984) 'Explaining commercial credit fraud', in D.J. Müller, D.E. Blackman, and A.J. Chapman (eds) *Psychology and Law*, Chichester: Wiley.

Levin, J. and Fox, A.F. (1985) *Mass Murder*, New York: Plenum.

Liberman, R.P., Ferris, C., Salgado, P., and Salgado, J. (1975) 'Replication of the Achievement Place model in California', *Journal of Applied Behavior Analysis 8*: 287–99.

Lipton, D., Martinson, R., and Wilks, D. (1975) *The Effectiveness of Correctional Treatment*, New York: Praeger.

Lipton, D.N., McDonel, E.C., and McFall, R.M. (1987) 'Heterosocial perception in rapists', *Journal of Consulting and Clinical Psychology 55*: 17–21.

Lipton, J.P. (1977) 'On the psychology of eyewitness testimony', *Journal of Applied Psychology 62*: 90–5.

Little, A. (1965) 'Parental deprivation, separation and crime: a test on adolescent recidivists', *British Journal of Criminology* 5: 419–30.

Litwack, T.R. and Schlesinger, L.B. (1987) 'Assessing and predicting violence: research, law, and applications', in I.B. Weiner and A.K. Hess (eds) *Handbook of Forensic Psychology*, New York: Wiley.

Lloyd-Bostock, S.M.A. and Clifford, B.R. (eds) (1983) *Evaluating Witness Evidence: Recent Psychological Research and New Perspectives*, Chichester: Wiley.

Lloyd-Bostock, S.M.A. and Shapland, J. (1986) 'The Police and Criminal Evidence Act, 1984: some continuing questions for psychologists', *Bulletin of the British Psychological Society* 39: 241–5.

Loftus, E.F. (1974) 'The incredible eyewitness', *Psychology Today* December: 117–19.

—— (1975) 'Leading questions and the eyewitness report', *Cognitive Psychology* 7: 560–72.

—— (1977) 'Shifting human colour memory', *Memory and Cognition* 5: 696–9.

—— (1979) *Eyewitness Testimony*, Cambridge, Mass: Harvard University Press.

—— (1980) 'Impact of expert psychological testimony on the unreliability of eyewitness identification', *Journal of Applied Psychology* 65: 9–15.

—— (1981) 'Eyewitness testimony: psychological research and legal thought', in M. Tonry and N. Morris (eds) *Crime and Justice: An Annual Review of Research*, Vol. 3, Chicago, Ill: University of Chicago Press.

—— (1986) 'Ten years in the life of an expert witness', *Law and Human Behavior* 10: 241–63.

Loftus, E.F. and Burns, T.E. (1982) 'Mental shock can produce retrograde amnesia', *Memory and Cognition* 10: 318–23.

Loftus, E.F. and Greene, E. (1980) 'Warning: even memory for faces may be contagious', *Law and Human Behavior* 4: 323–34.

Loftus, E.F. and Ketcham, K.E. (1983) 'The malleability of eyewitness accounts', in S.M.A. Lloyd-Bostock and B.R. Clifford (eds) *Evaluating Eyewitness Evidence: Recent Psychological Research and New Perspectives*, Chichester: Wiley.

Loftus, E.F. and Loftus, G.R. (1980) 'On the permanence of stored information in the human brain', *American Psychologist* 35: 409–20.

Loftus, E.F. and Palmer, J.C. (1974) 'Reconstruction of automobile destruction: an example of the interaction between language and memory', *Journal of Verbal Learning and Verbal Behavior* 13: 585–9.

Loftus, E.F. and Zanni, G.R. (1975) 'Eyewitness testimony: the influence of the wording of the question', *Bulletin of the Psychonomic Society* 5: 86–8.

Loftus, E.F., Altman, D., and Geballe, R. (1975) 'Effects of questioning upon a witness's later recollections', *Journal of Police Science and Administration* 3: 162–5.

Loftus, E.F., Miller, D.G., and Burns, H.J. (1978) 'Semantic integration of verbal information into a visual memory', *Journal of Experimental Psychology: Human Learning and Memory* 4: 19–31.

Loftus, E.F., Schooler, J., and Wagenaar, W.A. (1985) 'The fate of memory: comment on McCloskey and Zaragoza', *Journal of Experimental Psychology: General* 114: 375–80.

Loftus, E.F., Loftus, G.R., and Messo, J. (1987) 'Some facts about "weapon focus" ', *Law and Human Behavior 11*: 55–62.

Loh, W.D. (1981) 'Perspectives on psychology and law', *Journal of Applied Social Psychology 11*: 314–55.

Loomis, S.D., Bohnert, P.J., and Huncke, S. (1967) 'Predictions of EEG abnormalities in adolescent delinquents', *Archives of General Psychiatry 17*: 494–7.

Lorenz, K. (1966) *On Aggression*, New York: Harcourt Brace World.

Lovegrove, S.A. (1984) 'Structuring judicial sentencing discretion', in D.J. Müller, D.E. Blackman, and A.J. Chapman (eds) *Psychology and Law*, Chichester: Wiley.

Lowe, C.F. (1983) 'Radical behaviourism and human psychology', in G.C.L. Davey (ed.) *Animal Models of Human Behaviour*, Chichester: Wiley.

Lowe, C.F. and Higson, P.J. (1981) 'Self-instructional training and cognitive behaviour modification: a behavioural analysis', in G. Davey (ed.) *Applications of Conditioning Theory*, London: Methuen.

Luckenbill, D.F. (1977) 'Criminal homicide as a situated transaction', *Social Problems 25*: 176–86.

Lykken, D.T. (1957) 'A study of anxiety in the sociopathic personality', *Journal of Abnormal and Social Psychology 55*: 6–10.

McAllister, H.A. and Bregman, N.J. (1986) 'Juror under-utilization of eyewitness non-identifications: theoretical and practical implications', *Journal of Applied Psychology 71*: 168–70.

McCandless, B.R., Parsons, W.S., and Roberts, A. (1972) 'Perceived opportunity, delinquency, race and body build among delinquent youth', *Journal of Consulting and Clinical Psychology 38*: 281–7.

McClintock, F.H. and Gibson, E. (1961) *Robbery in London*, London: Macmillan.

McClintock, F.H., Avison, N.H., Savill, N.C., and Worthington, V.L. (1963) *Crimes of Violence*, London: Macmillan.

McCloskey, M. and Egeth, H.E. (1983) 'Eyewitness identification: what can a psychologist tell a jury?', *American Psychologist 38*; 550–63.

McCloskey, M. and Zaragoza, M. (1985a) 'Misleading post-event information and memory for events: arguments and evidence against the memory impairment hypotheses', *Journal of Experimental Psychology: General 114*: 375–80.

—— (1985b) 'Post-event information and memory: reply to Loftus, Schooler and Wagenaar', *Journal of Experimental Psychology: General 114*: 381–7.

McCord, J. (1978) 'A thirty-year follow-up of treatment effects', *American Psychologist 33*: 284–9.

McCord, W. and McCord, J. (1964) *The Psychopath: An Essay on the Criminal Mind*, New York: Van Nostrand Reinhold.

McCulloch, J.W. and Prins, H. (1978) *Signs of Stress: The Social Problem of Psychiatric Illness*, London: Woburn.

MacDonald, J.M. (1973) *Indecent Exposure*, Springfield, Ill: C.C. Thomas.

—— (1977) *Bombers and Firesetters*, Springfield, Ill: C.C. Thomas.

MacEachron, A.E. (1979) 'Mentally retarded offenders: prevalence and characteristics', *American Journal of Mental Deficiency 84*: 165–76.

McEwan, A.W. (1983) 'Eysenck's theory of criminality and the personality types and offences of young delinquents', *Personality and Individual Differences* 4: 201–4.

McEwan, A.W. and Knowles, C. (1984) 'Delinquent personality types and the situational contexts of their crimes', *Personality and Individual Differences* 5: 339–44.

McFall, R.M. (1976) *Behavioral Training: A Skill-Acquisition Approach to Clinical Problems*, Morristown, NJ: General Learning Press.

McGuire, J. and Priestley, P. (1983) 'Life skills training in prison and the community', in S. Spence and G. Shepherd (eds) *Developments in Social Skills Training*, London: Academic Press.

McGurk, B.J. (1978) 'Personality types among normal homicides', *British Journal of Criminology 19*: 31–49.

McGurk, B.J. and McDougall, C. (1981) 'A new approach to Eysenck's theory of criminality', *Personality and Individual Differences 2*: 338–40.

McGurk, B.J. and McGurk, R.E. (1979) 'Personality types among prisoners and prison officers — an investigation of Megargee's theory of control', *British Journal of Criminology 19*: 31–49.

McGurk, B.J. and Newell, T.C. (1987) 'Social skills training: case study with a sex offender', in B.J. McGurk, D.M. Thornton, and M. Williams (eds) *Applying Psychology to Imprisonment: Theory & Practice*, London: HMSO.

McGurk, B.J., McEwan, A.W., and Graham, F. (1981) 'Personality types and recidivism among young delinquents', *British Journal of Criminology 21*: 159–65.

McGurk, B.J., Thornton, D.M., and Williams, M. (1987) *Applying Psychology to Imprisonment: Theory & Practice*, London: HMSO.

McKenzie, I.K. (1984) 'Psychology and police education: a reply to Taylor', *Bulletin of the British Psychological Society 37*: 145–7.

—— (1985) 'Hostage incidents: fostering the psychological bonds', *Policing 1*: 284–94.

McLean, A. (1979) *Work Stress*, Reading, Mass: Addison-Wesley.

Maher, P. (ed.) (1987) *Child Abuse: An Educational Perspective*, Oxford: Blackwell.

Malamuth, N.M. (1981) 'Rape proclivity among males', *Journal of Social Issues 37*: 138–57.

Malamuth, N.M. and Check, J.V.P. (1980) 'Sexual arousal to rape and consenting depictions: the importance of the woman's sexual arousal', *Journal of Abnormal Psychology 89*: 763–6.

Malamuth, N.M. and Donnerstein, E. (1982) 'The effects of aggressive-pornographic mass media stimuli', in L. Berkowitz (ed.) *Advances in Experimental Social Psychology*, Vol. 15, New York: Academic Press.

Malamuth, N.M., Heim, M., and Feshbach, S. (1980) 'The sexual responsiveness of college students to rape depictions: inhibitory and disinhibitory effects', *Journal of Personality and Social Psychology 38*: 399–408.

Malcolm, P.B., Davidson, P.R., and Marshall, W.L. (1985) 'Control of penile tumescence: the effects of arousal level and stimulus content', *Behaviour Research and Therapy 23*: 273–80.

Malpass, R.S. (1981) 'Training in face recognition', in G.M. Davies, H.D. Ellis, and J.W. Shepherd (eds) *Perceiving and Remembering Faces*, London: Academic Press.

Malpass, R.S. and Devine, P.G. (1983) 'Measuring the fairness of eyewitness identification lineups', in S.M.A. Lloyd-Bostock and B.R. Clifford (eds) *Evaluating Witness Evidence: Recent Psychological Research and New Perspectives*, Chichester: Wiley.

Marcus, B. (1982) 'Psychologists in the Prison Department', in S. Canter and D. Canter (eds) *Psychology in Practice*, Chichester: Wiley.

Mark, R. (1978) *In the Office of Constable*, London: Collins.

Marsh, P. and Campbell, A. (eds) (1982) *Aggression and Violence*, Oxford: Blackwell.

Marsh, P., Rosser, E., and Harré, R. (1978) *The Rules of Disorder*, London: Routledge & Kegan Paul.

Marshall, J. (1966) *Law and Psychology in Conflict*, New York: Anchor.

Marshall, J. and Cooper, C.L. (eds) (1981) *Coping with Stress at Work*, Aldershot, Hants: Gower.

Marshall, J., Marquis, K.H., and Oskamp, S. (1972) 'Testimony validity as a function of question form, atmosphere and item difficulty', *Journal of Applied Social Psychology* 2: 167–86.

Marshall, R.J. (1983) 'A psychoanalytic perspective on the diagnosis and development of juvenile delinquents', in W.S. Laufer and J.M. Day (eds) *Personality Theory, Moral Development, and Criminal Behavior*, Lexington, Mass: Lexington Books.

Marshall, W.L. and Barbaree, H.E. (1984) 'A behavioral view of rape', *International Journal of Law and Psychiatry* 7: 51–77.

Martinson, R. (1974) 'What works? — Questions and answers about prison reform', *The Public Interest* 35: 22–54.

Mawson, A.R. and Jacobs, K.J. (1978) 'Corn consumption, tryptophan, and cross-national homicide rates', *Journal of Orthomolecular Psychiatry* 7: 227–30.

Mayhew, P. (1979) 'Defensible space: the current status of crime prevention theory', *Howard Journal of Penology and Crime Prevention 18*: 150–9.

Mayhew, P., Clarke, R.V.G., Sturman, A., and Hough, J.M. (1976) *Crime as Opportunity*, Home Office Research Study 34, London: HMSO.

Mayhew, P., Clarke, R.V.G., Burrows, J.N., Hough, J.M., and Winchester, S.W.C. (1979) *Crime in Public View*, London: HMSO.

Mayhew, P., Clarke, R.V.G., and Hough, J.M. (1980a) 'Steering column locks and car theft', in R.V.G. Clarke and P. Mayhew (eds) *Designing out Crime*, London: HMSO.

Mayhew, P., Clarke, R.V.G., Hough, J.M. and Winchester, S.W.C. (1980b) 'Natural surveillance and vandalism to telephone kiosks', in R.V.G. Clarke and P. Mayhew (eds) *Designing out Crime*, London: HMSO.

Mednick, S.A., Pollock, V., Volavka, J., and Gabrielli, W.F. (1982) 'Biology and violence', in M.E. Wolfgang and N.A. Weiner (eds) *Criminal Violence*, Beverly Hills, Calif: Sage.

Mednick, S.A., Gabrielli, W.F., and Hutchings, B. (1983a) 'Genetic influences in criminal behavior: evidence from an adoption cohort', in K.T. VanDusen and S.A. Mednick (eds) *Prospective Studies of Crime and Delinquency*,

The Hague: Kluwer-Nijhoff Publishing.

Mednick, S.A., Moffit, T.E., Pollock, V., Talovic, S., Gabrielli, W.F., and VanDusen, K.T. (1983b) 'The inheritance of human deviance', in D. Magnusson and V.L. Allen (eds) *Human Development: An Interactional Perspective*, London: Academic Press.

Megargee, E.I. (1966) 'Undercontrolled and overcontrolled personality types in extreme antisocial aggression', *Psychological Monographs 80* (3, whole no. 611).

—— (1982) 'Psychological determinants and correlates of criminal violence', in M.E. Wolfgang and N.A. Weiner (eds) *Criminal Violence*, Beverly Hills, Calif: Sage.

Meiselman, K. (1978) *Incest: A Psychological Study of Causes and Effects with Treatment Recommendations*, San Francisco, Calif: Jossey-Bass.

Merikangas, J.R. (1981) 'The neurology of violence', in J.R. Merikangas (ed.) *Brain-Behavior Relationships*, Lexington, Mass: Lexington Books.

Milan, M.A., Wood. L.F., Williams, R.L., Rogers, J.G., Hampton, L.R., and McKee, J.M. (1974) *Applied Behavior Analysis and the Imprisoned Adult Felon Project I: The Cellblock Token Economy*, Montgomery, Ala: Experimental Manpower Laboratory for Corrections.

Milgram, S. (1963) 'Behavioral study of obedience', *Journal of Abnormal and Social Psychology 67*: 371-8.

Miller, A. (1984) *Thou Shalt Not Be Aware: Society's Betrayal of the Child*, New York: Farrar, Straus, & Giroux.

Miller, A.D., Ohlin, L.E., and Coates, R.B. (1977) *A Theory of Social Reform: Correctional Change Processes in Two States*, Cambridge, Mass: Ballinger.

Miller, C.K., Zumoff, L., and Stephens, B.A. (1974) 'A comparison of reasoning skills and moral judgements in delinquent, retarded, and normal adolescent girls', *Journal of Psychology 86*: 261-8.

Miller, D.G. and Loftus, E.F. (1976) 'Influencing memory for people and their actions', *Bulletin of the Psychonomic Society 7*: 9-11.

Miller, G. (1962) *Psychology: The Science of Mental Life*, Harmondsworth: Pelican.

Miller, N.E. (1941) 'The frustration-aggression hypothesis', *Psychological Review 48*: 337-42.

—— (1960) 'Learning resistance to pain and fear: effects of overlearning, exposure, and rewarded exposure in context', *Journal of Experimental Psychology 60*: 137-45.

Miller, P. and Rose, N. (1986) *The Power in Psychiatry*, Cambridge: Polity Press.

Miller, W. (1976) 'Youth gangs in the urban crisis era', in J.F. Short (ed.) *Delinquency, Crime and Society*, Chicago: University of Chicago Press.

Mills, R.B. (1976) 'Simulated stress in a police recruit selection', *Journal of Police Science and Administration 4*: 179-86.

Mirels, H.L. (1970) 'Dimensions of internal versus external control', *Journal of Consulting and Clinical Psychology 34*: 226-8.

Mischel, W. (1968) *Personality and Assessment*, New York: Wiley.

Modgil, S. and Modgil, C. (eds) (1987) *B.F. Skinner: Consensus and Controversy*, New York: Falmer Press.

Moffitt, T., Gabrielli, W., Mednick, S., and Schulsinger, F. (1981) 'Socioeconomic status, IQ, and delinquency', *Journal of Abnormal Psychology 90*: 152-6.

Monahan, J. (1981) *Predicting Violent Behavior*, Beverly Hills, Calif: Sage.

Monahan, J. and Klassen, D. (1982) 'Situational approaches to understanding and predicting individual violent behavior', in M.E. Wolfgang and N.A. Winer (eds) *Criminal Violence*, Beverly Hills, Calif: Sage.

Monahan, J. and Loftus, E.F. (1982) 'The psychology of law', *Annual Review of Psychology 33*: 441–75.

Monahan, J. and Steadman, H.J. (eds) (1983) *Mentally Disordered Offenders: Perspectives from Law and Social Science*, New York: Plenum.

Monroe, R.R. (1978) *Brain Dysfunction in Aggressive Criminals*, Lexington, Mass: D.C. Heath.

Moore, C.C. (1907) 'Yellow psychology', *Law Notes 11*: 125–7.

Morash, M. (1983) 'An explanation of juvenile delinquency: the integration of moral-reasoning theory and sociological knowledge', in W.S. Laufer and J.M. Day (eds) *Personality Theory, Moral Development and Criminal Behavior*, Toronto: Lexington Books.

Morgan, P. (1975) *Child Care: Sense and Fable*, London: Temple Smith.

Morris, E.K. and Braukmann, C.J. (eds) (1987) *Behavioral Approaches to Crime and Delinquency: A Handbook of Application, Research, and Concepts*, New York: Plenum.

Morris, N. and Hawkins, G. (1970) *The Honest Politician's Guide to Crime Control*, Chicago, Ill: University of Chicago Press.

Moskowitz, M.J. (1977) 'Hugo Münsterberg: a study in the history of applied psychology', *American Psychologist 32*: 824–42.

Moxon, D. and Jones, P. (1984) 'Public reactions to police behaviour: some findings from the British Crime Survey', *Policing 1*: 49–56.

Moyer, K.E. (1976) *The Psychobiology of Aggression*, New York: Harper & Row.

Mrazek, F.J. (1984) 'Sexual abuse of children', in B. Lahey and A.E. Kazdin (eds), *Advances in Clinical Child Psychology*, Vol. 6, New York: Plenum.

Mulvey, E.P. and LaRosa, J.F. (1986) 'Delinquency cessation and adolescent development', *American Journal of Orthopsychiatry 56*: 212–24.

Münsterberg, H. (1908) *On the Witness Stand: Essays on Psychology and Crime*, New York: Clark, Boardman.

—— (1914) *Psychology: General and Applied*, New York: Appleton.

Myers, M. (1979) 'Rule departure and making law: juries and their verdicts', *Law and Society Review 13*: 861–90.

Neale, J.M. and Oltmanns, T.F. (1980) *Schizophrenia*, New York: Wiley.

Newman, J.P. and Kosson, D.S. (1986) 'Passive avoidance learning in psychopathic and nonpsychopathic offenders', *Journal of Abnormal Psychology 95*: 252–6.

Newman, J.P., Widom, C.S., and Nathan, S. (1985) 'Passive avoidance in syndromes of disinhibition: psychopathy and extraversion', *Journal of Personality and Social Psychology 48*: 1,316–27.

Newman, J.P., Patterson, C.M., and Kosson, D.S. (1987) 'Response preservation in psychopaths', *Journal of Abnormal Psychology 96*: 145–8.

Newman, O. (1972) *Defensible Space: Crime Prevention through Urban Design*, New York: Macmillan.

—— (1980) *Community of Interest*, New York: Anchor.

Niederhoffer, A. (1967) *Behind the Shield: The Police in Urban Society*, Garden City, NY: Doubleday.

Nietzel, M.T. (1979) *Crime and its Modification: A Social Learning Perspective*, Oxford: Pergamon.

Nizer, L. (1978) *My Life in Court*, New York: Jove.

Noon, E. and Hollin, C.R. (1987) 'Lay knowledge of eyewitness behaviour: a British survey', *Applied Cognitive Psychology 1*: 143-53.

Novaco, R.W. (1976) 'The functions and regulation of the arousal of anger', *American Journal of Psychiatry 133*: 1,124-8.

—— (1978) 'Anger and coping with stress', in J.P. Foreyt and D.P. Rathjen (eds) *Cognitive Behavior Therapy*, New York: Plenum.

Offord, D.R. (1982) 'Family backgrounds of male and female offenders', in J. Gunn and D.P. Farrington (eds) *Abnormal Offenders, Delinquency, and the Criminal Justice System*, Chichester: Wiley.

Offord, D.R., Poushinsky, M.F., and Sullivan, K. (1978) 'School performance, IQ and delinquency', *British Journal of Criminology 18*: 110-27.

Opton, E. (1974) 'Psychiatric violence against prisoners: when therapy is punishment', *Mississippi Law Journal 45*: 605-44.

Orne, M.T., Soskis, D.A., Dinges, D.F., and Orne, E.C. (1984) 'Hypnotically induced testimony', in G.L. Wells and E.F. Loftus (eds) *Eyewitness Testimony: Psychological Perspectives*, Cambridge: Cambridge University Press.

Osborn, S.G. and West, D.J. (1979) 'Conviction records of fathers and sons compared', *British Journal of Criminology 19*: 120-33.

Osborne, K. (1982) 'Sexual violence', in M. Feldman (ed.) *Developments in the Study of Criminal Behaviour, vol. 2: Violence*, Chichester: Wiley.

Ostapiuk, E.B. (1982) 'Strategies for community intervention in offender rehabilitation: an overview', in M.P. Feldman (ed.) *Developments in the Study of Criminal Behaviour, vol. 1: The Prevention and Control of Offending*, Chichester: Wiley.

Ostapiuk, E.B. and Westwood, S. (1986) 'Glenthorne Youth Treatment Centre: working with adolescents in gradations of security', in C.R. Hollin and K. Howells (eds) *Clinical Approaches to Criminal Behaviour, Issues in Criminological and Legal Psychology, No. 9*, Leicester: British Psychological Society.

Overholser, J.C. and Beck, S. (1986) 'Multimethod assessment of rapists, child molesters and three control groups on behavioral and psychological measures', *Journal of Consulting and Clinical Psychology 54*: 682-7.

Owen, D.R. (1972) 'The 47, XYY male: a review', *Psychological Bulletin 78*: 209-33.

Pachella, R.G. (1986) 'Personal values and the value of expert testimony', *Law and Human Behavior 10*: 145-50.

Padawer-Singer, A.M. and Barton, A. (1974) 'The impact of pre-trial publicity on jurors' verdicts', in R.J. Simon (ed.) *The Jury System in America: A Critical Overview*, Beverly Hills, Calif: Sage.

Palamara, F., Cullen, F.T., and Gersten, J.C. (1986) 'The effect of police and mental health intervention on juvenile deviance: specifying contingencies in the impact of formal reaction', *Journal of Health and Social Behavior 27*: 90-105.

247

Parker, E. (1985) 'The development of secure provision', in L. Gostin (ed.) *Secure Provision: A Review of Special Services for the Mentally Ill and Mentally Handicapped in England and Wales*, London: Tavistock.

Parker, H. (1987) 'The use of expert reports in juvenile and magistrates' courts', in G. Gudjonsson and J. Drinkwater (eds) *Psychological Evidence in Court, Issues in Criminological and Legal Psychology, No. 11*, Leicester: British Psychological Society.

Patterson, K.E. and Baddeley, A.D. (1977) 'When face recognition fails', *Journal of Experimental Psychology: Human Learning and Memory 3*: 406–17.

Peay, J. (1982) ' "Dangerousness" — ascription or description?', in M. Feldman (ed.) *Developments in the Study of Criminal Behavior, vol. 2: Violence*, Chichester: Wiley.

Penrod, S.D. and Cutler, B.L. (1987) 'Assessing the competence of juries', in I.B. Weiner and A.K. Hess (eds) *Handbook of Forensic Psychology*, New York: Wiley.

Penrod, S.D., Loftus, E., and Winkler, J. (1982) 'The reliability of eyewitness testimony: a psychological perspective', in N.L. Kerr and R.M. Bray (eds) *The Psychology of the Courtroom*, New York: Academic Press.

Perkins, D.E. (1982) 'The treatment of sex offenders', in P. Feldman (ed.) *Developments in the Study of Criminal Behaviour, vol. 1: The Prevention and Control of Offending*, Chichester: Wiley.

—— (1987) 'A psychological treatment programme for sex offenders', in B.J. McGurk, D.M. Thornton, and M. Williams (eds) *Applying Psychology to Imprisonment: Theory and Practice*, London: HMSO.

Peterson, D.M. (ed.) (1979) *Police Work: Strategies and Outcomes in Law Enforcement*, Beverly Hills, Calif: Sage.

Peterson, J.L., Mihajlovic, S., and Gilliland, M. (1984) *Forensic Evidence and the Police: The Effects of Scientific Evidence on Criminal Investigations*, Washington, DC: US Department of Justice, National Institute of Justice.

Phares, E.J. (1984) *Introduction to Personality*, Columbus, Ohio: Charles E. Merrill.

Phillips, E.L. (1968) 'Achievement Place: token reinforcement procedures in a homestyle rehabilitation setting for "pre-delinquent" boys', *Journal of Applied Behavior Analysis 1*: 213–33.

—— (1978) *Progress Report: A 1977 Evaluation of Boys Town Youth Care Department Program*, Monograph Series: Boys Town Community-Based Programs.

Phillips, E.L., Phillips, E.A., Fixsen, D.L., and Wolf, M.M. (1971) 'Achievement Place: modification of behaviors of pre-delinquent boys within a token economy', *Journal of Applied Behavior Analysis 4*: 45–59.

Phillips, E.L., Phillips, E.A., Wolf, M.M., and Fixsen, D.L. (1973) 'Achievement Place: development of the elected manager system', *Journal of Applied Behavior Analysis 6*: 541–61.

Phillips, E.L., Phillips E.A., Fixsen, D.L., and Wolf, M.M. (1974) *The Teaching-Family Handbook*, Lawrence, Kan: University of Kansas Printing Service.

Piaget, J. (1932) *The Moral Judgement of the Child*, London: Kegan Paul.

Planansky, K. and Johnston, R. (1977) 'Homicidal aggression in schizophrenic men', *Acta Psychiatrica Scandinavia 55*: 65–73.

Platt, J.J., Scura, W., and Hannon, J.R. (1973) 'Problem-solving thinking of youthful incarcerated heroin addicts', *Journal of Community Psychology 1*: 278–81.

Platt, T. (1985) 'Criminology in the 1980s: progressive alternatives to "Law and Order" ', *Crime and Social Justice 22*: 191–9.

Ploughman, P. and Stensrud, J. (1986) 'The ecology of rape victimization: a case study of Buffalo, New York', *Genetic, Social, and General Psychology Monographs 112*: 303–25.

Pointing, J. (ed.) (1986) *Alternatives to Custody*, Oxford: Blackwell.

Pomerantz, A. and Atkinson, J.M. (1984) 'Ethnomethodology, conversation analysis, and the study of courtroom interaction', in D.J. Müller, D.E. Blackman, and A.J. Chapman (eds) *Psychology and Law*, Chichester: Wiley.

Poole, L. (1986) 'The contribution of psychology to the development of police training in Britain (with particular emphasis on Metropolitan London)', in J.C. Yuille (ed.) *Police Selection and Training: The Role of Psychology*, Dordrecht: Martinus Nijhoff.

Pope, D.W. and Weiner, N.L. (1981) *Modern Policing*, London: Croom Helm.

Porporino, F.J. and Zamble, E. (1984) 'Coping with imprisonment', *Canadian Journal of Criminology 26*: 403–21.

Powell, G.E. (1977) 'Psychoticism and social deviancy in children', *Advances in Behaviour Research and Therapy 1*: 27–56.

Powers, E. and Witmar, H. (1951) *An Experiment in the Prevention of Delinquency: The Cambridge-Somerville Youth Study*, New York: Columbia University Press.

Poyner, B. (1981) 'Crime prevention and the environment: street attacks in city centres', *Police Research Bulletin 37*: 10–18.

Pratt, P. (ed.) (1986) *Sexual Assessment: Issues and Radical Alternatives, Issues in Criminological and Legal Psychology, No. 8*, Leicester: British Psychological Society.

Prentky, R., Cohen, M., and Seghorn, T. (1985) 'Development of a rational taxonomy for the classification of rapists: the Massachusetts treatment center system', *Bulletin of the American Academy of Psychiatry and Law 13*: 39–70.

Preston, M.A. (1982) 'Intermediate treatment: a new approach to community care', in M.P. Feldman (ed.) *Developments in the Study of Criminal Behaviour, Vol. 1: The Prevention and Control of Offending*, Chichester: Wiley.

Price, R.H. (1978) *Abnormal Behavior: Perspectives in Conflict* (2nd edn), New York: Holt, Rinehart, & Winston.

Priestley, P. and McGuire, J. (1985) *Offending Behaviour: Skills and Stratagems for Going Straight*, London: Batsford.

Prins, H. (1980) *Offenders, Deviants, or Patients? An Introduction to the Study of Socio-Forensic Problems*, London: Tavistock.

—— (1982) *Criminal Behaviour: An Introduction to Criminology and the Penal System* (2nd edn), London: Tavistock.

—— (1983) 'Diminished responsibility and the Sutcliffe case: legal, psychiatric and social aspects', *Medicine, Science and the Law 23*: 17–24.

—— (1986) *Dangerous Behaviour, the Law and Mental Disorder*, London: Tavistock.

Quinney, R. (1970) *The Social Reality of Crime*, Boston, Mass: Little, Brown.
—— (1975) *Criminology*, Boston, Mass: Little, Brown.
Quinsey, V.L. (1983) 'Prediction of recidivism and the evaluation of treatment programs for sex offenders', in S.N. Vernon-Jones and A.A. Keltner (eds) *Sexual Aggression and the Law*, Criminology Research Center: Simon Fraser University.
Quinsey, V.L., Chaplin, T.C., and Upfold, D. (1984) 'Sexual arousal to nonsexual violence and sadomasochistic themes among rapists and non-sex offenders', *Journal of Consulting and Clinical Psychology 52*: 651-7.
Quinsey, V.L., Chaplin, T.C., and Varney, G. (1981) 'A comparison of rapists' and non-sex offenders' sexual preferences for mutually consenting sex, rape, and physical abuse of women', *Behavioral Assessment 3*: 127-35.
Quinsey, V.L., Maguire, A., and Varney, G.W. (1983) 'Assertion and over-controlled hostility among mentally disorded murderers', *Journal of Consulting and Clinical Psychology 51*: 550-6.
Quinsey, V.L., Steinman, C.M., Bergersen, S.G., and Holmes, T.F. (1975) 'Sexual preferences among incestuous and non-incestuous child molesters', *Behavior Therapy 10*: 562-5.
Rabkin, J.G. (1979) 'Criminal behavior of discharged mental patients: a critical appraisal of the research', *Psychological Bulletin 86*: 1-27.
Rada, R.T. (1978) 'Classification of the rapist', in R.T. Rada (ed.) *Clinical Aspects of the Rapist*, New York: Grune & Stratton.
—— (1983) 'Plasma androgens in violent and non-violent sex offenders', *Bulletin of the American Academy of Psychiatry and the Law 11*: 149-58.
Radford, J. and Govier, E. (1980) *A Textbook of Psychology*, London: Sheldon Press.
Raine, A. (1985) 'Antisocial behaviour and social psychophysiology', in H. Wagner (ed.) *Bodily Changes and Social Behaviour: Theory and Experiment in Social Psychophysiology*, Chichester: Wiley.
Raine, A. and Venables, P.H. (1981) 'Classical conditioning and socialization — a biosocial interaction', *Personality and Individual Differences 2*: 273-83.
Rapoport, R. (1960) *The Community as Doctor*, London: Tavistock.
Rappeport, J.R. and Lassen, G. (1967) 'Dangerousness — arrest rate comparisons of discharged patients and the general population', in J.R. Rappeport (ed.) *Evaluation of the Dangerousness of the Mentally Ill*, Springfield, Ill: C.C. Thomas.
Rappeport, J.R., Lassen, G., and Hay, N.B. (1967) 'A review of the literature on dangerousness of the mentally ill', in J.R. Rappeport (ed.) *Evaluation of the Dangerousness of the Mentally Ill*, Springfield, Ill: C.C. Thomas.
Read, J.D., Barnsley, R.H., Ankers, K.S., and Whisham, I.Q. (1978) 'Variations in severity of verbs and eyewitnesses' testimony: an alternative explanation', *Perceptual and Motor Skills 46*: 795-800.
Read, J.D. and Bruce, D. (1984) 'On the external validity of questioning effects in eyewitness testimony', *International Review of Applied Psychology 33*: 33-49.
Reckless, W.C. (1967) *The Crime Problem*, New York: Appleton-Century-Crofts.
Reckless, W.C. and Dintz, S. (1967) 'Pioneering with self-concept as a vulnerability factor in delinquency', *Journal of Criminal Law, Criminology and Police Science 58*: 515-23.

Redl, F. and Toch, H. (1979) 'The psychoanalytic perspective', in H. Toch (ed.) *Psychology of Crime and Justice*, New York: Holt, Rinehart, & Winston.

Rees, L. (1973) 'Constitutional factors and abnormal behaviour', in H.J. Eysenck (ed.) *Handbook of Abnormal Psychology*, London: Pitman Medical.

Regoli, R.M., Poole, E.D., and Hewitt, J.D. (1979) 'Refining police cynicism theory: an empirical assessment, evaluation and implications', in D.M. Peterson (ed.) *Police Work: Strategies and Outcomes in Law Enforcement*, Beverly Hills, Calif: Sage.

Reid, I.D. (1982) 'The development and maintenance of a behavioural regime in a secure Youth Treatment Centre', in M.P. Feldman (ed.) *Developments in the Study of Criminal Behaviour, vol. 1: The Prevention and Control of Offending*, Chichester: Wiley.

Reid, I.D., Feldman, M.P., and Ostapiuk, E.B. (1980) 'The Shape Project for young offenders: introduction and overview', *Journal of Offender Counseling, Services and Rehabilitation 4*: 233–46.

Reiner, R. (1979) 'Police unionism', in S. Holdaway (ed.) *The British Police*, London: Edward Arnold.

Reiser, M. (1972) *The Police Department Psychologist*, Springfield, Ill: C.C. Thomas.

—— (1973) *Practical Psychology for Police Officers*, Springfield, Ill: C.C. Thomas.

—— (1982) *Police Psychology — Collected Papers*, Los Angeles, Calif: LEHI Publishing.

Reiser, M. and Klyver, N. (1987) 'Consulting with the police', in I.B. Weiner and A.K. Hess (eds) *Handbook of Forensic Psychology*, New York: Wiley.

Reiss, A.J. (1967) *Studies in Crime and Law Enforcement in a Major Metropolitan Area*, Washington, DC: US Government Printing Office.

Reppetto, T.A. (1976) 'Crime prevention and the displacement phenomenon', *Crime and Delinquency 22*: 166–77.

Riches, D. (ed.) (1986) *The Anthropology of Violence*, Oxford: Blackwell.

Richman, N., Stevenson, J., and Graham, P.J. (1982) *Pre-School to School: A Behavioural Study*, London: Academic Press.

Roach, J. and Thomaneck, J. (eds) (1985) *Police and Public Order in Europe*, London: Croom Helm.

Robertson, G. (1981) 'The extent and pattern of crime amongst mentally handicapped offenders', *Apex: Journal of the British Institute of Mental Handicap 9*: 100–3.

Robins, L. (1966) *Deviant Children Grown Up*, Baltimore, Md: Williams & Wilkins.

Rokeach, M. (1973) *The Nature of Human Values*, New York: Free Press.

Rokeach, M., Miller, M.G., and Snyder, J. (1971) 'The value gap between police and policed', *Journal of Social Issues 27*: 155–71.

Romero, J.J. and Williams, L.M. (1983) 'Group psychotherapy and intensive probation supervision with sex offenders: a comparative study', *Federal Probation 47*: 36–42.

—— (1985) 'Recidivism among convicted sex offenders: a 10-year follow-up study', *Federal Probation 49*: 58–64.

Rosanoff, A.J., Handy, L.M., and Rosanoff, F.A. (1934) 'Crime and delinquency in twins', *Journal of Criminal Law and Criminology 24*: 923–34.

Rosanoff, A.J., Handy, L.M., and Plesset, I. (1941) 'The etiology of child behavior difficulties, juvenile delinquency and adult criminality with special reference to their occurrence in twins', *Psychiatric Monographs* (California) No. 1, Sacramento Department of Institutions.

Ross, R.R. and Fabiano, E.A. (1985) *Time to Think: A Cognitive Model of Delinquency Prevention and Offender Rehabilitation*, Johnson City, Tenn: Institute of Social Sciences and Arts.

Rotenberg, M. and Nachshon, I. (1979) 'Impulsiveness and aggression among Israeli delinquents', *British Journal of Social and Clinical Psychology 18*: 59–63.

Rotter, J.B. (1954) *Social Learning and Clinical Psychology*, Englewood Cliffs, NJ: Prentice-Hall.

—— (1966) 'Generalized expectancies for internal versus external control of reinforcement', *Psychological Monographs 80* (whole no. 609).

Rotton, J. and Frey, J. (1985) 'Air pollution, weather, and violent crimes: concomitant time-series analysis of archival data', *Journal of Personality and Social Psychology 49*: 1,207–20.

Rouke, F.L. (1957) 'Psychological research on problems of testimony', *Social Issues 13*: 50–9.

Rowe, D.C. (1983) 'Biometrical genetic models of self-reported delinquent behaviour: a twin study', *Behavior Genetics 13*: 473–89.

Rowe, D.C. and Osgood, D.W. (1984) 'Heredity and sociological theories of delinquency: a reconsideration', *American Sociological Review 49*: 526–40.

Russell, D.E.H. (1975) *The Politics of Rape*, New York: Stein & Day.

—— (1982) *Rape and Women's Identity*, London: Sage.

—— (1986) *The Secret Trauma: Incest in the Lives of Girls and Women*, New York: Basic Books.

Russo, P.A., Engel, A.S., and Hatting, S.H. (1983) 'Police and occupational stress: an empirical investigation', in R.R. Bennett (ed.) *Police at Work: Policy Issues and Analysis*, Beverly Hills, Calif: Sage.

Rutherford, A. (1978) 'Decarceration of young offenders in Massachusetts', in N. Tutt (ed.) *Alternative Strategies for Coping with Crime*, Oxford: Blackwell.

—— (1986) *Growing Out of Crime: Society and Young People in Trouble*, Harmondsworth: Pelican.

Rutter, M. (1972) *Maternal Deprivation Reassessed*, Harmondsworth: Penguin.

—— (1981) *Maternal Deprivation Reassessed* (2nd edn), Harmondsworth: Penguin.

Rutter, M. and Giller, H. (1983) *Juvenile Delinquency: Trends and Perspectives*, Harmondsworth: Penguin.

Saks, M. (1977) *Jury Verdicts*, Lexington, Mass: Heath.

Sales, B.D. and Hafemeister, T.L. (1985) 'Law and psychology', in E.M. Altmaier and M.E. Meyer (eds) *Applied Specialities in Psychology*, London: Lawrence Erlbaum.

Samenow, S.E. (1983) 'Violence in every soul?', in W.S. Laufer and J.M. Day (eds) *Personality Theory, Moral Development, and Criminal Behavior*, Lexington, Mass: Lexington Books.

—— (1984) *Inside the Criminal Mind*, New York: Time Books.

Samuels, A. (1975) 'Mental illness and criminal liability', *Medicine, Science and the Law 15*: 198–204.

Sanday, P.R. (1981) 'The socio-cultural context of rape: a cross-cultural study', *Journal of Social Issues 37*: 5–27.

Sandberg, A.A., Koepf, G.F., Ishiara, T., and Hauschka, T.S. (1961) 'An XYY human male', *Lancet 262*: 488–9.

Sanders, G.S. and Simmons, W.L. (1983) 'Use of hypnosis to enhance eyewitness accuracy: does it work?', *Journal of Applied Psychology 68*: 70–7.

Sanders, G.S. and Warnick, D.H. (1981) 'Truth and consequences: the effect of responsibility on eyewitness behavior', *Basic and Applied Social Psychology* 2: 67–79.

Sarason, I.G. (1968) 'Verbal learning, modeling and juvenile delinquency', *American Psychologist 23*: 254–66.

—— (1978) 'A cognitive social learning approach to juvenile delinquency', in R.D. Hare and D. Schalling (eds) *Psychopathic Behavior: Approaches to Research*, Chichester: Wiley.

Sarason, I.G., Johnson, J.H., Berberich, J.P., and Siegal, J.M. (1979) 'Helping police officers to cope with stress: a cognitive-behavioral approach', *American Journal of Community Psychology 7*: 593–603.

Saunders, D.M., Vidmar, N., and Hewitt, E.C. (1983) 'Eyewitness testimony and the discrediting effect', in S.M.A. Lloyd-Bostock and B.R. Clifford (eds) *Evaluating Witness Evidence: Recent Psychological Research and New Perspectives*, Chichester: Wiley.

Saunders, J.T., Reppuci, N.D., and Sarata, B.P. (1973) 'An examination of impulsivity as a trait characterizing delinquent youth', *American Journal of Orthopsychiatry 43*: 789–95.

Scaplehorn, C. (1974) 'Piaget's cognitive-developmental approach to morality', in S. Mogdil (ed.) *Piagetian Research: A Handbook of Recent Studies*, Slough: NFER.

Schachter, S. and Latané, B. (1964) 'Crime, cognition and the autonomic nervous system', in D. Levine (ed.) *Nebraska Symposium on Motivation*, Lincoln, Nebr: University of Nebraska Press.

Schafer, S. (1976) *Introduction to Criminology*, New York: McGraw-Hill.

—— (1977) 'The problem of free will in criminology', *Journal of Criminal Law and Criminology 67*: 481–5.

Schlesinger, L.B. and Revitch, E. (1983) 'Sexual dynamics in homicide and assault', in L.B. Schlesinger and E. Revitch (eds) *Sexual Dynamics of Anti-Social Behavior*, Springfield, Ill: C.C. Thomas.

Schmauk, F.J. (1970) 'Punishment, arousal, and avoidance learning in sociopaths', *Journal of Abnormal Psychology 76*: 325–35.

Schoenthaler, S. and Doraz, W. (1983) 'Types of offenses which can be reduced in an institutional setting using nutritional intervention', *International Journal of Biosocial Research 4*: 74–84.

Scholder, M.H. (1982) 'The argument against the use of hypnosis to improve or enhance the memory of courtroom witnesses', *Law and Psychology Review* 7: 71–86.

Schonebaum, R.M. and Zinober, J.W. (1977) 'Learning and memory in mental retardation: the defective-developmental distinction re-evaluated', in I. Bialer and M. Sternlicht (eds) *The Psychology of Mental Retardation*, New York: Psychological Dimensions.

Schooler, J.W., Gerhard, D., and Loftus, E.F. (1986) 'Qualities of the unreal', *Journal of Experimental Psychology: Learning, Memory, and Cognition 12*: 171–81.

Schwendinger, H. and Schwendinger, J. (1979) 'Delinquency and social reform: a radical perspective', in L. Empry (ed.) *Juvenile Justice*, Charlottesville, Va: University of Viriginia Press.

Scully, D. and Marolla, J. (1985) ' "Riding the bull at Gilley's": convicted rapists describe the rewards of rape', *Social Problems 32*: 251–63.

Segal, Z.V. and Marshall, W.L. (1985a) 'Heterosexual social skills in a population of rapists and child molesters', *Journal of Consulting and Clinical Psychology 53*: 55–63.

—— (1985b) 'Self-report and behavioral assertion in two groups of sexual offenders', *Journal of Behavior Therapy and Experimental Psychiatry 16*: 223–9.

—— (1986) 'Discrepancies between self-efficacy predictions and actual performance in a population of rapists and child molesters', *Cognitive Therapy and Research 10*: 363–76.

Segal, Z.V. and Stermac, L. (1984) 'The measure of rapists' attitudes towards women', *International Journal of Law and Psychiatry 7*: 437–40.

Sepejak, D., Menzies, R.J., Webster, C.D., and Jensen, F.A.S. (1983) 'Clinical predictions of dangerousness: two-year follow-up of 408 pretrial forensic cases', *Bulletin of the American Academy of Psychiatry and the Law 11*: 171–82.

Sewell, J.D. (1983) 'The development of a critical life events scale for law enforcement', *Journal of Police Science and Administration 11*: 113–14.

Shaffer, D.R. (1985) 'The defendant's testimony', in S.M. Kassin and L.S. Wrightsman (eds) *The Psychology of Evidence and Trial Procedure*, Beverly Hills, Calif: Sage.

Shapiro, A. (1969) 'Delinquent and disturbed behaviour within the field of mental deficiency', in A.V.S. De Rueck and R. Porter (eds) *The Mentally Abnormal Offender*, London: J.& A. Churchill.

Shapiro, P.N. and Penrod, S. (1986) 'Meta-analysis of facial identification studies', *Psychological Bulletin 100*: 139–56.

Shapland, J. and Williams, T. (eds) (1983) *Mental Disorder and the Law: Effects of the New Legislation, Issues in Criminological and Legal Psychology, No. 4*, Leicester: British Psychological Society.

Shealy, A.E. (1979) 'Police corruption: screening and high-risk applicants', in C.D. Speilberger (ed.) *Police Selection and Evaluation*, New York: Praeger.

Sheldon, W.H. (1942) *The Varieties of Temperament: A Psychology of Constitutional Differences*, New York: Harper & Row.

—— (1949) *Varieties of Delinquent Youth: An Introduction to Constitutional Psychiatry*, New York: Harper & Row.

Shepherd, J. (1981) *Sociology*, St Paul, Minn: West Publishing.

Shepherd, J.W. (1981) 'Social factors in face recognition', in G.M. Davies, H.D. Ellis, and J.W. Shepherd (eds) *Perceiving and Remembering Faces*, London: Academic Press.

—— (1983) 'Identification after long delays', in S.M.A. Lloyd-Bostock and B.R. Clifford (eds) *Evaluating Witness Evidence: Recent Psychological Research and New Perspectives*, Chichester: Wiley.

Shepherd, J.W., Ellis, H.D., and Davies, G.M. (1982) *Identification Evidence: A Psychological Evaluation*, Aberdeen: University of Aberdeen Press.

Short, J.F. (ed.) (1968) *Gang Delinquency and Delinquent Subcultures*, New York: Harper & Row.

Siann, G. (1985) *Accounting for Aggression: Perspectives on Aggression and Violence*, London: Allen & Unwin.

Siegal, L.J. (1986) *Criminology* (2nd edn), St Paul, Minn: West Publishing.

Sinclair, I. and Clarke, R. (1982) 'Predicting, treating, and explaining delinquency: the lessons from research on institutions', in M.P. Feldman (ed.) *Developments in the Study of Criminal Behaviour, vol. 1: The Prevention and Control of Offending*, Chichester: Wiley.

Singer, M.T. and Nievod, A. (1987) 'Consulting and testifying in court', in I.B. Weiner and A.K. Hess (eds) *Handbook of Forensic Psychology*, New York: Wiley.

Skinner, B.F. (1938) *The Behavior of Organisms*, New York: Appleton-Century-Crofts.

—— (1953) *Science and Human Behavior*, New York: Macmillan.

—— (1974) *About Behaviourism*, London: Cape.

—— (1985) 'Cognitive science and behaviourism', *British Journal of Psychology* 76: 291–301.

Sluckin, W., Herbert, M., and Sluckin, A. (1983) *Maternal Bonding*, Oxford: Blackwell.

Sosowsky, L. (1978) 'Crime and violence amongst mental patients reconsidered in view of the new legal relationship between the State and the mentally ill', *American Journal of Psychiatry 135*: 33–42.

Sparks, R.F. (1981) 'Surveys of victimization — an optimistic assessment', in M. Tonry and N. Morris (eds) *Crime and Justice: An Annual Review of Research*, vol. 3, Chicago, Ill: University of Chicago Press.

Sparks, R.F., Genn, H.G., and Dodd, D.J. (1977) *Surveying Victims: A Study of the Measurement of Criminal Victimization, Perceptions of Crime, and Attitudes to Criminal Justice*, Chichester: Wiley.

Sparrow, S.S., Ballo, D.A., and Cicchetti, D.V. (1984) *Vineland Adaptive Behavior Scales*, Circle Pines, Minn: American Guidance Service.

Spence, S.H. (1981) 'Differences in social skills performance between institutionalized juvenile male offenders and a comparable group of boys without offence records', *British Journal of Clinical Psychology 20*: 163–71.

—— (1982) 'Social skills training with young offenders', in P. Feldman (ed.) *Developments in the Study of Delinquent Behaviour, vol. 1: The Prevention and Control of Offending*, Chichester: Wiley.

Spence, S.H. and Marzillier, J.S. (1981) 'Social skills training with adolescent male offenders: II. Short-term, long-term and generalized effects', *Behaviour Research and Therapy 19*: 349–68.

Spencer, S. (1984) 'Homicide, mental abnormality and offence', in M.Craft and A. Craft (eds) *Mentally Abnormal Offenders*, London: Baillière Tindall.

Spielberger, C.D., Spaulding, H.C., Jolley, M.T., and Ward, J.C. (1979a) 'Selection of effective law enforcement officers', in C.D. Spielberger (ed.) *Police Selection and Evaluation*, New York: Praeger.

Spielberger, C.D., Ward, J.C., and Spaulding, H.C. (1979b) 'A model for the selection of law enforcement officers', in C.D. Spielberger (ed.) *Police Selection and Evaluation*, New York: Praeger.

Spitzer, S. (1975) 'Toward a Marxian theory of deviance', *Social Problems 22*: 638–51.

Spivack, G., Platt, J.J., and Shure, M.B. (1976) *The Problem-Solving Approach to Adjustment: A Guide to Research and Intervention*, San Francisco, Calif: Jossey-Bass.

Sporer, S.L. (1982) 'A brief history of the psychology of testimony', *Current Psychological Reviews 2*: 323–40.

Spry, W.B. (1984) 'Schizophrenia and crime', in M. Craft and A. Craft (eds) *Mentally Abnormal Offenders*, London: Baillière Tindall.

Stephenson, G.M. (1984) 'Accuracy and confidence in testimony: a critical review and some fresh evidence', in D.J. Müller, D.E. Blackman, and A.J. Chapman (eds) *Psychology and Law*, Chichester: Wiley.

Stermac, L.E. and Quinsey, V.L. (1986) 'Social competence among rapists', *Behavioral Assessment 8*: 171–85.

Stern, L.W. (1939) 'The psychology of testimony', *Journal of Abnormal and Social Psychology 34*: 3–20.

Stewart, C.H.M. and Hemsley, D.R. (1979) 'Risk perception and likelihood of action in criminal offenders', *British Journal of Criminology 19*: 105–19.

Storr, A. (1970) *Human Aggression*, Harmondsworth: Penguin.

Strasser, G., Kerr, N.L., and Bray, R.M. (1982) 'The social psychology of jury deliberations: structure, process, and product', in N.L. Kerr and R.M. Bray (eds) *The Psychology of the Courtroom*, New York: Academic Press.

Straus, M.A., Gelles, R., and Steinmetz, S. (1980) *Behind Closed Doors: Violence in the American Family*, Garden City, NY: Doubleday.

Stuart, R.B. (ed.) (1981) *Violent Behavior: Social Learning Approaches to Prediction, Management and Treatment*, New York: Brunner/Mazel.

Stumpfl, F. (1936) *Die Ursprunge des Verbrechens om Lebenshauf von Zwillingen*, Leipzig: Georg Thieme Verlag.

Stumphauzer, J.S. (1972) 'Increased delay of gratification in young prison inmates through imitation of high delay peer models', *Journal of Personality and Social Psychology 21*: 10–17.

Sturman, A. (1980) 'Damage on buses: the effects of supervision', in R.V.G. Clarke and P. Mayhew (eds) *Designing out Crime*, London: HMSO.

Sue, S., Smith, R.E., and Pedroza, G. (1975) 'Authoritarianism, pretrial publicity and awareness of bias in simulated jurors', *Psychological Reports 37*: 1,299–1,302.

Sutherland, E.H. (1939) *Principles of Criminology*, Philadelphia, Pa: Lippincott.

—— (1947) *Principles of Criminology* (4th edn), Philadelphia, Pa: Lippincott.

Sutherland, E.H. and Cressey, D.R. (1960) *Principles of Criminology* (6th edn), Philadelphia, Pa: Lippincott.

—— (1970) *Criminology* (8th edn), Philadelphia, Pa: Lippincott.

—— (1974) *Criminology* (9th edn), Philadelphia, Pa: Lippincott.

Sykes, G. (1974) 'The rise of critical criminology', *Journal of Criminal Law and Criminology 65*: 206–13.

Syndulko, K. (1978) 'Electrocortical investigations of sociopathy', in R.D. Hare and D. Schalling (eds) *Psychopathic Behaviour: Approaches to Research*, Chichester: Wiley.

Szasz, T.S. (1961) *The Myth of Mental Illness*, New York: Dell.

—— (1970) *The Manufacture of Madness*, New York: Dell.

Tanford, S. and Penrod, S.D. (1982) 'Biases in trials involving defendants charged with multiple offenses', *Journal of Applied Social Psychology 12*: 453–80.

Taylor, I., Walton, P., and Young, J. (1973) *The New Criminology: For a Social Theory of Deviance*, London: Routledge & Kegan Paul.

Taylor, L. (1984) *Born to Crime: The Genetic Causes of Criminal Behaviour*, London: Greenwood Press.

Taylor, M. (1983) 'Psychology and police education', *Bulletin of the British Psychological Society 36*: 406–8.

Taylor, P.J. (1982) 'Schizophrenia and violence', in J. Gunn and D.P. Farrington (eds) *Abnormal Offenders, Delinquency, and the Criminal Justice System*, Chichester: Wiley.

—— (1985) 'Motives for offending among violent and psychotic men', *British Journal of Psychiatry 147*: 491–8.

—— (1986) 'Psychiatric disorder in London's life-sentenced offenders', *British Journal of Criminology 26*: 63–78.

Taylor, P.J. and Gunn, J. (1984) 'Violence and psychosis II — effect of psychiatric diagnosis on conviction and sentencing of offenders', *British Medical Journal 289*: 9–12.

Teplin, L.A. (1984) 'Criminalizing mental disorder: the comparative arrest rate of the mentally ill', *American Psychologist 39*: 794–803.

Territo, L. and Vetter, H.J. (1981) *Stress and Police Personnel*, Boston, Mass: Allyn & Bacon.

Terry, W.C. (1981) 'Police stress: the empirical evidence', *Journal of Police Science and Administration 9*: 61–75.

Tharp, R.G. and Wetzel, R.H. (1969) *Behavior Modification in the Natural Environment*, New York: Academic Press.

Thornton, D.M. (1987) 'Treatment effects on recidivism: a reappraisal of the "nothing works" doctrine', in B.J. McGurk, D.M. Thornton, and M. Williams (eds) *Applying Psychology to Imprisonment: Theory & Practice*, London: HMSO.

Thornton, D.M. and Reid, R.L. (1982) 'Moral reasoning and type of criminal offence', *British Journal of Social Psychology 21*: 231–8.

Thornton, D.M., Curran, L., Grayson, D., and Holloway, V. (1984) *Tougher Regimes in Detention Centres: Report of an Evaluation by the Young Offender Psychology Unit*, London: HMSO.

Thorpe, D. (1978) 'Intermediate treatment', in N. Tutt (ed.) *Alternative Strategies for Coping with Crime*, Oxford: Blackwell.

Tickner, A.H. and Poulton, E.C. (1975) 'Watching for people and actions', *Ergonomics 18*: 35–51.

Tidmarsh, D. (1982) 'Implications from research studies', in J.R. Hamilton and H. Freeman (eds) *Dangerousness: Psychiatric Assessment and Management*, London: Gaskell.

Tittle, C. (1975) 'Labelling and crime: an empirical evaluation', in W. Gove (ed.) *Deviance: Evaluating a Perspective*, New York: Wiley.

Toch, H. (1969) *Violent Men*, Chicago, Ill: Aldine.

—— (1979) 'Perspectives on the offender', in H. Toch (ed.) *Psychology of Crime and Criminal Justice*, London: Holt, Rinehart, & Winston.

Tomaselli, S. and Porter, R. (eds) (1986) *Rape*, Oxford: Blackwell.

Toner, B. (1982) *The Facts of Rape* (2nd edn), London: Arrow Books.

Trasler, G. (1986) 'Situational crime control and rational choice: a critique', in K. Heal and G. Laycock (eds) *Situational Crime Prevention: From Theory into Practice*, London: HMSO.

Treasaden, I.H. (1985) 'Current practice in regional interim secure units', in L. Gostin (ed.) *Secure Provision: A Review of Services for the Mentally Ill and Mentally Handicapped in England and Wales*, London: Tavistock.

Tully, B. and Cahill, D. (1984) *Police Interviewing of the Mentally Handicapped: An Experimental Study*, London: Police Foundation.

Tunstall, O., Gudjonsson, G., Eysenck, H., and Haward, L. (1982a) 'Professional issues arising from psychological evidence presented in court', *Bulletin of the British Psychological Society 35*: 329–31.

—— (1982b) 'Response to professional issues arising from psychological evidence presented in court: a reply to Dr Heim', *Bulletin of the British Psychological Society 35*: 333.

Turk, A. (1969) *Criminality and Legal Order*, Chicago, Ill: Rand McNally.

Tutt, N. (1971) 'The subnormal offender', *British Journal of Mental Subnormality 17*: 42–7.

Ullmann, L. and Krasner, L. (1975) *A Psychological Approach to Abnormal Behavior* (2nd edn), Englewood Cliffs, NJ: Prentice-Hall.

Van Den Haag, E. (1982) 'Could successful rehabilitation reduce the crime rate?', *Journal of Criminal Law and Criminology 73*: 1,022–35.

Van Dusen, K.T., Mednick, S.A., Gabrielli, W.F., and Hutchings, B. (1983) 'Social class and crime in an adoption cohort', *Journal of Criminal Law and Criminology 74*: 249–69.

Vernis, J.S. and Walker, V. (1970) 'Policemen and the recall of criminal details', *Journal of Social Psychology 81*: 217–21.

Visher, C.A. (1983) 'Gender, police arrest decisions, and notions of chivalry', *Criminology 21*: 5–28.

—— (1987) 'Juror decision-making: the importance of evidence', *Law and Human Behavior 11*: 1–17.

Vold, G. (1958) *Theoretical Criminology*, Oxford: Oxford University Press.

Waddington, P.A.J. (1982) 'Conservatism, dogmatism, and authoritarianism in British police officers: a comment', *Sociology 16*: 591–4.

Walker, M.J. and Brodsky, S.L. (eds) (1976) *Sexual Assault: The Victims and the Rapist*, Lexington, Mass: Lexington Books.

Walker, N. (1965) *Crime and Punishment in Great Britain*, Edinburgh: Edinburgh University Press.

—— (1968) *Crime and Insanity in England*, vol. 1, Edinburgh: Edinburgh University Press.

Wall, P.M. (1965) *Eyewitness Identification in Criminal Cases*, Springfield, Ill: C.C. Thomas.

Waller, I. and Okihiro, N. (1978) *Burglary: The Victim and the Public*, Toronto: University of Toronto Press.

Walsh, D.P. (1978) *Shoplifting: Controlling a Major Crime*, London: Macmillan.

Ward, E. (1982) 'Clinical psychology as evidence', in J. Shapland (ed.) *Lawyers and Psychologists — Gathering and Giving Evidence, Issues in Criminological and Legal Psychology, No. 3*, Leicester: British Psychological Society.

Warnick, D.H. and Sanders, G.S. (1980) 'The effects of group discussion on eyewitness accuracy', *Journal of Applied Social Psychology 10*: 249–59.

Warren, M.Q. (1983) 'Applications of interpersonal-maturity theory to offender populations', in W.S. Laufer and J.M. Day (eds) *Personality Theory, Moral Development, and Criminal Behavior*, Lexington, Mass: Lexington Books.

Washbrook, R.A.H. (1981) 'Neuroticism and offenders', *International Journal of Offender Therapy and Comparative Criminology 24*: 122–9.

Weber, D.E. and Burke, W.H. (1986) 'An alternative approach to treating delinquent youth', *Residential Group Care and Treatment 3*: 65–85.

Weinberg, H.I. and Baron, R.S. (1982) 'The discredible eyewitness', *Personality and Social Psychology Bulletin 8*: 60–7.

Weiner, B.A. (1985) 'Legal issues raised in treating sex offenders', *Behavioral Sciences and the Law 3*: 325–40.

Weiner, I.B. (1987) 'Writing forensic reports', in I.B. Weiner and A.K. Hess (eds) *Handbook of Forensic Psychology*, New York: Wiley.

Weiner, N.A. and Wolfgang, M. (1985) 'The extent and character of violent crime in America, 1969–1982', in L. Curtis (ed.) *American Violence and Public Policy*, New Haven, Conn: Yale University Press.

Weiner, N.L. (1981) 'Policing in America', in D.W. Pope and N.L. Weiner (eds) *Modern Policing*, London: Croom Helm.

Weinrott, M.R., Jones, R.R., and Howard, J.R. (1982) 'Cost effectiveness of teaching family programs for delinquents: results of a national evaluation', *Evaluation Review 6*: 173–201.

Weiss, G. (1983) 'Long-term outcome: findings, concepts and practical implications', in M. Rutter (ed.) *Developmental Neuropsychiatry*, New York: Guilford Press.

Weissman, M.M. and Myers, J.K. (1978) 'Affective disorders in a US urban community', *Archives of General Psychiatry 35*: 1,304–10.

Welch, G.J. (1985) 'Contingency contracting with a delinquent and his family', *Journal of Behavior Therapy and Experimental Psychiatry 16*: 253–9.

Wellford, C. (1975) 'Labeling theory and criminology: an assessment', *Criminology 16*: 513–26.

Wells, G.L. (1984) 'How adequate is human intuition for judging eyewitness testimony?', in G.L. Wells and E.F. Loftus (eds) *Eyewitness Testimony: Psychological Perspectives*, Cambridge: Cambridge University Press.

—— (1986) 'Expert psychological testimony: empirical and conceptual analyses of effects', *Law and Human Behavior 10*: 83–95.

Wells, G.L. and Lindsay, R.C.L. (1980) 'On estimating the diagnosticity of eyewitness non-identifications', *Psychological Bulletin 88*: 776–84.

—— (1983) 'How do people judge the accuracys of eyewitness identifications?', in S.M.A. Lloyd-Bostock and B.R. Clifford (eds) *Evaluating Witness Evidence: Recent Psychological Research and New Perspectives*, Chichester: Wiley.

Wells, G.L. and Loftus, E.F. (eds) (1984) *Eyewitness Testimony: Psychological Perspectives*, Cambridge: Cambridge University Press.

Wells, G.L. and Murray, D.M. (1984) 'Eyewitness confidence', in G.L. Wells and E.F. Loftus (eds) *Eyewitness Testimony: Psychological Perspectives*, Cambridge: Cambridge University Press.

Wells, G.L., Leippe, M.R., and Ostrom, T.M. (1979a) 'Guidelines for empirically assessing the fairness of a lineup', *Law and Human Behavior 3*: 285–93.

Wells, G.L., Lindsay, R.C.L., and Ferguson, T.J. (1979b) 'Accuracy, confidence and juror perceptions in eyewitness identification', *Journal of Applied Psychology 64*: 440–8.

Wells, G.L., Lindsay, R.C.L., and Tousignant, J.P. (1980) 'Effects of expert psychological advice on human performance in judging the validity of eyewitness testimony', *Law and Human Behavior 4*: 275–85.

West, D.J. (1965) *Murder Followed by Suicide*, London: Heinemann.

—— (1967) *The Young Offender*, London: Pelican.

—— (1980) 'The clinical approach to criminology', *Psychological Medicine 10*: 619–31.

—— (1982) *Delinquency: Its Roots, Careers and Prospects*, London: Heinemann.

—— (1984) 'The victim's contribution to sexual offences', in J. Hopkins (ed.) *Perspectives on Rape and Sexual Assault*, London: Harper & Row.

—— (1986) 'Clinical approaches to criminology', in C.R. Hollin and K. Howells (eds) *Clinical Approaches to Criminal Behaviour, Issues in Criminological and Legal Psychology, No. 9*, Leicester: British Psychological Society.

—— (1987) *Sexual Crimes and Confrontations*, Aldershot, Hants: Gower.

West, D.J. and Farrington, D.P. (1973) *Who Becomes Delinquent?*, London: Heinemann Educational.

—— (1977) *The Delinquent Way of Life*, London: Heinemann.

Westly, W. (1970) *Violence and the Police: A Sociological Study of Law, Custom and Morality*, Cambridge, Mass: MIT Press.

Whipple, G.M. (1909) 'The observer as reporter: a survey of "the psychology of testimony" ', *Psychological Bulletin 6*: 153–70.

—— (1910) 'Recent literature on the psychology of testimony', *Psychological Bulletin 7*: 365–8.

—— (1911) 'Psychology of testimony', *Psychological Bulletin 8*: 307–9.

—— (1912) 'Psychology of testimony and report', *Psychological Bulletin 9*: 264–9.

—— (1913) 'Psychology of testimony and report', *Psychological Bulletin 10*: 264–8.

—— (1914) 'Psychology of testimony and report', *Psychological Bulletin 11*: 245–50.

—— (1915) 'Psychology of testimony', *Psychological Bulletin 12*: 221–4.

—— (1917) 'Psychology of testimony', *Psychological Bulletin 14*: 234–6.

—— (1918) 'The obtaining of information: psychology of observation and report', *Psychological Bulletin 15*: 217–48.

Whitley, B.E. (1986) 'The effects of discredited eyewitness testimony: a meta-analysis', *Journal of Social Psychology 127*: 215–17.

Widom, C.S. (1978) 'An empirical classification of female offenders, *Criminal Justice and Behavior 5*: 35–52.

Wigmore, J.H. (1909) 'Professor Münsterberg and the psychology of testimony:

being a report of the case of *Cokestone v. Münsterberg'*, *Illinois Law Review* 3: 399–445.

Wilkinson, P. (1977) *Terrorism and the Liberal State*, London: Macmillan.

Williams, D. (1969) 'Neural factors relating to habitual aggression — consideration of differences between habitual aggressives and others who have committed crimes of violence', *Brain* 92: 503–20.

Williams, G. (1955) 'The definition of crime', in J. Smith and B. Hogan (eds) *Criminal Law* (2nd edn), London: Butterworths.

Williams, L.S. (1984) 'The classic rape: when do victims report?', *Social Problems* 31: 459–67.

Williams, T., Alves, E., and Shapland, J. (eds) (1984) *Options for the Mentally Abnormal Offender: A Linked System of Prisons, Hospitals, Secure Units and the Community?*, Issues in Criminological and Legal Psychology, No. 6, Leicester: British Psychological Society.

Willis, A. (1986) 'Help and control in probation: an empirical assessment of probation practice', in J. Pointing (ed.) *Alternatives to Custody*, Oxford: Blackwell.

Wilson, J.Q. (1975) *Thinking about Crime*, New York: Basic Books.

Wilson, S. (1980) 'Vandalism and "defensible space" on London housing estates', in R.V.G. Clarke and P. Mayhew (eds) *Designing out Crime*, London: HMSO.

Windlesham, Lord (1987) *Responses to Crime*, Oxford: Clarendon.

Winick, C. (1979) 'The psychology of the courtroom', in H. Toch (ed.) *Psychology of Crime and Criminal Justice*, New York:. Holt, Rinehart, & Winston.

Witkin, H.A., Mednick, S.A., Schulsinger, F., Bakkstrøm, E., Christiansen, K.O., Goodenough, D.R., Hirschhorn, K., Lundsteen, C., Owen, D.R., Philip, J., Rubin, D.B., and Stocking, M. (1976) 'Criminality in XYY and XXY men', *Science* 193: 547–55.

Wolfgang, M.E. (1958) *Patterns in Criminal Homicide*, Philadelphia, Pa: University of Pennsylvania Press.

—— (1971) 'Why criminal statistics?', in L. Radzinowicz and M.E. Wolfgang (eds) *Crime and Justice, vol. 1: The Criminal in Society*, New York: Basic Books.

Wolfgang, M.E. and Ferracuti, F. (1967) *The Subculture of Violence: Towards an Integrated Theory in Criminology*, London: Tavistock.

Wood, R. and Flynn, J.M. (1978) 'A self-evaluation token system versus an external evaluation token system alone in a residential setting with pre-delinquent youth', *Journal of Applied Behavior Analysis* 11: 503–12.

Woodward, M. (1955) 'The role of low intelligence in delinquency', *British Journal of Delinquency* 6: 281–303.

Wootton, B. (1959) *Social Science and Social Pathology*, London: Allen & Unwin.

Wormith, J.S. (1984) 'The controversy over the effects of long-term incarceration', *Canadian Journal of Criminology* 26: 423–37.

Wright, R. (1980) 'Rape and physical violence', in D.J. West (ed.) *Sex Offenders in the Criminal Justice System*, Cambridge: University of Cambridge, Institute of Criminology.

Yarmey, A.D. (1979) *The Psychology of Eyewitness Testimony*, New York: Free Press.

—— (1984) 'Age as a factor in eyewitness memory', in G.L. Wells and E.F. Loftus (eds) *Eyewitness Testimony: Psychological Perspectives*, Cambridge: Cambridge University Press.

—— (1986a) 'Perceived expertness and credibility of police officers as eyewitnesses', *Canadian Police College Journal 10*: 31-52.

—— (1986b) 'Verbal, visual, and voice identification of a rape suspect under different levels of illumination', *Journal of Applied Psychology 71*: 363-70.

Yarmey, A.D. and Tressillian Jones, H.P. (1983) 'Is the psychology of eyewitness identification a matter of common sense?', in S.M.A. Lloyd-Bostock and B.R. Clifford (eds) *Evaluating Witness Evidence: Recent Psychological Research and New Perspectives*, Chichester: Wiley.

Yates, E., Barbaree, H.E., and Marshall, W.L. (1984) 'Anger and deviant sexual arousal', *Behavior Therapy 15*: 287-94.

Yochelson, S. and Samenow, S.E. (1976) *The Criminal Personality, vol. 1: A Profile for Change*, New York: Jason Aronsen.

Yoshimasu, S. (1961) 'The criminological significance of the family in the light of the studies of criminal twins', *Acta Criminologiae et Medicinae Legalis Japanica 27*: 117-41.

—— (1965) 'Criminal life curves of monozygotic twin-pairs', *Acta Criminologiae et Medicinae Legalis Japanica 31*: 9-20.

Young, J. (1986) 'The failure of criminology: the need for a radical realism', in R. Matthews and J. Young (eds) *Confronting Crime*, Beverly Hills, Calif: Sage.

Yuille, J.C. (1980) 'A critical examination of the psychological and practical implications of eyewitness research', *Law and Human Behavior 4*: 335-45.

—— (1986) *Police Selection and Training: The Role of Psychology*, Dordrecht: Martinus Nijhoff.

Yuille, J.C. and Cutshall, J.L. (1986) 'A case study of eyewitness memory to a crime', *Journal of Applied Psychology 71*: 291-301.

Yuille, J.C. and McEwan, N.H. (1985) 'Use of hypnosis as an aid to eyewitness memory', *Journal of Applied Psychology 70*: 389-400.

Zanni, G.R. and Offerman, J.T. (1978) 'Eyewitness testimony: an exploration of question wording upon recall as a function of neuroticism', *Perceptual and Motor Skills 46*: 163-6.

Zaragoza, M.S., McCloskey, M., and Jarvis, M. (1987) 'Misleading post-event information and recall of the original event: further evidence against the memory impairment hypothesis', *Journal of Experimental Psychology: Learning, Memory, and Cognition 13*: 36-44.

Zellweger, H. and Simpson, J. (1977) *Chromosomes of Man*, London: Heinemann/SIMP.

Zillman, D. (1979) *Hostility and Aggression*, Hillsdale, NJ: Lawrence Erlbaum.

Ziskin, J. (1981) *Coping with Psychiatric and Psychological Testimony* (3rd edn), Venice, Calif: Law and Psychology.

Zuriff, G.E. (1985) *Behaviorism: A Conceptual Reconstruction*, New York: Columbia University Press.

Name index

Abel, G.G. 85, 86, 92–3
Abrahamson, D. 35
Adlam, R.C.A. 127, 133
Adlam, K.R.C. 130, 141–4
Adler, A. 34
Ahlstrom, W.M. 48
Aichhorn, A. 34-5
Ainsworth, P.B. 126, 136–7, 144, 151, 176
Akers, R.L. 43
Alban Metcalfe, B.M. 151
Alder, C. 81, 94
Alexander, F. 35
Alexander, J.F. 195
Alexander, R.N. 190
Allen, J.V. 186
Allsopp, J.F. 57
Alper, A. 156
Alterman, A.I. 52
Alter-Reid, K. 89
Alves, E.A. 186
Amir, M. 78, 80, 81, 82
Anderson, C.A. 66
Andrew, J.M. 48
Arbuthnot, J. 49, 53, 195
Argyle, M. 3, 43
Aromaa, K. 17
Aronfreed, J. 51
Aronson, E. 177
Aronstam, D. 160
Asch, S.E. 53
Ashmore, Z. 183
Ashworth, A. 105, 108, 115,

161, 173
Atkinson, J.M. 153
Atkinson, R.L. 2
Austin, T.L. 131
Ausubel, D. 46
Avery-Clark, C.A. 92

Baddeley, A.D. 156
Bailey, W. 204
Baldwin, J. 162, 163, 167, 171
Bales, K.B. 12
Ball, I. 106
Bandura, A. 3, 42–3, 66, 78
Barbaree, H.E. 85, 86, 97
Barlow, G. 191
Barnes, C. 111
Baron, R.A. 64
Baron, R.S. 162
Barth, R.P. 208
Bartol, A.M. 152
Bartol, C.R. 22, 31, 54, 56, 77, 80, 152, 183, 186
Barton, A. 164
Baxter, D.J. 86-7
Bayer, R. 9, 207
Bean, P.T. 125
Beccaria, C. 9
Beck, S. 87, 88, 93, 94
Beck, S.J. 48
Becker, H. 8, 11
Becker, J.V. 92
Bekerian, D.A. 159
Belson, W. 15, 200

Subject index